Dragon's Uproar Over Hills

China's Intrusion in North East Asia

R.K. Pandey

Gaurav Book Centre Pvt Ltd

Delhi

Publisher
GAURAV BOOK CENTRE PVT LTD
4832/24,Prahlad Lane,S-207 Ansari
Road, Daryaganj, Delhi-110002
Ph.: 43570976, 23278261
Email: gauravbookcentre@gmail.com

Edition: 2025

ISBN: 978-93-83316-94-6

Laser Typesetting
JEE-VEE Graphics, Delhi

Price: 1295/-

Printed
Vikas Computers, Delhi

Contents

Preface

As China continues to apply sustained military pressure on India's borders in the midst of visits exchanged between the two countries' leaders and senior officials, China's official media continues to publicise articles intended to caution India that China retains the option of initiating military hostilities. The number of articles stating that China will have to resort to military force to settle outstanding border disputes has increased since 2010, with the intensification of the disputes in the South China Sea and especially with Japan. They coincide with the 'rise' in China's economic and military might. Interestingly, Chinese officials routinely advise their Indian counterparts to rein in the Indian media whose 'jingoistic' tenor apparently imposes strains on India-China relations.

China has been claiming about 90,000 sq km of Arunachal Pradesh along its 1,080-km LAC contiguous with Tibet as its own, even referring to the Indian side as South Tibet. The Chinese are also wary of India's advantage in Chushul-Chumar sector. "Obviously, the Chinese Army was trying to stop India from developing border military infrastructure in Daulat Beg Oldi in April. There the Chinese are at a disadvantage, primarily due to the terrain," a serving Major General of the Indian Army said. During the tense 21-day confrontation, Indian troops were "eye-to-eye" with the PLA, pitching tents opposite Chinese tents 19 km inside Indian territory.

Tensions are rising in Northeast Asia, threatening more than a generation of peace and prosperity that has made the region's growth and development the envy of the world. Regional reaction to China's declaration of an "air defense identification zone" encompassing areas controlled by South Korea and Japan is the latest sign that longstanding rivalries, territorial disputes, and historical antagonisms increasingly have the potential to result in conflict.

The downturn in relations between China and Japan and between Japan and South Korea represents a serious challenge to regional stability and a deep concern to the United States, which has a major stake in the region and important alliances with both Seoul and Tokyo.

Many of the Northeast Asia region's problems have deep roots and long histories, and emotion and resentment play a significant role in keeping old disputes alive. If the region is to avoid conflict, it must find a way to move past the often-tragic legacy of its history. China, Japan, and Korea must understand the seriousness of the situation and share responsibility for addressing it. Failure to do so is not an option, since the region's stability and prosperity are at stake.

North East Asia has been forcefully thrust in the global strategic consciousness as in the run-up to 2014 China has switched over from its much publicised and much trumpeted 'peaceful rise of China' to a robust and unabashed use of China's 'hard power' accumulated in the last decade without any checkmating. Gone are the US think tanks treatises emphasising and glorifying the use of China's 'soft power'.

China after signalling the world in 2009 with its public display of its stupendous military might felt strong enough to indulge in its use of 'hard power' first in the South China Sea against Vietnam and the Philippines and now in the East China Sea against Japan. Both South China Sea and East China Sea conflict escalations by China have now emerged as global 'flash-points'. Concurrently, China also started displaying its use of 'hard power' on the India-Tibet border encouraged by India's timid strategic responses.

The ripostes to China's military rise in North East Asia and its wider strategic impact, and so also its threatening contours, have emerged in the shape of the United States Strategic Pivot to Asia in2009 and Russia's Strategic Pivot to Asia Pacific in 2012. Both implicitly are targeted at checkmating China's unrestrained military adventurism in Asia Pacific.

As the book addresses this crucial issue quite deftly, it is hoped that it would prove to be a source of great information for the reader.

—*Auther*

1

The Entering Dragon

The traveller, who passes through the tranquil Himalayan vista of Tawang in summer when the snows have melted and the Nurangang waterfall is a distant roar, will come across a small temple named Jaswant Garh situated between Se La and Jang. It is dedicated to a baba who bore the name Jaswant Singh Rawat in another life. Behind every canonisation lies a myth. Behind the baba's myth is a soldier called Rifleman (RFN) Jaswant Singh, Number 4039009, serving with the 4th Battalion of the Garhwal Rifles on India's eastern border with China in the winter of 1962. The legend was born at the spot where he fell fighting the Chinese Army, defending his post. All the company he had was two local Monpa girls named Sela and Nura. On the morning of November 17, a Chinese machine gun had opened up, pinning a company down. Jaswant and his friends crawled up to the machine gun nest and blew it up with grenades, charging into the smoke permeated with the smell of cordite, bayoneting to death the Chinese soldiers inside. They grabbed the gun as a prize, and began to crawl back towards the Indian lines. The Chinese resumed firing, and Jaswant was hit.

One of his comrades died and Jaswant motioned the other wounded jawan, Gopal Gusain, to take the gun back to the Indian side as a trophy of war. The order to withdraw was given, but Number 4039009, refused. Along with Sela and Nura, he set up interspaced guns and directed a stream of fire at Chinese positions that made the enemy think an entire Indian division was firing at them. Finally a local betrayed the three; the Chinese threw their entire might against Jaswant's position. Sela was killed by a grenade, Nura was captured and Jaswant turned his gun on himself when only one cartridge was left, realising that he was about to be taken prisoner. It is claimed that he killed more than 300 Chinese soldiers in his last stand. A brass bust of Jaswant made by the Indians in his honour stands at the site he fell. It is kept inside the small temple that bears his name, along with other personal possessions. A marble plaque honours him and 161 other soldiers of his battalion who died in the battle of Nuranang, in which the Garhwal Rifles was awarded the battle honour. Whether it is a high-ranking General or a mere jawan, all soldiers stop to pay their respects at Jaswant Garh. The soldiers posted there treat Jaswant as if he is still alive; his boots are spit shined and his uniform is pressed and folded. He has also been promoted, and is now an Honorary Captain in the Indian Army.

EYEBALL TO EYEBALL

Fifty-six years later, on April 15, Jaswant Singh wasn't around when 30-odd Chinese troopers pitched tents in Debsang Bulge in northern Ladakh and refused to leave for three weeks. It came as a surprise to India, considering that since February, the Chinese had not ventured that far into the Indian side of the Line of Actual Control (LAC). Temperatures soared in the tracts around Shyok River in eastern Ladakh, not far from the famously grassless Aksai Chin when the People's Liberation Army (PLA) of China made its audacious and taunting demonstration of aggressive intent. It was reminiscent of the shadow game played between the two countries in 1950, when China expressed its gratitude for Indian "stabilising the Indo-Chinese border" but continued its military buildup in Aksai Chin. Then Prime Minister Nehru had declared in Parliament that "Our maps show that the McMahon Line is our boundary and that is our boundary...we stand by that boundary and we will not let anyone else come across that boundary". But they did.

On August 13, Indian soldiers at Anjaw in Arunachal Pradesh were getting ready for dinner after a gruelling physical training session. Unknown to them, a patrol team of 60 Chinese Army personnel entered about 30 km into Indian territory across the

LAC up to Fishtail in Chaglagam sector. They set up temporary shelters at Plam Plam, an Indian post after crossing the Tashitara Gompa monastery. After two days and nights, the patrol folded up their tents to return to base 20 kilometres from the 1,080-km LAC along Arunachal Pradesh.

Another Chinese long-distance patrol team reached the spot their comrades had vacated. It was detected within a few hours by an Indian patrol. The face-off lasted for about a week. The Indian government did not wish to escalate the situation. After a flag meeting and some diplomacy, the Chinese withdrew without much fuss.

When Prime Minister Manmohan Singh visits Beijing next month, he will be signing a new peace pact—the Border Defence Cooperation Agreement (BDCA), which is a Chinese initiative. A senior visiting PLA official gave the draft to India in March. It took the Depsang intrusion to bring the BDCA to India's attention, after a theory surfaced in South Block corridors mentioning that China staged the border faceoff to ensure that New Delhi gave requisite respect to its draft. Former ambassador and strategic expert Phunchok Stobdan pointed out that Ladakh was a major bone of contention between China and India, unlike Arunachal Pradesh, where Indian political control over the territory is strong and the local people's connect with India is strong. In contrast, its political hold in Ladakh is weak and even local perception has been changing in China's favour, which Beijing is aware of.

Thwarting Efforts

It was in the summer of 1986 when China showed its ugly face for the second time to India. Along the banks of the Sumdorong Chu rivulet in what was then known as the North East Frontier Agency (NEFA), now Arunachal Pradesh, Chinese troopers were feverishly building permanent military structures. On June 26 that year, a month ahead of the 7th round of border talks between the two countries, India lodged a formal protest with China against the intrusion. The Chinese intentions then were clear to India. It wanted to occupy that territory and lay claim to it during the border talks of July 1986.

It took the genius of the then Indian Army chief, General K Sunderji, to undo what Beijing was trying to inflict on India. What the Indian patrol team on that June day in 1986 noticed was two platoons of the PLA raising permanent structures and another 200 reinforcements joining the two platoons to provide them protection.

Within two months, China had also built a helipad, which led to Sundarji taking a tough stand and using the Air Force's transporters to airlift a brigade-sized force to counter the Chinese. Indian forces occupied positions on Hathung La ridge over the Namka Chu River and set up manned defences across the McMahon Line, shocking the Chinese. Their counter was moving eight divisions to eastern Tibet, which was seen by global observers as a sign of possible 1962 repeat.

However, diplomacy came into play and the matter was resolved following the external affairs minister's visit in May 1987 and followed up with then Prime Minister Rajiv Gandhi's visit to Beijing in September 1988, the first after Nehru's.

Hitting Indian Pride

China has been claiming about 90,000 sq km of Arunachal Pradesh along its 1,080-km LAC contiguous with Tibet as its own, even referring to the Indian side as South Tibet. The Chinese are also wary of India's advantage in Chushul-Chumar sector. "Obviously, the Chinese Army was trying to stop India from developing border military infrastructure in Daulat Beg Oldi in April. There the Chinese are at a disadvantage, primarily due to the terrain," a serving Major General of the Indian Army said. During the tense 21-day confrontation, Indian troops were "eye-to-eye" with the PLA, pitching tents opposite Chinese tents 19 km inside Indian territory.

It was a wake-up call. China currently holds 43,000-sq km of eastern Ladakh—Aksai Chin—which the PLA captured in 1962. In hindsight, military experts say that Aksai Chin seems to be China's only strategic objective since 1962, considering that its soldiers withdrew from other areas they had occupied, including Arunachal Pradesh. In 1962, when the Indian Army made its last stand across the frozen river at the 5,411-metre Saser-La pass, armed with only 100 rifle rounds each and a few machine guns, the advancing Chinese army stopped at the McMahon Line. In 2013, too, the Chinese intrusions were meant to be a demonstration of military machismo, for they withdrew after making their point. As if to keep the kettle boiling, the PLA kept up exhibitions of hostility along the LAC periodically—the last one a day before Independence Day.

As the Indian media kept up a never-before focus on the "Chinese threat", it articulated the concern that China had eaten into Indian territory over a period of time. All hell broke loose in New Delhi, when a newspaper reported an official confirmation of a "640 sq km loss", according to a report by National Security Advisory Board convener Shyam Saran. The Opposition immediately raised the issue. BJP's Yashwant Sinha was one of the most vociferous critics. "This is a very serious concern. The government has not taken the Opposition and Parliament into confidence," he said. Mulayam Singh Yadav of the Samajwadi Party—who has been defence minister—has been belligerent on the issue. Defence Minister A K Antony denied the existence of the Saran report. However, he also admitted that the "Chinese build-up of infrastructure is more superior." He added that the Indian side had not created matching infrastructure for long. In 1949, China militarized the Aksai Chin border while India was engaged in preventing Ladakh from being taken by Pakistan.

Ready to Strike

On an average, there are around 250 incidents of Chinese transgressions into the Indian side every year. The Indian defence establishment has no counter move or means to prevent the transgressions, till the time the border dispute is resolved by the special representatives who have talked 16 rounds till date. To be prepared for any eventuality, India has strengthened its military infrastructure along LAC in the last decade. India's Cabinet Committee on Security has given approval for raising a mountain strike corps, with over 50,000 troopers at a cost of '64,000 crore, with special mountain warfare equipment and transport helicopter units. It was in 2010 that India realised the need for more specialised troops to fight the Chinese and two new mountain divisions, with

20,000 troopers each, were raised. India is also building new advanced landing grounds for the Air Force to operate its troop transport aircraft and helicopters from, in both Ladakh and in the North-east.

Already three ALGs have come up in Ladakh—at Daulat Beg Oldi, Fuk Che and Nyoma—apart from developing eight new ALGs at Aalo, Ziro, Mechuka, Tuting Walong, Passighat, Vijoynagar and Tawang. It has deployed two regiments of the Akash air defence missile systems in the North-east facing China, apart from raising two squadrons of its front line Sukhoi Su-30MKI fighter planes at Tezpur and Chabua. Retired Brigadier Arun Sahgal noted that the PLA is concerned over India matching China's military infrastructure in Ladakh at the Lanzhou Military Area Command. India had long realised its folly over ignoring the military infrastructure and the force levels along the LAC. Pakistan is militarily on the wane and its threat to India's western theatre is blunted over its engagement in anti-terror operations on its Afghan border. Defence experts say Pakistan's military infirmity is the reason why India is building roads, bridges and advanced landing grounds, so that mobilisation is easier during any conflict. Of its total of 13 army corps, the Indian Army has four corps with 45,000 soldiers each, facing China—14 Corps at Leh; 33 Corps at Sukna; 4 Corps at Tezpur and 3 Corps at Dimapur, all defensive formations. All its offensive Strike Corps—1 Corps based at Mathura; 2 Corps based at Ambala and 21 Corps in Bhopal focus on Pakistan. The raising of a new Mountain Strike Corps is the first time India has created an offensive formation aimed at China. In the Central Sector, where Uttarakhand's border which China falls, the Indian Army has based three Brigades facing its neighbour.

Strategy in Adversity

The current Indian strategic thought on China and the threat it poses to national security is driven by the China Study Group, a high-powered committee comprising the Foreign Secretary, Defence Secretary, Home Secretary and the Indian Armed Forces chiefs as members. It is supervised and guided by National Security Adviser Shivshankar Menon. The Group is so powerful that not one decision, including the patrol pattern of the Indian troopers and the Indo-Tibetan Border Police (ITBP) men guarding the LAC, the territorial limit up to which they would venture, is taken by local military commanders without its permission. The group worked overtime in April-May during the Debsang face-off. As the three flag meetings of local commanders took place at Spanggur Gap in Ladakh, the Group strove to resolve the issue through diplomacy. In short, it explains the Indian official thought process on how to counter China, which is fast modernising its armed forces and developing military infrastructure on LAC.

However, the Left, accused of being "pro-China", has its own analysis. "Both India and China are emerging economies," says D Raja of CPI. "To that extent, there is a natural competition among them." Advocating dialogue to keep tempers down, Raja points to the possible use of trade to accomplish dominion. "China floods India with cheap goods, which is a problem for us. But China needs the Indian market, and more than that, it needs Indian iron ore," he says, suggesting that border destinies can be dictated by this interdependence, since war is not an option. Like the Left, the NCP, led by Sharad Pawar, calls for dialogue at the defence ministers' level as well as the NSA.

Says NCP ideologue D P Tripathi, "China's perception of an unfavourable strategic Indo-US alliance is what prompts it to keep India under pressure. It also wants to be accepted as a leading axis in world politics." The historical precedents of this fear go back to the days of Chairman Mao. In 1956, the CIA began to recruit and train Tibetan guerrillas at camps in Kalimpong. This was the start of Mao's India paranoia. Says Indo-China expert Swaran Singh, "We are so focused with the US that we have less time for other countries. But, China believes that we are ganging up with the US. So, they are upping the ante." Mao doused the Chinese Army's enthusiasm for action against India on Aksai Chin front fearing that India would allow American U-2 surveillance aircraft to photograph China's nuclear test site at Lop Nor. By then, Mao had begun to see India as an "imperialist" state and wished for Tibet "to remain in a backward state, becoming a 'buffer state' between China and India."

POLITICAL GAMES

Fifty-one years later, a senior Congress minister described the new Chinese premier, Xi Jinping, as a pragmatic leader and dismissed a serious flare-up at the political level. "His first phone call after taking over as prime minister was to Manmohan, and India was one of his first foreign destinations. This shows that he wants to take Indo-China relations to the next level," the minister said.

However, the power structure in China is changing. "The hawks in the PLA want to exacerbate the Sino-Indian border situation, they are the ones ordering the muscle-flexing, which is often without the knowledge or support of Beijing," the minister said. This is parallel to the situation in Pakistan, where a gap of strategic intent exists between the army and the political leadership, and India is perennially caught in this tug-of-war.

The minister pointed out that during the UPA's first tenure, there was much engagement at the informal political level with China. Sonia Gandhi had made a high-profile visit to China, which was not followed up. "The first serious steps towards normalisation of ties were taken during the reign of Rajiv Gandhi, and a systematic border dispute settlement architecture was created," he said. The UPA II, caught up as it was in serious political flux, besides Sonia's own preoccupation with her health, slowed the urgent imperative of building on those interactions.

China watchers speculate on the political weather along the border after the general elections are over in 2014. They do not expect that, if the BJP comes to power, Sino-Indian relations will become skewed.

Conflict Redux

The past continues to live on in the bleak salt flats landscape along India's border with China 5,000 feet above sea level, where six decades ago an Indian patrol discovered signs of heavy construction. Concrete mixers were churning, road rollers were spewing diesel smoke and engineers were shouting out instructions. Labourers were busy like ants, carrying pans of cement on their heads. Along the Aksai-Chin Plain connecting Xinjiang and Tibet, the Chinese were constructing an all-weather road. There was uproar in India and the government immediately issued strong diplomatic protests accusing the Chinese of violating India's territorial integrity. In return, the northern neighbour insisted that Aksai-Chin has always been in its dominion. A flurry of diplomatic activities followed, but India refused to engage in negotiations until the Chinese Army completely withdrew from Aksai-Chin. It was 1957, five years before the night of October 19, 1962, when Chinese artillery opened fire on Indian posts east of India's northern-most military base and India lost its first war since Independence. Much has changed since then, militarily, economically and diplomatically. At stake now is a loss of face at home and abroad, as India faces more and more Chinese incursions along the LAC. The ghosts of 1962 may have been appeased, but they have ever quite left.

INDIA-CHINA BORDER TUSSLE: THE DRAGON IS DREAMING BIG

As China continues to apply sustained military pressure on India's borders in the midst of visits exchanged between the two countries' leaders and senior officials, China's official media continues to publicise articles intended to caution India that China retains the option of initiating military hostilities. The number of articles stating that China will have to resort to military force to settle outstanding border disputes has increased since 2010, with the intensification of the disputes in the South China Sea and especially with Japan. They coincide with the 'rise' in China's economic and military might. Interestingly, Chinese officials routinely advise their Indian counterparts to rein in the Indian media whose 'jingoistic' tenor apparently imposes strains on India-China relations.

In this backdrop the Hong Kong-based daily, Wen Wei Po, published an article in June this year captioned 'Six Wars to be fought by China in the next Fifty Years'. It was re-posted on a Hong Kong website around mid-September. While the author's background is not yet known, the article's layout suggests he has been briefed by some Chinese analysts with extreme nationalist views.

The Wen Wei Po is owned by the People's Republic of China (PRC) and its editor-in-chief is a Chinese Communist Party (CCP) cadre who is often also a member of the Chinese People's Political Consultative Conference (CPPCC). It is part of China's tightly controlled propaganda apparatus. The CPPCC is headed by one of the seven members of the ruling Politburo Standing Committee (PBSC).

Asserting that China can wipe out past humiliations and regain dignity only once it achieves national reunification, the article avers that China will have to fight six wars in the next 50 years to achieve this. It lists these as for the: "unification" of Taiwan which will be fought between 2020-2025; "reconquest" of the Spratlys which will occur between 2025 and 2030; "reconquest of Southern Tibet" which will take place between 2035-2040; "reconquest" of Diaoyu Island and Ryukyu Islands between 2040 and 2045; "unification of Outer Mongolia" between 2045 to 2050; and taking back of the "lands lost to Russia" for which a war will be fought between 2055 and 2060.

The article is confident that China will be victorious, noting additionally that the war for unification with Taiwan will be the first for "New China" and will test the development of the People's Liberation Army (PLA) in modern warfare. It states that China will emerge as the real world power by the mid-21st century. It views the role of the US and Japan as important in determining the duration of the wars to be fought, but assesses that the US will be reluctant to overtly intervene in any military hostilities with Taiwan or Japan. The scenario envisages Japan and Russia as on the decline, the US and India as stagnant, and Central Europe as on the rise consequent to the integration of Europe. It recommends this period as ideal for the "reconquest" of the Diaoyu and Ryukyu Islands.

Relevant for India is the so-called third war for the "reconquest of southern Tibet" projected to take place between 2035-2040. The article states that after taking back Taiwan and the Spratly Islands by 2030, China's military power would have increased substantially in army, navy, air force and space warfare. China will then be a power second only to the US and India will, therefore, lose this war.

Describing "southern Tibet" as the only point of conflict between the two countries, the article observes that India has for long imagined China as an enemy. It takes note of India's close military and economic ties with the US, Russia and Europe, adding that the attitude of Indian officials and media is more friendly towards these countries and "repellent or even hostile" to China. It emphasises that though after 20 years India will lag further behind China in military power, it will nevertheless still be one of the few world powers. If, therefore, China uses military force to "conquer Southern Tibet" then it will have to suffer some losses.

The article recommended that the best strategy and first option for China is to incite India's disintegration. China should try its best to incite Assam and Sikkim to fight for independence. The second option is to export advanced weapons to Pakistan thus helping it to conquer the southern Kashmir region in 2035 and effect the unification of Kashmir. While India and Pakistan are busy fighting each other in Kashmir, Chinese forces should initiate a 'blitz' attack to "conquer southern Tibet". Unable to fight a two-front war, India will lose both. China can then retake Southern Tibet easily, while Pakistan can control the whole of Kashmir. If this plan cannot be adopted, the final and least preferred option is to take direct military action to take back "southern Tibet".

While this article is unlikely to have emanated from high levels in China's military establishment, it does reiterate a theme often articulated in the official Chinese media that China will have to finally resort to the use of armed force to settle outstanding border disputes. Such articles have been appearing after China completed the review of its Asia policy in 2011. A publication of the official CCP mouthpiece in November 2011, for example, recommended that "China adopt new approaches in dealing with its neighbours". It said "goodwill that is one-sided may not bring about harmony with our neighbours" and "sometimes certain altercations (with the neighbours) are appropriate and can foster the return of peace."

"HISSING DRAGON - SQUIRMING TIGER" CHINA'S SUCCESSFUL STRATEGIC ENCIRCLEMENT OF INDIA

Sino Indian relations have been frosty at best and chilly at worst. Besides a brief period of bonhomie between 1954 and 1958, India and China have spent a bulk of their 53 year diplomatic history countering each other. While China perceives itself as the de-facto regional power and a rising global power, India has never conceded to China, either regional superiority or acknowledged its global preeminence. Today, Chinese assistance to Pakistan's nuclear and missile program only adds to Indian notions of Chinese perfidy since the border war of 1962. China's decision to attack India has its origins, in Mao's personality as much as Nehru's forward policy. The objective of this chapter is to assess the nature of the Chinese threat to India. After 1962, China has diligently charted India's strategic encirclement with a high degree of success. India is therefore justifiably concerned about Chinese intentions. China as much as Pakistan, is set to pose a daunting challenge to Indian strategic interests.

After independence, the struggle for regional supremacy began in earnest. Liberal and democratic Nehruvian India was the antithesis of totalitarian and repressive Maoist China. Reclusive and introspective Mao contrasted with gregarious and outgoing Nehru. While Mao grappled with China's internal unrest and political chaos, Nehru played an architect's role in founding The Non-Aligned Movement (NAM). Indeed, the brief border war gave Mao an unprecedented opportunity to "cut India to size and undermine India as an alternative model for the developing world. The swiftness and brute power with which Mao managed to humiliate India not only boosted China's image internationally, but also helped Mao to consolidate domestically when his political fortunes were weakening"

"The question remains, if Mao had still been in retirement, would Liu Shaoqi and Zhou Enlai have chosen to teach Nehru a lesson in quite so a brutal fashion? Probably not, in the light of their support to a conciliatory policy only four months earlier". The former Indian Charge d' affairs, P.K. Banerjee gives the benefit of doubt to Premier Zhou even though he was personally responsible for war preparations against India.

1962 was a watershed in Sino-Indian relations and Mao made good his threat of "teaching India a lesson." That, Mao never entertained serious territorial designs on the Indian North East emerges from recent disclosures in the Bulletin of the Cold War International History Project. In a conversation with Soviet Diplomat S.F. Antonov, Mao said, "We never, under any circumstances, will move beyond the Himalayas. This is completely ruled out. This is an argument over inconsequential pieces of territory."

While it is undeniable that Nehru, guided by faulty intelligence and poor international political assessments adopted a "forward policy" and precipitated the war, contemporary studies have ignored the impact of domestic Chinese politics, personality cults and the international environment that were crucial to the Chinese decision. Indeed, Chairman Mao and his enigmatic personality were central to the decision to attack and humiliate India in October - November, 1962. Mao's behavior towards India flies in face of his engagement tactics with other more powerful nations from which China faced equal if not grater threat.

The fortuitous international environment also aided Mao's decision to cross the Himalayan divide. The Cuban missile crisis in October and the declining threat of KMT invasion in 1962 was central to the timing of the attack. On 26 June, 1962 President Kennedy declared that the US was determined to defend Taiwanese integrity, but in a secret State Department communication, he assured China of not supporting a KMT invasion of the mainland.

With nearly 500,000 troops amassed opposite the Quemoy Islands to repel a KMT assault, it is highly unlikely that Mao would have contemplated a two front war. India's long standing Cold War friend, USSR too, played an unbecoming role. The Soviet nod for the attack on India came on October 14, 1962 at the dinner hosted by Khrushchev for departing Chinese Ambassador Liu Xiao.

So here was India in November 1962, thrashed and beaten lock, stock and barrel by China. Following the war, China relinquished its gains in North East India but retained its gains in North West India in the Aksai Chin Plateau where it had built an all weather road connecting Xianjian to Tibet.

Spurred by these events, India went nuclear on May 8, 1974 and Pakistan followed suit. Even though Pakistan became an overt nuclear weapon state in May 1998, it had acquired nuclear weapons capability in the mid 1980's. Chinese support to Pakistan's nuclear weapons program is unprecedented because this is the only case of a state consciously assisting weaponization of another state. Though blue prints and plans for Pakistan's nuclear program were stolen by Dr. A.Q. Khan from URENCO plant in Almeo Netherlands, it is subsequent Chinese scientific and technological support from China that nurtured the fledgling Pakistani program and prevented it from fizzling out.

The origins of Sino-Pak defense cooperation lie in a comprehensive nuclear cooperation agreement signed in 1986. Chinese assistance to Pakistan's nuclear aspirations predate and post date China's accession to the NPT in 1992, and the signing of the IAEA safeguards agreement in 1993. The Chinese involvement has been meticulously documented by the US Intelligence community and several Non Governmental Organizations. Chinese assistance ranges from provision of special industrial machine tools and gadgets like ring magnets, required for nuclear weapon fabrication to other ingredients like Tritium gas essential for achieving fusion in thermonuclear weapons and boosting nuclear yields. As early as 1983, China had transferred weapon design and fissile material, sufficient for 2 devices with an estimated yield of 20-25 KT. From pressurized water reactors to unsafe-guarded plutonium reprocessing facilities, China has systematically planned, directed, encouraged and eventually ensured a modicum of reliability and survivability to the Pakistani nuclear weapon program.

China's assistance to Pakistan has extended to short and medium range ballistic missile capability acquisition as well. Like its assistance in the nuclear field, China's generosity in sharing missile technology is well documented too. In fact, the US imposed sanctions on China in 1991 and 1993 for sale of the DF-11 / CSS-7 related technology to Pakistan. The Hatf-1, Hatf-2 and Shaheen bear uncanny resemblance to Chinese M-11 and M-9 series.

Central to China's strategic encirclement strategy of India are the SAARC (South Asian Association for Regional Cooperation) states including Myanmar. In this regard, China's liaisons with Bangladesh, Nepal, Bhutan and Myanmar deserve close scrutiny. A perilous quadrangular nuclear situation seems to be developing in Myanmar involving 3 other nuclear powers- China, Pakistan and Russia. Myanmar officially confirmed on January 21, 2002 that it is building a nuclear reactor with Russian assistance. Two Pakistani nuclear scientists Suleiman Asad and Mohammed Ali Mukhtar are known to have visited Myanmar in an advisory capacity in November 2001. This came to light when US officials were investigating the Al Qaida infrastructure in that region.

India's relationship with Myanmar's military junta has largely been antagonistic. For example, former First Lady, Mrs. Usha Narayanan, wife of President R.K Narayanan is a close friend of incarcerated Burmese democratic icon, Aung San Suu Kyi. The current Indian Defense Minister, George Fernandes has long allowed exiled Burmese students to operate out of his 3 Krishna Menon Marg residence even before he assumed that post as India's Defence Minister.

India's key concern about Chinese activity in Myanmar stems from Chinese activity in the Coco Islands. The island was gifted to Burma by Nehru. Air strip, signal intelligence nodes and an 85 meter jetty under construction pose an emerging threat to the Indian tri services command in Port Blair, Andaman Islands about 190 nautical miles (300 Kilometers) away. With a distance of only 22 nautical miles from Landfall, the northernmost island of the Andaman archipelago, the Coco's pose a significant ELINT (Electronic Intelligence) and SIGINT (Signal Intelligence) threat to India's missile testing range, Chandipur-on-Sea and The Sriharikota Launching Range designed to assemble, test, launch large Indian multi-stage rockets. The launch range is situated in Sriharikota Island about 62 miles, north of the South Indian city of Chennai.

Chinese listening posts in Sittwe (Aykab) and Zedetkyi Kyun (St. Luke's) off the Terrasserim coast in Southern Myanmar enable China to monitor traffic in the Straits of Malacca and Phillips Channel prior to entering South China Sea. China has also pledged about US$ 1.2 Billion worth of military hardware to Myanmar. The expansion of the naval base at Hainggyi Island could on completion support an infrastructure capable of docking Chinese SSN and SSBN submarines, including those being procured from Russia. Indian suspicions are well founded because the current ELITN, SIGINT and burgeoning naval infrastructure exceeds Myanmar's legitimate security concerns. In effect, the ongoing Chinese activity in Myanmar seems to give corroborate a statement attributed to PLAN General Staff Logistics Department Director, Zhao Nanqi, "We can no longer accept the Indian ocean as India's ocean". Indeed, China is trying hard to live up to the Myanmarese adulation, "paukphaw" (full brothers).

Like Myanmar, Bangladesh too is emerging as a frontline state in China's effort to strategically suffocate India. Ironically, Bangladesh in spite of Indian military intervention in 1971 to avert its humanitarian tragedy and facilitate its independence, remains categorically anti Indian. In deferment to the sensitivities of Pakistan, China refused diplomatic recognition to Bangladesh until four years after its birth in 1975. Beijing described Bangladesh's emergence as a product of Indo-Soviet machinations and consistently called for an "independent foreign policy" and "opposition to outside interference" . Only on the assassination of the pro India, Bangladeshi Prime Minister, Sheikh Mujib on August 31, 1975, did China accord diplomatic recognition to Bangladesh, 15 days thence.

The principal bone of contention between the two countries is illegal immigration. According to Lt. Gen (retd.) S.K. Sinha, former Governor of the North Eastern State of Assam, illegal migration from Bangladesh accounted for approximately 22% of the growth differential between the Islamic community in the Assam (77%) and the rest of India (55%) between 1971 and 1991. Given the problem of religious fundamentalism, the presence of an estimated 5 million illegal Bangladeshi migrants and the right wing Hindu BJP, the problem of illegal migration has assumed destabilizing proportions. It is against this backdrop that Bangladesh's first and only Defense Cooperation Agreement was signed during the visit of the current Prime Minister, Begum Khalida Zia in December 2002. "This agreement ambiguous in wording includes at least military training and defense production without specifying as to whom China and Bangladesh might be cooperating against or what weapons are sought for joint production."

The Dragon has not left any unturned stones. In stalking India, it has made assiduous efforts to cultivate the remaining SAARC countries of Nepal, Bhutan and Sri Lanka. Nepal despite its strong cultural affinity to India has sought to remain equidistant between the India and China. On more than one occasion in its history, Nepal has played one country against the other, complicating India's National Security Management Strategy. In the 1960's, King Mahendra agreed to the construction of Kathmandu-Kodari highway linking Tibetan Lhasa with Nepalese Kathmandu. Though the Chinese proposal may have been presented to bait Nepalese acceptance of Chinese proposals on the Sino-Nepalese border issue, the strategic ramifications for India was immense. Bounded by India on three sides and high Himalayas on the fourth, the Lhasa-Kathmandu highway freed landlocked Nepal of its India dependence for trade and commerce. The new highway provided China with its second all weather strategic road access to South Asia. The first one being Karakorum Highway, linking the Pakistani city of Rawalpindi to the Kashgar in the Xinjiang Autonomous Region of China. The importance that China attaches to Nepal is self evident from examining the level and frequency of CCP functionaries visiting Nepal since the diplomatic relations were established on August 1, 1955.

The reclusive Kingdom of Bhutan, too hasn't escaped China's overtures. However, the effects, thus far have remained benign largely due to India's scrupulous adherence to Indo-Bhutan Treaty of Friendship and Cooperation, 1949. Being adjacent to the disputed Tawang Tract, in Indian state of Arunachal Pradesh, also claimed by China, Bhutan serves a buffer function. Bhutan therefore has significant strategic leverage with India. In return for acceptance of India's advice on external relations, as per Article 2 of the 1949 Treaty, the Bhutanese Kingdom remains free to pursue a domestic policy of its liking. Bhutan, like India has unresolved border issues with China. Given the 1949 treaty, Chinese efforts in solving the border problem directly with Bhutan are unlikely to succeed. The Northern Bhutanese border is an extension of The McMahon line, acceptable to India but unacceptable to China. Until the seventies, Bhutan's border issues with China were incorporated with in the scope of Sino-Indian border discussion. The Chinese stand remained that the Sino-Bhutanese border has never been officially demarcated and it would like to do so "through friendly consultations", the matter "concerns China and Bhutan alone" and "the Indian government has no right to intervene in it". Since 1984, the two countries commenced direct border talks. In 1998, during the twelfth round of border talks, the two countries signed "Agreement to Maintain Peace and Tranquility on the Bhutan-China Border". After 16 rounds of border talks, the Sino-Bhutan border remains tranquil yet under dispute.

Thus we have seen that the "Ghost of 1962" is yet to be exorcised. Following the flight of the Dalai Lama in 1959 and India's crushing defeat in 1962, it seems concerns of Tibetan nationalism has driven China to adopt a policy of unremitting hostility towards India. Like an iron hand clothed in a velvet glove, China's success has been the successful petrifaction of the Indian strategic community. By flouting international nuclear and missile proliferation protocols, China is singularly responsible for the nuclearizing Pakistan, which defines its raison-d-etre in anti Indian terms. China has actively courted a strategic relationship with India's satellite neighbors like Nepal, Bangladesh, Bhutan and Myanmar. Of all regional states, Myanmar is emerging as the single largest threat to Indian strategic interests in South East Asia. Burgeoning Chinese naval capability in Myanmar, may in a few years allow China to interdict regional Sea Lanes of Communication (SLOC). It is also possible that China will persuade Bangladesh to develop Chittagong as a deep water port on the lines of Gwadar in East Pakistan.

Chinese aims have not fully succeeded in the SAARC region because of the geographical location of these states. No matter what, China's efforts are at a conventional level, Indian leverage in facilitating overland trade and commerce, vital to SAARC countries is a geographical reality. The dependence on India ensures a degree of leverage that China will find hard to match. Having said that, the long- term trend indicates a growing penetration of what once was an undisputed Indian sphere of influence.

After 14 rounds of border talks between India and China, The Joint Working Group has not produced any progress except meaningless platitudes It is surprising that, in spite of vigorous affirmations after every round of a Joint Working Group meeting, The McMahon Line comes no closer to resolution in 2003 than it was in 1914, when Lonchen Shatra, the Tibetan Plenipotentiary and Sir Henry McMahon, Secretary to the British Indian Government initiated the fateful documents.

Though maps of the least disputed "middle sector" falling under the newly formed Indian state of Uttaranchal have been exchanged, it seems China is on the look out for unilateral concessions that it has in the past. During the Indian Foreign Minister Jaswant Singh's visit to Beijing in March 2002, it was decided to complete delineation of the LAC (Line of Actual Control) in the western sector by the year end. Yet no progress has been made. India's bugbear Pakistan seems to have crept into the picture again. The western sector is complicated by Pakistan's secession of 5180 sq km Indian territory to China in 1962. By discussing this sector, China risks opening up the Sino-Pakistan Boundary Agreement, which it ostensibly will try to avoid. India on its part has steadfastly refused Chinese hints that the western sector be considered sans the Pakistan ceded territory. Nothing seems to have happened in the 40 years since the ill-fated border war to indicate Chinese intentions toward India have turned benign. The Dragon is on the move in Tibet also. In December 2001, China successfully completed two sections of the first railway tunnel of the Qinghai-Tibet link, in pursuit of the 1118 Km Gormu-Lhasa railway line. The railway link while connection Lhasa-Beijing and Shanghai, will reduce travel time between Gormu to Lhasa from

72 to 16 hours. Furthermore, the railway link provides the first reliable transportation means to haul back Tibetan mineral resources to mainland China. Militarily, on completion of the railway line, China can mobilize approximately 12 Divisions or 120,000 men in less than 2 days. Thus, India's strategic future is fraught with great danger.

India's problem remains its discomfiture with its preeminent size and its false pretensions of being an "emerging great power". Sadly, India lacks the stomach and the spine to be one. Under these circumstances, I am, but, forced to conclude that the Chinese containment efforts shall continue till India concedes or India miraculously grows a part of its autonomy that its seems to have lost since 1971. Between the two scenarios, it is likely that India will continue her pathetic existence, scorned, abused and treated inconsequentially by great and small powers alike.

DRAGON FIRE IN HIMALAYAS FLUSTERS INDIA

Indian analysts are in two minds whether the tensions were precipitated at a local level on the Chinese side or were part of a deliberate move calibrated from Beijing with a political or diplomatic objective.

The tension in the Ladakh sector of India's disputed border with China subsided after some four weeks of suspense and high drama as unobtrusively as it first appeared in mid-April. The only difference between the beginning and the end is that while the Indians were taken by surprise by the Chinese troop "intrusion," the withdrawal has been a negotiated affair.

This difference underscores three things. One, China's intention was not belligerent. Two, the negotiations for the easing of the tension took place through the existing mechanism for the resolution of such precipitate situations. Three, negotiations would have resulted in some sort of understanding, which in turn helped defuse the situation.

The Indian analysts are in two minds whether the tensions were precipitated at a local level on the Chinese side or were part of a deliberate move calibrated from Beijing with a political or diplomatic objective. When it comes to the "inscrutable" Chinese, there is scope for seamless speculations.

It stands to reason that given the high sensitivity of the border dispute with India and the volatility of the situation in Tibet and their centrality for the Chinese foreign policy as a whole, the local units of the People's Liberation Army deployed to Tibet and the China-India border region could not have acted thoughtlessly. Besides, taking into account the way the Chinese political system works, a new leadership in Beijing was just about setting out on a ten-year long journey and a misstep by the caravan was highly improbable.

What might have been the Chinese objective? The Chinese have said very, very little – nothing, in fact, in comparison with the high-decibel rhetoric on the Philippines, Vietnam or Japan. Evidently, they were chary of inflaming passions.

The Indian establishment too – that is, the political and foreign policy establishment – also kept a "blackout" on the negotiations leading to the easing of the tension. What really caused the tension? Was the tension eased as a result of an understanding reached? If so, what was the deal? But matters have been left to conjecture.

Putting together the bits and pieces of whatever percolated through the secrecy veil, this was indeed a "localized affair," as Prime Minister Manmohan Singh put it. Delhi cauterized the wound and went about with the business of life – an Indian military delegation visited Beijing as originally scheduled; External Affairs Minister Salman Khurshid paid an official visit to China; and, a cordial and ceremonial welcome was given to the visiting Chinese Premier Li Keqiang.

In a nutshell, it would appear that the Chinese side compelled Delhi to intervene at the highest level to remove certain Indian deployments to the hotly contested eastern Ladakh sector of the border through the recent period, which they found objectionable and threatening their sensitive communication links in the region, after having failed to resolve the issue at the local level. And in the bargain, the border dispute itself has come to the front burner, something which the Chinese side had been wanting and the

Indians were reluctant about. The Special Representatives of the two countries who are entrusted with the responsibility to negotiate a settlement of the border dispute are to meet in Beijing next month.

However, if it seems a happy denouement, nothing could be further from the truth. The question that begs an answer is why the Chinese resorted to pressure tactic at a time when the ties with India seemed on an upward curve as signified by the extraordinary gesture by Li to make India his first visit abroad after assuming office. Curiously, these are times when Beijing has its plate full already with acrimonies, friction and tensions with a number of its neighbours and it didn't look good to pick up yet another row with yet another neighbour.

All in all, the Chinese may have made a point to the Indian leadership that war is far too serious a matter to be left to soldiers. Put differently, they may have drawn attention to the danger that any "forward policy" with a view to secure unilateral advantages on the ground along the disputed Line of Actual Control [LoAC] that separates the two countries' armed forces could lead to ugly situations, fraught with high risk of confrontation.

The heart of the matter is that there is an eerie similarity between what happened last month and the action-reaction syndrome ensuing from India's "forward policy" in the run-up to the 1962 conflict. From the Chinese perspective, it is advantageous to "freeze" the situation as of now since they already enjoy many tactical advantages on the ground in terms of the geography and logistics and communication links.

The Indians, on the other hand, are acutely conscious of their disadvantages and would like to do something about it on a priority basis to bring about some parity. Clearly, there is plenty of scope for flashpoints arising in the future too unless there is a conscious political attempt on both sides to ensure that peace and tranquility prevails on the LoAC.

The 1962 conflict with China still rankles in the Indian consciousness and the security analysts acknowledge the existence of a "revenge" mentality. Of course, that is plainly jingoistic and cannot be injected into the policymaking processes in Delhi. Neither the present climate in world politics and the co-relation of forces internationally nor the dismal state of India's political economy allows Delhi the latitude to contemplate settling scores with China through coercive methods.

But what is most certainly going to happen is that the Indian policymakers will hunker down. To be sure, they have gone through Li's visit with impeccable dignity and composure. They didn't mind that after all that happened so very recently the Chinese dignitary reached out to the Indian public opinion showering petals of goodwill all around. They even talked trade issues with Li.

But deep down there is a profound sense of disquiet. The impression is sinking in that there has been a breach of trust on the part of the Chinese. The detractors of the government's policy of constructive engagement of China smell blood. The Chinese incursion is being projected into the public discourse as yet another manifestation of Beijing's malfeasance toward India.

How this plays out on the geopolitical plane will bear watch. India will at all times want to retain its strategic autonomy, but, equally, a credible enough case can be made out that given the uncertainties in the ties with China, India needs to be part of an alliance system involving other like-minded countries that are wary of Chinese intentions. The current visit of Manmohan Singh to Japan assumes added significance from this perspective. The Indian defence minister A.K. Antony is also due to visit Australia. The US-India Strategic Dialogue is scheduled to take place in Delhi in June, which also involves secretary of state John Kerry's first official visit to India and his talks with the Indian leadership at the highest level will dwell upon the US' rebalancing strategy in Asia.

The "pro-US" lobby in the Indian media and think tanks has resuscitated the thesis (which didn't find acceptance so far at the policy level) that India should tap into the US' rebalancing strategy and build up its strategic capabilities. Indeed, the tensions with China become a powerful argument for India to develop close military ties with the US, Japan and Australia.

Having said that, there are overlapping templates in the geopolitics of Asia-Pacific, which complicate India's policy options – for instance, Obama administration's determined push to make China's new leadership a "stakeholder" in the international system as evident in the initiative to hold the forthcoming summit with President Xi Jinping in California on June 7-8; Asian countries' reticence to be part of any containment strategy toward China; the steady deepening and growing interplay between the ASEAN economies and China's growth strategy. Even with Japan, the caveat must be added that Manmohan Singh is visiting Shinzo Abe's Japan. Again, the US' capacity to commit to a long-term "pivot to Asia" is itself in doubt, given the imponderables in the recovery of its economy and the decline in its global influence.

Paradoxically, Beijing has weakened those very power centres in Delhi, which were working to usher in a brave new world of India-China partnership against some very heavy odds, whereby the two countries would work together on their convergences and shared interests even as they work on the border problem.

2

Chinese Intrusions Across the LAC

Reacting to President Pranab Mukherjee's visit to Arunachal Pradesh in November of this year, the Chinese foreign ministry spokesperson Qin Gang stated that "We hope that India will proceed along with China, protecting our broad relationship, and will not take any measures that could complicate the problem, and together we can protect peace and security in the border regions". China has routinely protested top Indian policymakers visiting Arunachal Pradesh which it claims as its territory along with Aksai Chin. In October 2009, China expressed deep dissatisfaction when Prime Minister Manmohan Singh visited Arunachal Pradesh as part of an election campaign for the state assembly elections. China again reacted sharply to the visit of the Indian Defence Minister, A K Antony to Arunachal Pradesh when on February 25, 2012, the Chinese foreign ministry spokesperson, Hong Lei stated that such visits create complications towards resolution of the border issues. This issue is further complicated by a 4, 000 km border dispute.

Recently, a Border Defence Cooperation Agreement (BDCA) was signed between China and India during the visit of Prime Minister Manmohan Singh to China. Both sides agreed to refrain from military offensives at the border and share information on military exercises near the Line of Actual Control (LAC) through regular border personnel meetings. The good news about the BDCA is that it institutionalizes the process of conflict management at the border, if and when intrusions take place. The bad news is that the agreement does not resolve the differing perceptions of the LAC itself. Hence, intrusions will continue to occur. The other critical issue which remains unresolved is China's claim over 90, 000 square kms of territory in India's eastern sector and 38, 000 square kms of territory in the Western sector. History will tell us that territorial disputes between major powers with geographic proximity have resulted in military conflict. Moreover, the likelihood of conflict is high when the political systems embroiled in territorial disputes differ: China's authoritarian system *versus* India's democracy.

The Pattern

What has been the pattern of China's border intrusions? For one, it has occurred on both sectors. Second, it has increased in the last few years. For instance, Chinese intrusions across the LAC totaled 180 in 2011 and had a rising trend in 2012 going forward. Third, these intrusions are determined to make China's presence felt at the LAC.

Tense and dangerous situations kept lurking on the LAC in 2012.[3] In May 2012, two PLA patrols comprising 50 soldiers reached Thangla, Chantze, in West Kameng District of the eastern sector only turning back after they met with Indian forces. 30 PLA soldiers crossed over to Asaphila in Arunachal Pradesh on May 19 and destroyed a patrol hut of the Indian forces. A PLA patrol painted China on the rocks near Charding-Nilung Nala in Demchok in Ladakh on July 8, 2012. Such events continued with further intrusions by China in the Trig Heights and Pangong Tso Lake.

In the spring of 2013, the border witnessed another altercation when a Chinese border patrol set up camp in the Ladakh sector of Jammu and Kashmir. The Chinese intrusion in the remote Daulat Beg Oldi sector may have, as evident from the flag meeting minutes, been in retaliation of the Indian Army's construction of a single watch tower along the LAC in Chumar division. Chumar, a remote village on Ladakh-Himachal Pradesh border, is claimed by the Chinese as its own territory and have been frequented by helicopter incursions almost every year. Chumar represents a

Chinese vulnerability as it is the only area across the LAC to which the Chinese do not have direct access. On July 16, 2013, 50 PLA soldiers riding on horses and ponies crossed over into Chumar and staked their claims to the territory and only went back after a banner drill with the Indian border troops. This had been preceded by two Chinese helicopters violating Indian air space over Chumar on July 11. This intrusion coincided with India's decision to raise a *Mountain Strike Corp* of 50, 000 along the China-India border. On August 13, 2013 Chinese troops intruded more than 20 kilometres inside the Chaglagam area of Arunachal Pradesh and stayed there for two days.

The Vortex

Bolstering such aggression at the border is China's steady expansion of military capabilities centered in the plateau of the Tibet Autonomous Region (TAR). China has been shooting for border dominance via military means and has built the required military infrastructure throughout the TAR. The operational objectives are to initiate and sustain intense 'shock and awe' type blitzkrieg short campaigns against India. The military machine to achieve these objectives consists of land and air forces backed by stockpiled logistics and supplies. China has built road and rail networks in Tibet, which provide ground mobility to 400,000 PLA soldiers in the two military regions opposite India. It has deployed upgraded ballistic missiles, added several new dual use airfields in Tibet and expanded its military assets transport capability. Advanced Chinese fighter aircraft stationed in TAR are capable of operating at high altitudes.

What is however interesting to note is that in the overall scheme of China's airpower there are no major air bases within short strike range of India. Rather, in the PLA's battle strategy, the Indian air force assets across the LAC will be ideal targets for the PLA ballistic missiles stockpiled in underground tunnels built into the mountainside in Xinjiang and Tibet. These missiles are located in proximity to the LAC with ready access from the Western Tibet highway. To destroy the supply logistics and transportation of Indian ground forces up to the LAC, the PLA plans include rocket artillery massed fire-assaults combined with air strikes. To war-game out such a theatre, the PLA conducted its first joint Army-Air Force live-fire exercise on the Qinghai-Tibet plateau simulating the higher altitudes of the Himalayas in 2010.[7] Interestingly, the Chinese military transported combat equipment for the exercise using the Qinghai-Tibet railroad, which was a first. The PLA and the PLAAF (PLA Air Force) followed up in 2011 with live-fire exercises on the lower plateau and higher mountains on the Qinghai-Tibet Plateau. For example, the PLAAF assets deployed in the Shigatse air base such as Su-27SKs, Su-27UBKs and J-10s engaged in air sorties in coordination with ground-based radar. Again a closer look at the level of PLAAF component in these exercises were limited to roughly platoon sized detachments reflecting the absence of offensive strike and power projection air capabilities in the TAR. But certainly these exercises threw up a lot of smoke and noise intended for the Indians who had their ears pressed to the ground not far away.

The real component of China's operational strategy vis-à-vis India at the border are its missiles deployed to the Tibetan vicinity. China replaced its old liquid fuelled, nuclear capable CSS-3 intermediate range ballistic missile with "more advanced CSS-5 MRBMs". Intercontinental missiles such as the DF-31 and DF-31A have been deployed by China at Delingha, north of Tibet. China has also deployed the solid fuelled DF-21 in Delingha with a range of 2, 150 kms, which is within striking distance of Delhi (2, 000 kms from Delingha). The DF-21 can be launched from either a 13 or 15 metres diameter pad difficult to detect by satellites because of its mobility. Missiles can also escape detection since they are housed in underground tunnels. Such tunnels exist in Yatung, in the Chumbi valley, close to Sikkim.

Motorized Capability

Tibet offers a flat surface which augments motorized mobility, which China has exploited fully. China has deployed Main Battle Tanks (MBT) and infantry combat vehicles in Tibet for defensive purposes in case there is a future conflict with India. As well as the mountainous region opposite Northeast India, MBTs have been hauled up and positioned along the LAC. On August 18,

2013, the Tibet Military Command (TMC) of the PLA conducted a wartime river-crossing support drill organized by an engineer regiment in the waters of the Yarlung Tsangpo River. The regiment conducted the drill with new-type heavy pontoon bridge equipment.

The PLA's ace card is however it's Construction Corps workforce, a highly efficient and disciplined force that can roll out metaled roads during war. Gravel roads on the LAC enable better water drainage during the monsoons as well as avoids Indian radar, which the PLA has taken full advantage of, having the quick capability of converting gravel roads to black topped. The PLA has an edge over the Indian Army at the LAC since it is not tasked to maintain a constant physical vigil, rather content with the usage of networked and remotely-controlled surveillance systems. These surveillance capabilities are augmented with strategically built barren flat ground patches along the LAC to serve as helipads for deploying Rapid Reaction Forces (RRF) whenever required. The RRF, also called the 'Resolving Emergency Mobile Combat Forces (REMCF)' is the PLA's rapid strike force. The airborne RRF are strategically located within TAR and can be rapidly deployed within 48 hours on the LAC through the network of medium-lift and attack helicopters. The PLA deployment on the LAC opposite Arunachal Pradesh is drawn from the General Army bases in Chengdu and Yunnan. Interestingly, the flanking maneuvers of airborne units combined with jungle warfare training of the PLA units have been strategized to unleash the localized blitzkrieg effect. These efforts are vindicated by dual-use airports near the LAC at Shigatse Pingan and Ngari Gunsa in addition to Lhasa, Nyingchi, and Qamdo airports. The surface transportation backbone in the TAR include highways, the railway line and oil pipeline from Gormo to Lhasa, the eastern highway from Chengdu to Lhasa and the western highway running along the LAC though Aksai Chin.

Policy Insights

Three critical policy insights can be drawn from China's intrusions across the LAC and military development in TAR and neighboring areas.

First, China's repeated intrusions are bolstered by its rapid military infrastructure development in its own border regions.

Second, China feels compelled to showcase its military presence to India across the LAC due to its own "vulnerability perception" and lack of political legitimacy in Tibet. China is deeply suspicious about the intentions of the Dalai Lama and the Tibetan-Government in Exile in India. China interprets India's support to the Dalai Lama as a long term Indian strategic objective to free Tibet from China. Hence, any increase in Indian military presence near the LAC is viewed, not only as Indian assertiveness on the border but also connected to plausible Indian plans to provide support to a restive Tibetan population in Tibet.

Third, the US "pivot to Asia" policy has only made China more aggressive with regard to its territorial claims as is seen by its unilateral declaration of an "Air Defence Identification Zone (ADIZ)" over the disputed islands in the East China Sea. The new President Xi Jinping is apparently following an aggressive Chinese posture with regard to its territorial claims. India must therefore remain alert to the fact that escalation across the LAC is likely despite the BDCA. Moreover, India must game out the likely security consequences if China decides to suddenly impose a similar unilateral ADIZ over Arunachal Pradesh.

CHINESE INTRUSIONS INTO INDIA'S BORDERS EVER END?

There has been a faceoff between the Chinese People's Liberation Army (PLA) troops and Indian soldiers in Burtse and Depsang in northern Ladakh, as late as March 20 and 28, 2015, according to press reports.

The two locations had been the targets of the PLA patrolling in the past also. The involved Chinese troops withdrew to their areas after being challenged by the Indian side. The reports are disquieting from India's point of view. The development, if confirmed, comes at a time close to the scheduled visit to China of the Indian Prime Minister Modi in May 2015. Modi had told China that if bilateral relations were to improve then border intrusions by PLA troops had to cease. Going by the India-China

Joint Statement issued at the end of President Xi Jinping's visit to India (September 2014) which laid stress on border tranquility, it appeared that the PRC understood what Modi said. Even then, the latest incident in Ladakh has happened. It will therefore be incumbent on the Chinese side to explain why there is still no let up in its transgressions across Indian borders.

India- China borders remain rather quiet without any serious military incident since last several years. The last major standoff between the troops of the two sides took place in 1987 in Sumdorong Chu valley in Arunachal Pradesh. It followed the veteran Chinese leader Deng Xiaoping's threat in October 1986, as reported in the press, to teach a lesson to India if it continued nibbling across the border. This being so, Chinese PLA intrusions into India's borders have been a regular feature in recent periods; the reported March 2015 border happenings are a case in point.

Are the continuing border incidents in the India-China border 'transgressions' or 'intrusions'? Each side interprets the border happenings differently. India alleges that the Chinese troops are carrying out 'transgressions' into the border which according to it means that they cross over to Indian territory only to eventually retreat to their side. India at the same time admits Chinese 'intrusions' are occurring some times which it sees as their crossing over to Indian side, but staying put. It says that no 'intrusion' has been reported or taken place on the border including Sikkim, during the five years since 2010. The People's Republic of China (PRC), on its part, refers in general only to occurrences of "isolated incidents" in the border. It however feels that India is also transgressing along the LAC and that such 'violations' against China could be more than double than that has been alleged by India. The intentions of the two parties in any case look to downplay the tensions along the LAC; both seem to be against attaching too much importance to border crossings in the interest of overall bilateral ties. Importantly, they agree on one point, i.e. Differing perceptions of each other on the LAC are contributing to border tensions. Given below, is data on notable Chinese intrusions into Indian borders in recent years, including on the PRC's relevant prominent statements and cartographic positions:

Feb 1997: Chinese PLA intruded 6 kms across India's Himachal Pradesh. It happened subsequent to former PRC President Jiang Zemin's visit to India in November 1996. The incident happened despite the 1993 India-China agreement for maintenance of peace and tranquility along the LAC and the November 1996 agreement on Confidence Building Measures in the Military Field along the LAC in the India-China Border areas.

26.6.2003: The PLA intruded in the Asaphila region of the upper Subansiri District of Arunachal Pradesh, which is one of the eight known pockets of dispute (In Arunachal: Thag La, Sumdorong Chu and Yangshi in Kameng, Asaphila in Subansiri and Madan Ridge in Lohit; in Ladakh and Uttarakhand: Trig Heights, Yakla and Barahoti). The incident happened when Indian Prime Minister Vajpayee was on an official visit to Beijing. 10 Indian soldiers were abducted by Chinese military according to reports.

May 2005: Chinese troops intruded into Asaphila again. The incident happened after former Chinese Prime Minister Wen Jiabao's visit to India in April 2005 and despite India-China Protocol on "Modalities for the Implementation of CBMs in the Military Field along the LAC in India-China Border Areas", signed during Wen's visit. As per protocol, settled population in the border is not to be disturbed. (The Chinese side denied the incident).

November 2006: The then PRC President Hu Jinato visited India. Prior to that, the PRC Ambassador to India Sun Yuxi affirmed that "the whole of the so-called state of Arunachal Pradesh is Chinese territory. Tawang is only one of the places in it. We are claiming all of that".

2009: Chinese Foreign Ministry protested the then Indian Prime Minister Dr Manmohan Singh's visit to Arunachal Pradesh.

December 2010: Former Chinese Prime Minister Wen Jiabao visited India. Prior to that, Beijing denied visa to India's Northern Army Commander and began issuing stapled visas to residents of Jammu and Kashmir.

2012: Chinese Foreign Ministry protested the visit to Arunachal Pradesh by the then Indian Defence Minister.

2013: Chinese Foreign Ministry protested the visit to Arunachal Pradesh by the Indian President Pranab Mukherjee.

April 2013 – early May 2013: Chinese intruded in Daulat Beg Oldi (DBO), Ladakh region, and Depsang plains of Aksai Chin. They set up camps in tents in Depsang valley. The PLA also intruded in Chaglagam area in Arunachal Pradesh. All such intrusions happened prior to Chinese Premier Li Keqiang's first visit to India (19-21 May 2013). Indian officials say Chinese Depsang intrusion was 19 km deep inside Indian Territory, ahead of even the Chinese perception of the LAC.

June 2014: Coinciding with Indian Vice President Ansari's visit to China, the PRC published a map showing the entire Arunachal Pradesh and large chunks of Jammu and Kashmir as Chinese territory.

24.6. 2014: The PLA intruded into Pangong Lake, Ladakh; Chinese troops made a 6 km deep incursion. Stayed for 2 hours in the high speed boats and went back.

September 2014: The Chinese troops intruded in Chumar area of Ladakh. Intrusion by Chinese civilians at Demchok along the LAC also took place. 1000 Chinese troops intruded into 3 kms inside India's Chumar territory. Chumar incident lasted for a week. It reflected a Chinese claim on a new area. It happened ahead of, during and beyond Chinese President Xi Jinping's visit to India (17 – 19 Sep. 2014). China however withdrew its troops from Chumar finally. China's objection was reportedly to India's construction of a road in the area.

January 2015: Chinese Foreign Ministry protested Japanese minister's recognition of Arunachal Pradesh as part of India (Japanese foreign minister Fumio Kishida, New Delhi, January 2015)

20.2.2015: China protested Indian Prime Minister Modi's visit to Arunachal Pradesh; Chinese Vice Foreign Minister summoned Indian envoy to protest; Chinese Foreign Ministry and the PRC embassy in New Delhi, also protested.

8.3.2015: Chinese Foreign Minister Wang Yi said that the Sino-Indian border dispute "has been contained. At the moment, the boundary negotiations are in the process of building up small positive developments. It is like climbing a mountain and the going is tough because we are on the way up."

20.3.2015 & 28.3.2015: The PLA intruded in Burtse and Depsang in Northern Ladakh.

2.4.2015: The PRC Foreign Ministry spokesperson said at a regular press briefing that China is ready to work with India to find a comprehensible and reasonable solution to the border dispute, adding that the dispute is a "huge" one in the eastern sector of the Sino-Indian border and is undeniable fact".

Intrusions- Broad Trend

A close examination of data given in paragraphs 4 & 5 above reveals a broad trend with respect to China's intrusions across Indian borders, as listed below:

- It can be seen that the intrusions have happened during or close to the periods of exchanges of high level visits between India and China. No doubt, the PRC's primary motive behind such acts is to reinforce its border claims against India on such important occasions; more importantly, China might also be hoping that the intrusions could push India into defensive positions during the crucial bilateral talks taking place during these visits on various strategic issues dividing them including the border.
- China's intrusions seem to be extending to new areas; this would mean expansion of its border claims. So far, there have been 8 areas of dispute in its thinking - Thagla, Sumdorongchu, Yangshi, Asaphila and Madan ridge (all in Arunachal Pradesh) and Trig Heights and Yakla (both in Ladakh region) and Barahoti (Uttarkhand). New additions being noticed are Chumar, Pangong, DBO and Depsang, all in Western Sector. Reports quoting Indian experts say that through incursions, China has been able to occupy 640 Sq kms of Indian territory in Eastern Ladakh. They have since been denied by the Indian government.

- 90% of Chinese intrusions since 2012 have happened in the Western Sector. This suggests China's priority to the defence of its perceived borders in the Western Sector in comparison to that of Eastern Sector. The PRC, in particular, may like to defend its position in the Aksai Chin region of the Western Sector, already being occupied by it, but claimed by India. The importance was also noticed in the PRC's past 'swap' formula which provided for its giving up claims in the Eastern Sector in return for India's recognition of Aksai Chin in the Western Sector (China no longer mentions this formula). For China, the Western Sector is of significant strategic value; the key Western Highway connecting Xinjiang and Tibet falls in it. Also, the PRC's intrusions into and apparent efforts to establish permanent facilities in the Indian border, may be aimed at linking the Aksai Chin with Gilgit-Baltistan region of Pakistan Occupied Kashmir where the Chinese military is engaged in construction activities. Another point with regard to China's importance to Western Sector, are some claims, not so far official, noticed in the PRC that Ladakh is a part of China's Tibet.
- It appears that the Chinese intrusions across Indian border have been gaining momentum ever since India carried out its nuclear tests in 1998 suggesting China's inclination to link the border dispute with India with geo-politics. Notable in the current context is that they almost doubled in 2012 in comparison to the figure for the previous year. The 2012 level has continued in 2013 and for 2014, the situation could be the same. A reason could be new compulsions being felt by China to respond to India's heightened activity close to the border, in particular to stop the latter's acceleration of military infrastructure up gradation in the border – troop buildup, establishment of new border posts, putting air strips into operations again such as DBO, building of border roads etc. Departing from their past practice, Indian security forces are now more aggressive with daily patrolling along certain areas on the border and ready to forbid Chinese troops along the LAC.

- Some Chinese intrusions have happened deep inside Indian Territory, for e.g. in the DBO sector, the presence of Chinese military is kilometers ahead of even the Chinese perception of the LAC. This and staying of Chinese troops in the intruded land in tents could mark a new trend and reveal the PRC's long term intentions. Indian experts (like Srikanth Kondapalli) feel that these intrusions could be meant for probing Indian defences and testing of India's vulnerabilities along the LAC. Indian experts (like Brahma Challaney) think that China may try to gain more Indian territory in the process, change ground realities in the border and redraw map in its favour. They call this as China's 'Salami Slice' strategy aimed at taking control of Indian territories by small maneuvers.
- On the question as to why the Chinese intruded while President Xi Jinping's visit to India was still in progress, a possible explanation could be that after Mr Modi's landslide election victory in India, the PRC was unhappy with his government's foreign policy moves; in particular, the Chinese could have been unhappy with Mr Modi's implied condemnation of it for having " 18th century expansionist mindset, encroaching upon other countries, intruding in other's waters, invading other countries and capturing territory". India's boost to ties with Japan and Vietnam, two China-wary nations, during days before Mr Xi's visit to Arunachal could also have contributed to China's unhappiness. Some analysts have raised a question whether or not the Chinese intrusion in September 2015 was known to President Xi Jinping who was still in Indian soil; they have argued that the People's Liberation Army (PLA) influences the country's foreign policy course. But it has to be acknowledged that the whole party and government including the military in China function under a unified command which decides the foreign policy of the country; any idea of isolating the PLA in the process could be wrong.
- The continuing Chinese intrusions across Indian border

may mean the ineffectiveness of the signed India-China Border Defence Cooperation Agreement (BDCA). It is possible that the PRC is taking advantage of the BDCA's silence about deployment of troops in the LAC and in particular on from how many kilometers from the LAC, the two countries are required to exchange information on troop movements. India may think that not all its troop movements near the border are its troop build ups.

- China's protests over visits of Indian leaders to Arunachal Pradesh could be because of another factor- the stand of the Dalai Lama set up in India on Arunachal Pradesh. The Dharamsala-based Tibetan government in exile has said that "they recognize the McMahon Line as international border and that as such, Arunachal Pradesh is a part of India. It is bound by the Simla Agreement signed with the British India in 1914 and that there is no reason to deviate from the agreement." Beijing seems to be wary of any attempt to link the Tibet issue with that concerning Sino-Indian border; it considers the former as an internal problem. For the outside world, however, the linkage is obvious.

PRC's suspicions of the roles of US and Japan on the border issue

Of special interest to observers are signs suggesting that the PRC may be becoming suspicious of the US support to India on the question of border issue. Influential Chinese writers (Professor Zhang Li, South Asia Research Center, Sichuan University) have said that the support of Washington "led to a hardening of India's position on disputed border with China like that in Aksai Chin, Sikkim and Arunachal Pradesh". They (Prof Wang Dehua) have remarked that the Indian army's intrusions into the Chinese side were encouraged by the US so as to make some noise to distract China from the South China Sea, where it is in a spat with its sea neighbors such as the Philippines and Vietnam over the disputed islands. But India is neither on the US side nor on China's side, but has its own agenda." Scholars have alleged (9.4.2015) that the US is provoking India in the latter's relation with China, by offering the bait of support to India's permanent membership in the UN Security Council, adding that India remains unmoved.

Chinese suspicions on US as above need to be understood in another context. For the first time, Japan has sided with India on Arunachal issue (Foreign Minister Kishida, New Delhi, January 2015, while offering Japan's support to India's development projects in the Eastern Sector). Also, for the first time in recent years, a foreign power seems to have come in open support of India on the issue. With apparent concern over any internationalization of Arunachal issue, the Chinese foreign ministry promptly conveyed its 'serious concern' to Japan on this count. A PRC scholar affirmed that Kishida's words had "unveiled Japan's intent of 'uniting' the countries that have territorial disputes with China, in an attempt to create a strong impression that Japan, along with China's other neighboring countries, is bullied by a rising China."

In connection with what has been said above, it will be useful to have a look into the existing official positions of the US and Japan on the Sino-Indian border issue. The official US line is that it accepts the McMahon line as defining the Sino-Indian border, as observed by former US Ambassador to India J.K. Galbraith in October 1962. Washington is however non-committal on the status of Aksai Chin. Japan's official position is that it does not take sides on the Sino-border issue; but definitely marking a departure from this position is the de facto recognition of the country's foreign minister that Arunachal Pradesh is part of India. Relevant is his clarification – India "basically and effectively controls [Arunachal], and China and India are continuing consultations on the border issue, I made the remark taking these facts into account". One can expect that at a time when the US and Japan are engaged in a geo-political contest with China in Asia-Pacific region, they may not like to further annoy China by giving open support to India on the Sino-Indian border issue; however, the two official positions mentioned above, seem to contain a message – US and Japan may not be averse to adopt a pro-India stand on the issue when the time comes.

India may have to watch closely for any evidence towards China's official perception about the intentions of the US and

Japan on the Sino-Indian border issue. As a consequence of any PRC feeling that the two powers are working in tandem with India on that issue, regional geopolitics may become a factor in Beijing-New Delhi relations, posing a challenge to the two sides on how to manage it.

Intrusions in a wider context

It will be a mistake to look at China's border transgressions into India in isolation; they need contextualization taking into account China's historical views of its boundaries, which expose the country's expansionist outlook. The PRC believes that it has 'historically lost' territories to foreign countries; it however says that it is not making such claims in the modern sense. Beijing connects the country's external boundary as existed during Qing dynasty period to the contemporary borders. The maps published in the PRC in end eighties and in first decade of the century encompassed vast areas belonging to neighboring countries (The Historical Atlas of China, 1982-1987 and History of China's Modern Borders, vol. 1, 2007). Parts of India's Northeast and Andamans were shown in the maps as 'historically lost territories' of China.

Meriting close attention is also the impact on the Chinese stand on border intrusions coming from the PRC's "core interests'-based foreign policy framework, visible since middle of 2008. Under this framework, China aims to promote 'win-win cooperation with outside world, but would not compromise its 'core interests', i.e on all matters concerning the country's territorial sovereignty.

China says that friendship and the 'no compromise' position are two 'pillars' of its diplomatic strategy. India should therefore expect China's adoption of a two pronged approach towards it, which simultaneously mixes elements of both cooperation and assertion. At this juncture, signs seem to be emerging towards a beginning by China to readjust its foreign policy through according priority to economic interests in comparison to core interests; India may have to wait for the impact of such readjustment on China's policy on borders with India; it may have to examine the probability of the level of PLA intrusions into the Indian border coming down as China starts reducing the importance of assertiveness and according priority to economic interests while making its foreign policy.

Can 1962 be repeated? The answer could be yes, but not in that scale. Despite the apparent success of several mutually agreed confidence building measures in keeping the borders peaceful, India should be alert on the eventuality of intrusions expanding further, leading to an India-China 'local war'. The PRC visualizes occurrence of 'local wars under informatisation conditions'. The belief is that such wars can be short and happen in China's periphery, enabling China to realize limited political objectives. Can China use force to settle borders with India? The answer is affirmative considering that China's 'Active Defence' strategy does not rule out the military resorting to 'offensive operational postures'. Forceful recovery of 'Southern Tibet' (as China calls Arunachal) and fighting a 'partial war' with India were topics in the Chinese blogs not very long ago. China's use of force to turn territorial conditions in its favour has precedence. Beijing launched 'counter attacks in self-defense' against Vietnam, India and former Soviet Union in 1979, 1962 and 1969 respectively. In the current period, China is indulging in a show of force in East and South China seas.

Bilaterally, China's keenness to get closer to India and vice versa at the present moment is beyond question. President Xi Jinping and Prime Minister Modi are taking a lead in this direction. The motivating factors for the two countries are obviously are mutual economic benefits. At the same time, they require to face the fact that the strategic mistrust between them is not going to disappear soon. A Chinese blog aptly describes such situation. It identifies the roots of misunderstandings between China and India and wants their removal. It says, "The Chinese people suspect that India is using US and Japan to contain China and the Indians believe that China is restraining India through its moves in Indian Ocean and building of ports in Pakistan, Bangladesh, and Sri Lanka etc. India also fears that China opposes India's nuclear policy".

India will have to be prepared for the Chinese border intrusions /transgressions to continue as it is not going to be easy to bridge the perceptional differences among the two on the LAC quickly. More important will be to find a permanent solution to the border issue; India and China find that it is complex and will be time consuming. This explains their current inclination to conduct bilateral relations looking beyond the border dispute and concentrate on working together in other fronts, especially by strengthening mutual economic cooperation. India-China border talks may prolong indefinitely as the PRC is going to persist with its principled position of not compromising on all sovereignty-related issues including that of "Southern Tibet", as it calls India's Arunachal Pradesh. In such a situation, the best way for India would be to continue the border talks with China, but without expecting any quick breakthrough in them. Its long term plans should take into account the likelihood of future border conflicts with China and the need to build its defense preparedness as an insurance against any misadventure by China, howsoever it may look illogical at present.

INDIA VOWS TO PROTECT BORDER AMID ALLEGED CHINESE INCURSION

India has vowed to protect its border, following reports that Chinese soldiers had set up a camp inside territory claimed by India in the Himalayas. The response from Indian Defense Minister, A.K. Antony, to reports that Chinese troops had set up a camp in the cold desert region of Ladakh was brief but firm.

"We are taking every care to protect our interests."

Indian officials say about 50 Chinese soldiers last week pitched tents about 10 kilometers inside what New Delhi says is its territory in the Ladakh region. It is close to an area where a landing strip was established by India during a brief war fought by the two sides in 1962. The airstrip is being refurbished. The officials say that following the movement by the Chinese, Indian troops also set up a temporary camp less than 500 meters away.

Sajjad Ahmed Kitchloo, the Home Minister in Jammu and Kashmir State where Ladakh is located, urged the federal government to take action against the movement of the Chinese troops, calling it a deep incursion.

The Chinese are making repeated efforts to push inside Indian territory, and this merits serious attention, Kitchloo said.

Officials in Beijing, however, denied the incursion and said conditions on the border were peaceful and stable. Hua Chun Ying, spokesman in the Chinese foreign ministry, said that China's troops have been abiding by the agreement between the two countries and the line of control as set by the two countries. Chinese troops have been patrolling behind China's line of control, he said.

Indian officials said that the two sides are in touch through diplomatic channels to defuse the latest confrontation. Military personnel from the two sides have met to address the matter. India and China's efforts to resolve their long-running border dispute have made little progress despite numerous rounds of talks. China claims the northeastern Indian state of Arunachal Pradesh, which shares cultural links with Tibet. India says China occupies large chunks of a barren plateau in Kashmir.

In recent years, there have been increasing reports in the Indian media of incursions by the Chinese along the border. Some Indian analysts attribute this to growing assertiveness by the Chinese.

India has also been beefing up its military presence along the border with China and much of its defense modernization plans are aimed at containing what is seen here as a potential threat from China.

ANOTHER CHINESE INCURSION ALONG LOC

In another incursion, Chinese troops intruded into the Chumar sector in Ladakh–the same area which had sparked off tensions in April–and smashed some bunkers besides cutting wires of cameras installed at the border post.

Official sources said today the intrusion took place when the troops of China's People's Liberation Army (PLA) entered Indian territory in the Chumar sector and started vandalising the observation bunkers besides cutting the wires which overlook the Chinese territory.

Chumar, located 300 km from here, has always been an area of discomfort for the Chinese troops as this is the only area along the Sino-Indian border where they do not have any direct access to the Line of Actual Control (LAC).

The 21-day face-off between the two sides in the remote Daulat Beg Oldi (DBO) sector on April 15 was triggered by construction of an observation tower in Chumar division which had to be subsequently dismantled by the Army on May 5 before the crisis was defused.

The Chinese side, according to the minutes of the flag meetings in the last week of March this year, had been objecting to the construction of the watch tower along the LAC in Chumar.

After dismantling the observation post and defence bunkers, Army had installed cameras to monitor movement of Chinese troops along the LAC, a step which had irked the PLA.

Chumar, a remote village on Ladakh-Himachal Pradesh border, is being claimed by China as its own territory. The Chinese side also reportedly resorted to helicopter incursions almost every year.

Last year, it dropped some of the soldiers of PLA in this region and dismantled the makeshift storage tents of the Army and ITBP.

This area is not accessible from the Chinese side whereas the Indian side has a road almost to the last point on which the Army can carry loads upto nine tonnes.

CHINESE VANDALISE INDIAN POSTS IN LADAKH

Chumar, in Ladakh's Daulat Beg Oldi sector/Depsang Valley seems to have become a compulsive preoccupation of Chinese Peoples Liberation Army (PLA)/China Border Police. In mid- April 2013 a platoon plus strength Chinese detachment made a most unusual kind of intrusion 19 kms across the Line of Actual Control (LAC) into Indian territory and camped there in tents with Molosser dogs for three weeks and departed after much diplomatic dialogue. On 17 June another detachment of Chinese troops came on horseback, demolished/ damaged some bunkers, cut some wires of cameras installed at the border post and took away some other visual equipment, broken remains of which were reportedly returned later.

Chumar, located 300 km from Leh, has always been an area of discomfort for the Chinese troops as this is the only location along the LAC, which they do not have easy/close access to. In the area of the April stand-off, Chinese troops came close to two km from the Indian posts in Burtse on 12 July, which is around 30 km from the perceived LAC. As per J&K media reports, this incursion was among five such incidents over 11 days. In Chumar, Chinese troops had entered the area on 16-17 and 18 July also and before that, on 11 July their helicopters violated Indian air space. On 20 July, a Chinese patrol came inside Chumar in the evening and after spending a few hours vandalizing visual equipment went back to their positions across the LAC. The 21-day face-off since April 15 was reportedly sparked off by the construction of an observation tower in Chumar division which had to be subsequently dismantled by the Army on May 5 before the crisis was defused. After dismantling the observation post and defence bunkers, Army had installed cameras to monitor movement of Chinese troops along the LAC, a step which had again irked the PLA.

Chumar, a remote village on Ladakh- Himachal Pradesh border, is being claimed by China as its own territory. The Chinese side also reportedly resort to helicopter incursions almost every year. In 2012, PLA troops were airdropped in this region, where they dismantled the storage tents of the Army and ITBP. This area is not accessible from the Chinese side whereas the Indian side has a road almost to the last point on which the Army can carry loads up to nine tonnes.

According to Maj Gen Ravi Arora (retd), in 2009, Indian Army recorded close to 100 "transgressions" on foot, motorised and boat patrols by PLA in the strategically located Pangong Tso area, on both north and south banks. Although the frequency of incursions by Chinese speedboats into Indian territory in and around the lake has not increased over the past few years, China has a stronger military presence on the lake and the Chinese Navy operates close to 22 armed patrol boats in the lake — mostly smaller vessels seating five to seven soldiers. Pangong Tso is one of the key border flashpoints between India and China.

In 1999, China took advantage of the Indian Army's buildup in Kargil and built a 5- km permanent track into Indian territory along the lake. Both sides now carry out routine patrols on the track and mark their presence, but avoid physical contact. Yet Chinese patrolling speedboats often swirl aggressively around Indian boats.

Chinese ire, already in plenty about India's support to Dalai Lama and Tibetans, shot up since 2008, when Prime Dr. Minister Manmohan Singh visited Arunachal Pradesh, soon after Defence Minister AK Antony's late 2007 visit there, when the latter exclaimed at China's huge infrastructural development. Dr. Singh referred to Arunachal Pradesh as "the land of India's rising sun" and promised a substantial long-overdue infrastructural development package to Arunachal Pradesh.

This was kickstarted by major mobilization and relocation of Border Roads Organisation's (BRO) resources. That was the spark-off point for the Chinese to focus their attention on the J&K part of the LAC by launching a series of multimode and multi-dimensional incursions involving camping, painting CHINA in Mandarin on rock faces, filching fuel and what not. And all these aggressive monkeytricks on the ground have continued along with visits by premiers/ministers/ delegations/working groups for trade and "defence cooperation". What certainly emerges from all these Chinese forays is that they are testing the resolve (or lack of it) of the Indian Government quite obvious from the statements of both Chinese and Indian leaders and officials- and also the fact that ITBP is manning many parts of the LAC is another factor. The working arrangement for guarding land and sea borders of India has generally been that undisputed international boundaries are guarded by Border Security Force (BSF)/Ladakh Scouts/ Assam Rifles (AR) under command of the Army and Coast Guard under Indian Navy. In fact for Coast Guard, it was decided at the outset itself that it would be under Ministry of Defence, unlike BSF, AR, which are under Ministry of Home Affairs (MHA). Of the two disputed borders, the Line of Control (LoC) with Pakistan and the

Line of Actual Control (LAC) with China, while both should be directly manned by 1999, China took advantage of the Indian Army's buildup in Kargil and built a 5- km permanent track into Indian territory along the lake. Both sides now carry out routine patrols on the track and mark their presence, but avoid physical contact. Yet Chinese patrolling speedboats often swirl aggressively around Indian boats.

Chinese ire, already in plenty about India's support to Dalai Lama and Tibetans, shot up since 2008, when Prime Dr. Minister Manmohan Singh visited Arunachal Pradesh, soon after Defence Minister AK Antony's late 2007 visit there, when the latter exclaimed at China's huge infrastructural Mandarin on rock faces, filching fuel and what not. And all these aggressive monkeytricks on the ground have continued along with visits by premiers/ministers/ delegations/working groups for trade and "defence cooperation". What certainly emerges from all these Chinese forays is that they are testing the resolve (or lack of it) of the Indian Governmentquite obvious from the statements of both Chinese and Indian leaders and officials- and also the fact that ITBP is manning many parts of the LAC is another factor.

The working arrangement for guarding land and sea borders of India has generally been that undisputed international boundaries are guarded by Border Security Force (BSF)/Ladakh Scouts/ Assam Rifles (AR) under command of the Army and Coast Guard under Indian Navy. In fact for Coast Guard, it was decided at the outset itself that it would be under Ministry of Defence, unlike BSF, AR, which are under Ministry of Home Affairs (MHA). Of the two disputed borders, the Line of Control (LoC) with Pakistan and the Line of Actual Control (LAC) with China, while both should be directly manned by the Army, with BSF/AR or the Indo- Tibetan Border Police (ITBP) in situ being under Army's command and control, the LoC is being guarded by Army.

However, in the case of the LAC, it is not known as to why any part of it has been allotted for guarding to ITBP and that too under direct control of MHA and not the Army, as in the case of South East Ladakh, where both major Chinese incursions of 2008-9 in the general area of the barren land at Chumar, East of the picturesque Tso Morari (lake), Zulung La (pass) and the 22, 420 feet high Mount Gya and the recent one in Daulat Beg Oldi occurred.

Interacting with this writer, Lt Gen JS Bajwa (R), author of Modernisation Of The PLA:Gauging its Latent Future Potential (Lancer) and Maj Gen Dhruv Katoch(R), Director, Centre for Land War Studies (CLAWS) both reiterated what they succinctly wrote about the drawbacks and disadvantages of deploying ITBP on the LAC.

While Bajwa has gone into details about various aspects of ITBP's lack of suitability for guarding the LAC, Katoch strongly recommends that Army must replace ITBP on the LAC and the latter be deployed against Left Wing Extremists (LWE), instead of requesting for Army's assistance, which the Defence Minister has correctly declined.

The Chinese have been very active on the LAC and those who camped in Depsang required more than a "police" force response. Deploying ITBP on the LAC sends the wrong message to the Chinese who interpret it as a tacit acceptance of the Indian Government that the LAC is not active or live and as such does not need to be guarded by Army. Bajwa states: "MHA's reluctance to place the ITBP under the Army is indicative of the underlying resistance of the IPS lobby to serve under any commander from the Army....".

Chinese only seem to understand the kind of message the Indian retaliation provided in Nathu La, Sikkim in 1967 and later in Arunachal Pradesh. In 1986, a PLA unit marched seven kilometres inside the Line of Actual Control at Somdurong Chu, Arunachal Pradesh. General K Sundarji airlifted troops and surrounded their camp; placed artillery on nearby heights and asked a unit to erect tents just 10 metres away. The Chinese withdrew.

3

Chinese Dragon and Indian Elephant: Trying to Reboot their Border Relations

Sino-Indian border talks are going on in New Delhi. India's National Security Adviser to the Prime Minister, Ajit Doval, and the Chinese State Councillor Yang Jiechi are going to try to reboot the tensed border relations in these two days. But, it is still too early to expect a breakthrough in resolving the conflict.

This is 18th such meeting between special representatives of China and India on border issues. It is mostly symbolic for several reasons. This is first such meeting after the visit of the Chinese President Xi Jinping's India visit last September. Since then, the sides have not shot at each other at the border. There has not been any open military confrontation also, which could have escalated into a military conflict. The last peak of tension on border was seen in August last year. But the armed forces quickly agreed to sheath their weapons. And China dismantled its military camps from the areas that the Indian side considers his own.

It was a good sign to the fact that both Beijing and New Delhi do not want the border problem, which cannot be resolved quickly, to mar their growing bilateral relationship.

These talks are being held in an atmosphere when economic interests are bringing the Chinese Dragon and the Indian elephant ever closer. Indian Prime Minister Narendra Modi has secured reliable support of his reforms from China. China with the entry into the large Indian market is expanding its global presence. China plans to invest in India's economy 20 billion dollars over five years. China will invest in 12 major projects in India and it is an unprecedented leap in Sino-Indian relations, because for the previous 14 years China has invested only 700 million dollars in India. From all this, it is very clear that any military activity on the disputed territories now won't be fruitful neither for China nor for India.

An expert of the International Economy & international relations institute at the Russian Academy of Sciences, Alexander Rogozhin believes that the pragmatism in bilateral relations has finally got the upper hand.

He says that both the sides want to strengthen ties and to overcome existing and intractable conflicts on the border. There also is a mutual economic interest. China pursues a policy of expanding economic expansion in all regions of the world without any exception. And India is a huge market, which China is trying to conquer. This is regarding road construction and water supply. India wants to sell its engineering products in China, which it finds difficult to penetrate into other markets. China is in need of average technology level products at affordable prices.

Accent now is in not letting the long-standing border issues to press underneath themselves the economic agenda. Beijing and New Delhi will try to strengthen this trend during the current consultations. By taking into account some geopolitical factors, such a possibility they definitely have.

One of those is accepting India as SCO (Shanghai Cooperation Organization) full member in Ufa summit this summer. China, after many years of hesitation, has given its initial approval.

Any new aggravation on the Sino-Indian border or being on the verge of balancing a military conflict is definitely not an agreeable scenario before the upcoming historic event. And leaders such as Xi Jinping, and Narendra Modi, who have political farsightedness, very well understand this. However, China is very well aware of the fact that India will not be given SCO full membership without its consent, neither this summer, nor later.

India wants to enter SCO along with Pakistan, and not a single day later.

China could take advantage of this trump card, but China will be careful to put it on the table of border talks. But, beneath the surface as an instrument to put pressure on India it will always be ready to trump this card.

CAN INDIAN ELEPHANT TAKE ON CHINESE DRAGON? 'NOT IN THE NEXT 20 YEARS'

- India predicted to outpace China as as world's fastest-growing economy in next year
- China's economy is slowing after over 25 years of breakneck growth
- But experts say India simply can't size up against China's raw economic might

In the latest "On China," which premieres Thursday, Kristie Lu Stout explores the rivalry between the world's two most populous nations. (4.30 a.m. ET and 11.30 p.m. ET)

Hong Kong (CNN) Chinese President Xi Jinping and Indian Prime Minister Narendra Modi are two dynamic leaders at the helm of the world's two most populous nations.

And one is particularly vocal about making his mark on history.

When India successfully placed a spacecraft into orbit around Mars last year, Modi revealed in the moment.

"History has been created today," he said. "We have dared to reach out into the unknown and have achieved the near impossible.

"The success of our space program is a shining symbol of what we are capable of as a nation."

Soon after the galactic feat, he took to the stage at New York's famous Madison Square Garden and received a welcome so rapturous that Jon Stewart called him "America's First Modi."

'Make in India'

And all along, Modi has issued his call to "Make in India," encouraging companies all over the world to manufacture their products in India where there is a vast talent pool and low-cost production.

While Modi's India is out to put its economy on the fast track, China's economy is slowing after over 25 years of breakneck growth. President Xi is managing the slowdown with efforts to boost domestic spending, while cracking down hard on corruption.

And it's been predicted that India could outpace China as the world's fastest growing economy as soon as this year.

Not so fast, says China watcher and India Today correspondent Ananth Krishnan.

"China is still pulling away from India," the Beijing-based reporter said. "If India grows 7.5% this year and China grows 7.4%, I think it makes a good headline. But I think people shouldn't get carried away about what it means in terms of a gap between China and India."

China's economy may be slowing down but India faces a longer list of economic challenges including higher unemployment, chronic inflation and an overwhelming lack of basic infrastructure.

"In terms of education, having access to different resources, and job creation, China has done well. It has progressed far better compared to India," said Infosys China CEO Rangarajan R. Vellamore.

"Even though there is free movement across the country (in India), the paradox is there are a lot of basic issues related to access to water and basic education."

In a recent budget, the Modi government announced plans to boost infrastructure spending as well as cut taxes on businesses among other initiatives to spur economic growth.

China's Economic Might

But despite Modi's big pro-business push, India simply can't size up against China's raw economic might.

"After 30 years of dedicated efforts in building China into a manufacturing powerhouse, it would take a long time for India to build that kind of manufacturing capability," said Haiyan Wang, Managing Partner of the China India Institute.

"It's not just about lower labor costs. You have to have a complex industry cluster of supply chains. You have to have the knowledge. You have to have the skills. You have to be connected to the international market," she said.

"So when you ask if India could compete with China, I don't think that is going to be happening — not in the next 20 years."

The Indian elephant may be charging ahead, but the sinewy dragon has the muscle to stay ahead. China has the capacity, the connectivity, and the capital to throw its weight around.

And being a single party state with no free elections, Xi can march toward a long-term goal without fretting about the next election.

Winning Hearts and Minds

But that's not to say the autocracy has the advantage on all fronts, especially when it comes to winning hearts and minds in the region.

"Even if China is putting money into the Asian Infrastructure Investment Bank (AIIB) and the Silk Road fund, it is also building airstrips on reclaimed islands on the South China Sea," said Krishnan.

"There no question that India's rise is far less threatening than China's rise."

With the 1962 border dispute still vividly remembered by many in India, the impression of China as a threat stands in the way of further economic integration between the two countries.

"If you look at India's seven northeastern states, which are probably in the most dire need of infrastructure, it's inconceivable for any of those states to allow a Chinese company to come and build roads," said Krishnan.

China and India: Mistrust?

So when Modi touches down in Beijing next month for his second meeting with Xi, can both leaders cast aside areas of political tension to get down to business? "As pragmatic as President Xi is, as pragmatic as Prime Minister Modi is, economic integration is going to happen regardless of 100% trust or not," said Haiyan Wang.

Eased by the pragmatism of two ambitious leaders, the elephant and the dragon could together leap at the opportunity for a strong economic alliance.

"If these two countries come together, 40% of the world's people are going to be prosperous," said Vellamore.

"If they are able to come together, there can be a new kind of world order in the entire region which is going to benefit all of Asia."

It's a moment for both leaders to make a lasting mark on history.

DRAGON'S GAME: INDIA NEEDS TO REFORMULATE ITS CHINA POLICY

The hype over Prime Minister Narendra Modi's China visit next month is likely to obscure the underlying strategic dissonance and tensions between the world's two most populous countries on issues extending from land and water to geopolitical aims.

Two issues stand out: An increasingly asymmetrical trade relationship and a gradually rising pattern of Chinese border incursions in several regions since 2006, when China for the first time claimed Arunachal Pradesh as 'South Tibet'.

India-China commerce constitutes one of the world's most lopsided trade relationships: China's exports are 3½ times greater in value than its imports, and it buys mainly primary commodities from India but exports value-added goods to it. For example, China's steel producers find India an easy dumping prey, with Chinese dumping of steel items rising almost fourfold under Modi's watch in 2014. New Delhi, by tamely allowing China to rake in growing profits through such trade, in effect funds the Chinese strategy to encircle India.

Despite rising border provocations, Indian policymakers have still to get their act together. To Modi's credit, he has stressed that border peace and tranquillity is a prerequisite to the continued growth of India-China relations. But with his government, like his predecessor's, preoccupied with fire-fighting on several fronts, policymakers are missing the significance of what China is up to.

There is a clear pattern, backed by an identifiable strategy, to the Chinese incursions. With the aid of progressively increasing or recurrent incursions in each coveted area, the strategy aims to create a dispute where no dispute has existed so that China can subsequently demand that it be settled 'peacefully' on give-and-take terms. This pattern and strategy are apparent, for example, from repeated Chinese intrusions in Ladakh's two strategic regions — Depsang and Chumar — where the geography favours Indian forces, lending a distinct military advantage.

Neither Chumar nor Depsang was in dispute earlier. Yet Chinese President Xi Jinping's India arrival last September coincided with a Chinese intrusion into Chumar — one of the biggest incursions ever, representing Xi's birthday gift for Modi, who turned 64 on that day. And Premier Li Keqiang's 2013 visit followed a Chinese encroachment into Depsang, with the intruding troops setting up camp in an area that extended beyond the 'line of actual control' (LAC) that China itself unilaterally drew when it defeated India in the 1962 Chinese-initiated war.

The tense, intrusion-triggered military standoffs notwithstanding, incursions remain business as usual for China. For example, on the eve of the recent border talks, and then soon thereafter, intruding Chinese forces had face-offs with Indian troops in two separate areas of the Depsang plateau. In both the cases on March 20 and March 28, the Chinese attempt to reach India's Old Patrol Point base was foiled. In response to an incursion, Indian forces hold a banner drill to get the intruding troops out — a task that might also necessitate one or more flag meetings. But no sooner has one face-off ended than another incursion occurs. After all, Chinese border 'transgressions', as government figures reveal, now exceed more than one per day.

One novel method the People's Liberation Army (PLA) has employed is to bring ethnic Han pastoralists to the valleys along the LAC and give them cover to range across it, thus driving Indian herdsmen from their traditional pasturelands. In the absence of a strategy to thwart such PLA-assisted 'civilian' encroachments (one of which occurred during Xi's visit), India has been incrementally losing land, especially in Arunachal and Ladakh.

Why blame China for employing means — fair or foul — to alter the LAC bit by bit when Indians remain confused as ever on how to respond? To thwart encroachment by regular PLA troops, India's first line of defence remains a thinly stretched police force. The home ministry-administered Indo-Tibetan Border Police is no match for the PLA guile and capability. Beefing up its strength alone won't suffice; it must be placed under the army's operational command.

The focus on high-level visits and the border talks proceeding for 34 years — a world record — distracts attention from India's strategic imperatives while emboldening China to furtively nibble at Indian territories.

The Modi government's recently concluded maiden border talks with China dashed hopes of these negotiations being reoriented to produce results. The two countries in September recommitted to 'an early settlement of the boundary question', with Modi urging Xi to "resume the stalled process of clarifying the LAC" — a process derailed by China's breaking of a 2001 promise to exchange maps with India. The recent discussions, however, represented no earnest effort to restructure the talks, under way since 1981.

India's choice is not between persisting with a weak-kneed policy and risking a war. India has a hundred different options between these extremities, as China's own actions attest. Yet national security adviser Ajit Doval said after the latest round that holding border negotiations was itself valuable, even if the talks yielded no progress, because their absence would mean "conflict is the only means of resolution". Such logic that the sole choice for India is between staying stuck in futile talks and entering into conflict only encourages a revanchist China to take India round and round the mulberry bush.

India must stop seeing options only at the extreme ends and build a credible counter-strategy. China indeed is trying to limit India's options by leveraging its economic clout, including as a major supplier of power and telecom equipment and active pharmaceutical ingredients and as a lender to financially troubled Indian firms. China is already India's largest source of imports.

With creative gradualism his forte, Modi must evolve a China policy that errs on the side of caution, not meekness. Caution averts problems but timidity, as the past decade has shown, invites more problems. Prudence demands denying China the leeway to continue distorting commerce and boosting its trade surplus year after year, even as it keeps India under mounting strategic pressure without incurring political costs.

ENGAGING THE DRAGON: INDIAN PRIME MINISTER MODI'S CHINA VISIT

Indian Prime Minister Narendra Modi's recent visit to China was certainly not short on grand gestures from his hosts. To begin with, the visit began in Xian, the hometown of Chinese President Xi Jinping, in a break with protocol. In fact, President Xi took his cue from his visit to India last September, when Modi received him in Ahmedabad, in his native state of Gujarat.

Important Takeaways

Modi's three-day visit to China produced some important takeaways. One was India's decision to grant electronic visas to Chinese tourists. This will help increase the number of Chinese tourists who visit the country, boosting tourism revenues. It was also decided to open a new Indian consulate in Chengdu, while China will open one in the southern Indian city of Chennai. Modi reached out to a who's who of Chinese industry when he visited Shanghai, and solicited Chinese investment in India as part of his "Make in India" initiative. In economic terms, Modi's visit was a success as deals worth nearly $22 billion were signed between Chinese and Indian companies.

Modi's visit was not marred by any unsavory incidents on the border, unlike last time when there were incursions from the Chinese side even as the Xi Jinping visit was on, raising doubts as to whether Beijing could be trusted to walk the talk.

China has already been cooperating with India in the railway sector, with projects to increase speed on some lines, while feasibility studies will be conducted for the introduction of high-speed railways in other areas, with Beijing's support. Agreements were also inked for provincial level partnerships between the south Indian state of Karnataka and the Chinese province of Sichuan, while sister city bonds were forged between Aurangabad and Dunhuang, Chennai and Chongqing, and Hyderabad and Qingdao.

India suffers from a huge trade deficit with China, and it is welcome that during the Modi visit "the two sides resolved to take joint measures to alleviate the skewed bilateral trade so as to realize its sustainability." Last year total bilateral trade stood at $70.65 billion although India reeled under a whopping trade deficit of $37.8 billion.

Problems Remain

Although Modi asked China to "reconsider its approach" on the issues that bedevil bilateral ties, it seems Beijing was in no mood to yield to any such talk from New Delhi. There are still many hard-liners in China who look down on India, as could be seen in an article in the state-run Global Times newspaper in the run-up to the Modi visit. The article said: "Modi has also been playing little tricks over border disputes and security issues, hoping to boost his domestic prestige, while increasing his leverage in negotiations with China."

Neither was India able to get unequivocal backing from China in its bid for permanent membership on the United Nations Security Council. The joint statement issued during Modi's visit merely mentioned that China "understands and supports India's aspiration to play a greater role in the United Nations, including in the Security Council." New Delhi was also unable to get Beijing's clear support for its bid to become a member of the Nuclear Suppliers Group, a multilateral organization that works to prevent proliferation of nuclear weapons.

Meanwhile, the absence of any mention of the Chinese "One Belt, One Road" initiative in the joint declaration shows that India is in no hurry to be a part of it. There was also no announcement on the border dispute, which clearly shows that the top leadership of the two countries would find it very difficult to sell any such deal to their domestic audiences. In addition, though the joint statement goes on to say that the two sides will "endeavour to operationalize the hotline between the two military headquarters," no deadline has been set as yet.

FUTURE PROSPECTS AND IMPACT ON INDIAN FOREIGN POLICY

While Modi's China visit has set the ball rolling for a new phase in ties between the two most populous nations in the world, what remains clear is that there still exist deep fissures between the two sides. It seems the ghosts of the 1962 Sino-Indian war, when China inflicted a humiliating defeat on India, refuse to be buried.

Modi's visit shows that although India's relations with the U.S. have improved by leaps and bounds since the end of the Cold War, New Delhi still feels it prudent to engage China in the economic realm. However, New Delhi would have to factor in China's close ties with Pakistan in any kind of engagement with Islamabad.

During Xi's visit to Pakistan in April, Beijing announced $46 billion in investment in Pakistan, the focus of which will be the China-Pakistan Economic Corridor. When completed, it will allow China to transport goods over land from Gwadar in Pakistan to Kashgar in western China, and from there to other parts of the country, thereby allowing China to bypass the Strait of Malacca.

Beijing would not like to see New Delhi getting too cosy with the U.S. and countries like Japan, and therein lies its rationale for engaging India. But as was clear from the Modi visit, it is unwilling to yield an inch on the boundary issue or on its claims over some parts of Indian territory like Arunachal Pradesh. It obviously sees benefits in keeping India on the back foot diplomatically.

New Delhi will also have to be careful not to miss the woods for the trees. China may have rolled out the red carpet for Modi during his visit, but that will not prevent it from using every trick in the book to undercut New Delhi's influence in its immediate neighbourhood and beyond. Decoding Beijing's Janus-faced policies is the key challenge for the Indian government and its policymakers.

INDIA-CHINA DISPUTES ON ARROGANCE OF INDIAN ELITES AND INFERIORITY OF ITS ORDINARY PEOPLE

An op-ed in the Chinese Communist Party's mouth piece calls Pm Modi "a pragmatist, rather than a visionary", questions his "little tricks" and asks if his visit to China can upgrade Sino-Indian ties.

The *Global Times* is a widely-read tabloid brought out by the *People's Daily* group, which is controlled by the Communist Party of China, and is said to be "close to the centre of Communist Party power" and one that "reflects the undertones of party policies". So when an op-ed appears in it, just before the visit of Indian Prime Minister Narendra Modi to China, calling him "a pragmatist, rather than a visionary" and charging him with "playing little tricks over border disputes and security issues, hoping to boost his domestic prestige while increasing his leverage in negotiations with China", it is bound to be noticed. And it was. Hu Zhiyong – a research fellow with the Institute of International Relations at the Shanghai Academy of Social Sciences – went on to also offer some dos and don'ts to the Indian prime minister.

Dos: The Indian government should loosen up on the limits of cross-border trade with China, reduce the trade deficit, improve the efficiency of government administrations, and relax the visa restrictions, in order to attract more Chinese companies to invest in India.

Don'ts: Modi should no longer visit the disputed border region in pursuit of his own political interests, nor should he deliver any remarks that infringe on the consensus on bilateral ties. Meanwhile, the Indian government should completely stop supporting the Dalai Lama, and stop making the Tibetan issue a stumbling block to the Sino-Indian relationship.

This assumes significance in the light of what former national security adviser Shivshankar Menon pointed out in an op-ed column:

First, both India and China have strong leaders whose primary appeal is to rising nationalist feeling in their countries. During Xi Jinping's September 2014 visit to India, the PLA in an unprecedented show of force (over 1000 troops) entered into one of the areas where there are differences in perception of where the Line of Actual Control lies, Chumar. Unlike in May 2013, when a similar incident before Premier Li Keqiang's visit was settled and the status quo restored within two weeks and before the visit, this time the Chinese took their own time. The timing of the intrusion and its duration made clear that it was deliberate — a signal at the least that China could embarrass the new Indian government when it wished, and that it was not so preoccupied with Japan and the South China Sea as to be unable to adopt a more robust posture on the India-China border.

Prime Minister Modi begins his China visit with a first stop at Xian on May 14 and in a rare break from precedent for Chinese leaders, President Xi Jinping is travelling there, his native town, to greet him. As the leaders get ready for a summit, the diplomatic back and forth has already begun. On May 12, Foreign Secretary S Jaishankar said India had lodged a protest against China's announcement of infrastructure projects in Pakistan-occupied Kashmir. India had so far kept a studied silence on Xi Jinping's Pakistan visit on April 20, where he had announced a $46-billion package that included highways and hydel power projects along the China-Pakistan Economic Corridor through PoK to the Gwadar port in Balochistan.

For the record, we give below the full text of the op-ed article by Hu Zhiyong published in the *Global Times* on May 11, 2015: Can Modi's visit upgrade Sino-Indian ties?

At the invitation by Chinese Premier Li Keqiang, Indian Prime Minister Narendra Modi will kick off his trip to China on Thursday. This is his very first state visit to China since Modi's inauguration in May 2014, as well as a return visit of Chinese President Xi Jinping's state visit to India in September last year.

Ever since Modi assumed office, he has taken the initiative to actively develop India's relationships with Japan, the US, and European countries in no time, in order to promote the country's poor infrastructure construction and economic development. But his diplomatic moves last year have proven that he is a pragmatist, rather than a visionary.

Modi has been busy strengthening India's ties with neighboring countries to compete with China, while trying to take advantage of the tremendous opportunities for economic development created by China, as Beijing is actively carrying forward the "One Belt and One Road" initiative. Modi has also been playing little tricks over border disputes and security issues, hoping to boost his domestic prestige while increasing his leverage in negotiations with China.

Therefore, the ball is in India's court to deepen the bilateral relations. For China, developing friendly cooperation with surrounding countries has always been the foothold of its diplomacy. Fostering close ties with India, China's largest neighbor in South Asia, is of great importance to China's perimeter security and stability.

However, a number of Indian elites deem the rise of Beijing as threat of New Delhi's development, and make comparisons between the two sides in every aspect, which risks dragging the bilateral ties into vicious competition, and severely constraining the further enhancement of Sino-Indian relations.

As a matter of fact, the development of China and India is at different levels with different characteristics, and there is simply no comparison between the two.

Due to historical feud and mutual mistrust that stems from geopolitics, the two sides have never established real strategic trust. Leaders from both China and India should not only strengthen mutual political trust, but also stick to a series of agreed principles and match their rhetoric with action. In light of this, Modi should no longer visit the disputed border region in pursuit of his own political interests, nor should he deliver any remarks that infringe on the consensus on bilateral ties. Meanwhile, the Indian government should completely stop supporting the Dalai Lama, and stop making the Tibetan issue a stumbling block to the Sino-Indian relationship. When it comes to the economic ties, despite the fact that China has already become India's largest trading partner, India's trade deficit with China keeps rising sharply. New Delhi is reluctant to admit the widening trade gap is its own fault, nor is it willing to examine its own economic structure and the quality of its exports to China. Instead, it has been repeatedly accusing or directing its anger at China.

The Indian government should loosen up on the limits of cross-border trade with China, reduce the trade deficit, improve the efficiency of government administrations, and relax the visa restrictions, in order to attract more Chinese companies to invest in India.

Furthermore, people-to-people and cultural exchanges between the two countries are far from enough. People from both China and India lack the most basic mutual understanding and interactions.

Due to the Indian elites' blind arrogance and confidence in their democracy, and the inferiority of its ordinary people, very few Indians are able to treat Sino-Indian relations accurately, objectively and rationally. Worse, some Indian media have been irresponsibly exaggerating the conflicts between the two sides, adding fuel to the hostility among the public.

Deepening bilateral relations requires concerted efforts of politicians from both sides. Modi should seize the chance of his China visit to enhance bilateral cooperation.

Increasing dialogues and communications is good for both sides, because only by improving communications can we reduce frictions and misunderstandings. This requires not only enhancement of political mutual trust between leaders, but also more intense people-to-people exchanges, and making the power of the public a driving force for the further development of Sino-Indian ties.

DRAGON'S MANIPULATION OF CROSS-BORDER RIVER FLOWS LIKELY TO BE THE SOURCE OF TENSION BETWEEN THE NATIONS

China is reluctant to accept other Asian powers as equals, but it lacks the power to impose its hegemony. China's power may be vast and still growing, yet it does not have the capability to enforce its writ on Asia.

Fifty years after China's invasion of India, the Dragon's manipulation of cross-border river flows is likely to be the source of tension between the nations.

Half a century after China's invasion of India - the only war it has won, despite its involvement in multiple military conflicts since the Communist 'revolution' - its relationship with New Delhi is more troubled than ever, with territorial disputes, trade friction and geopolitical competition roiling the ties.

Although China waged war to "teach India a lesson," in the words of its then premier, the real lesson that can be drawn today is that the aggression failed to achieve any lasting political objectives for Beijing and only fuelled enduring enmity with India.

If anything, the 42-day war helped to discard India's pacifist blinkers and spur the modernisation of its fledging military - developments that enabled India to fend off Pakistan's aggression less than three years later and, subsequently, to carve out an independent Bangladesh in a 13-day conflict that ranks as one of the 20th century's swiftest decisive wars. China did teach India a "lesson", but not the intended one.

The world has fundamentally changed since then. But not the India-China relationship, which remains weighed down by the bitter legacy of that war and by China's increasingly muscular approach in recent years - apparent from its overt refusal to accept the territorial status quo.

In other words, China, far from being content with the territorial gains it made in the period up to 1962, covets additional Indian administered land.

The issue up to the 1962 war was the Switzerland- size Aksai Chin plateau, now firmly in Chinese control. But the issue since 2006 - thanks to China's new assertiveness - is Arunachal Pradesh, which is three times larger than Taiwan and represents the largest Asian real estate coveted by Beijing.

India's meekness has effectively allowed China to shape the agenda and define Arunachal as the "dispute".

Dependent India

China, significantly, is seeking to disturb the status quo not just on land but also on cross- border river flows. Although a number of nations, stretching from Afghanistan to Vietnam, receive waters from the vast Tibetan plateau, India's dependence on Tibetan waters is greater than that of any other country.

With about a dozen important rivers flowing in from the Tibetan Himalayan region, India gets almost one-third of all its yearly water supplies of 1,911 billion cubic metres from Tibet, according to United Nations data. Put simply, India is most vulnerable to China's manipulation of cross-border river flows.

After unilaterally building a cascade of megadams on the Mekong - the lifeline of continental Southeast Asia - Beijing has unveiled plans to build a series of dams on the rivers flowing into India directly or via Nepal.

For example, five major dams have been planned on the Arun (known as Kosi in India) near the Tibet-Nepal frontier, with the uppermost dam to be located at Kanggong and the lowest at Shali, almost on the international boundary.

And in addition to the current construction of six new dams on the Brahmaputra, China proposes to build the world's largest dam at Metog ('Motuo' in Chinese), just before this river enters India. The dam, by impounding water on a gargantuan scale, will generate, according to the state-run Hydro China Corporation, 38,000MW of power, or nearly twice the installed capacity of the Three Gorges Dam.

India has signed generous water- sharing treaties with both the countries located downstream to it - Pakistan and Bangladesh - but China rejects the very concept of water sharing.

It does not have a single water- sharing pact with any neighbor, although, owing to its occupation of Tibet and Xinjiang, it has become the source of cross- border flows to more countries than any other riparian power in the world.

China's hydrological aggression in the form of projects to re-engineer cross-border flows unilaterally is an extension of its demographic aggression in Tibet, Xinjiang and Inner Mongolia, and its ongoing cartographic aggression against India, Japan, Vietnam and the Philippines. Acceptance of the status quo is a prerequisite to peace on any continent, but China is working to alter the status quo in Asia on the strength of its rapidly accumulating power.

China's predicament

The dramatic ascent of China parallels Japan's phenomenal rise as a major power during the Meiji era in the second half of the 19th century. Yet China's predicament today is similar more to the one Germany faced in the 19th century and the first half of the 20th century: Germany was too strong in a multi-polar Europe to accept a role for itself as one among equals, yet too weak to enforce its will on the other European powers.

China, too, is reluctant to accept other Asian powers as equals, but it lacks the power to impose its hegemony on Asia.

China's power may be vast and still growing, yet it lacks sufficient capability to enforce its writ on Asia or forcibly seize any of the territories it covets. Defence, after all, is easier than offence.

Against this background, the China-India equation will remain tense. India can expect no respite from Chinese strategic pressure.

Whether Beijing actually sets out to teach India "the final lesson" by launching a 1962-style surprise war will depend on several calculations, including India's defence preparedness to repel such an attack, domestic factors within China - such as economic and social unrest threatening the communist hold on power - and the availability of a propitious international timing of the type the US-Soviet Cuban missile crisis had provided in 1962.

But if India is not to be caught napping again, it has to inject greater realism into its China policy by shedding self-deluding shibboleths, shoring up its deterrent capabilities, and putting premium on leveraged diplomacy.

The larger Asian balance of power will be shaped by developments not only in East Asia but also in the Indian Ocean

- a crucial international passageway for oil deliveries and other trade.

Non-traditional security issues in the Indian Ocean region - from energy and climate security to transnational terrorism and environmental degradation - have become as important as traditional security issues, like freedom of navigation, security of sea lanes, maritime security, proliferation of weapons of mass destruction, and ocean piracy. The Indian Ocean region indeed is becoming a new global centre of trade and energy flows and geopolitics.

Ocean of Supremacy

If China were to gain the upper hand in the Indian Ocean region at India's expense, it will mark the end of India's world-power ambitions.

Thereafter, India will be seen as merely a sub-regional power whose clout does not extend to even entire South Asia, with Pakistan challenging it in the west and China in the north and south.

Unlike the strategic disadvantage India faces along the land frontier, with Chinese troops in most areas perched on the upper heights of the Himalayas, it enjoys a natural geographic advantage in the Indian Ocean region. The Chinese navy's operational disadvantages in the Indian Ocean are so glaring that a strong Indian naval force, by safeguarding the various 'gates' to the ocean, can seriously threaten China's trade and energy arteries, especially if the People's Liberation Army were to dare to launch another land aggression.

In 1962, the political and psychological shock from China's surprise invasion rattled India to such an extent that it did not use its air power to halt the Chinese advance, although Beijing lacked the air capability to protect its invading forces, let alone to bomb Calcutta.

If a 1962-style aggression is to be averted, India must invest in building a sophisticated, powerful navy with the capability to throttle the Chinese economy's lifeline through the Indian Ocean.

In any event, how the India- China relationship evolves will have an important bearing on Asian and wider international security. China seems to be signalling that its real, long-term rivalry is not so much with the US as with India. It clearly looks at India as a potential peer rival.

India's great-power ambitions depend on how it is able to manage the rise of China - both independently and in partnership with other powers. A stable equation with China is more likely to be realised if India develops a credible deterrent capability on land and at sea.

4

The Elephant, the Dragon and the Asian Century

When Rajiv Gandhi visited China in 1989, Deng Xiao Ping said to him: "An Asian Century is only possible when India and China come together".

The significance of this statement must not be under stated as mere political rhetoric. China and India are the two largest economies and militaries in Asia. In terms of human capital, together, the two nations account for almost 40% of the world's population. Given these figures, if the dream of the 'Asian Century' is to be realized, then India and China would have to radically alter their bilateral equation and follow a co-operative rather than confrontational policy toward each other.

Prime Minister Narendra Modi's government has renewed India's foreign policy focus toward India's immediate neighbourhood. When he was elected as the PM in May last year, Sino-Indian relations were at a significant low point due to tensions at the borders in Arunachal Pradesh and Jammu and Kashmir's Ladakh region.

In the last eight months, several high profile visits between Indian and Chinese officials have begun changing mutual perceptions on both sides. The Chinese President's visit in September last year marked a significant improvement in bilateral relations. During the visit, PM Modi statedthat "a climate of mutual trust and confidence; respect for each other's sensitivities and concerns; and, peace and stability in our relations and along our borders are essential for us to realize the enormous potential in our relations."

A framework for effective negotiations on the border issue was also discussed and NSA Ajit Doval was ultimately appointed as India's emissary for border talks in November. He met his counterpart, State Councillor Yang Jiechi earlier this month on the sidelines of the Munich Security Conference and talks are said to have begun progressing smoothly.

This month, Indian Foreign Minister Sushma Swaraj visited China to inaugurate the India-China Media Forum. She put forward a six point plan to broaden India's bilateral engagement with China which involved developing new areas of co-operation and finding a way to converge both countries' regional and international interests.

The points mentioned were – an action-based approach; broad–based bilateral engagement; identifying new areas of cooperation; expanding strategic communication; fulfilling common aspirations to usher in Asian century and setting up of industrial parks and projects in India that would contribute to PM Modi's "Make in India" campaign. President Xi Jinping broke protocol and held a rare meeting with Sushma Swaraj during her visit.

It is likely that this visit will pave the way for more fruitful discussions when Prime Minister Modi will visit China in May. Another interesting development from the visit was the Joint Communiqeissued after the RIC summit in which, China's Foreign Ministry spokesperson Hua Chunying stated that China had no reservations against India and Brazil getting a permanent seat in the United Nations Security Council (UNSC). Rhetorical though this statement may be, it is still a significant softening of stance from China's usual position.

Global geopolitical upheavals have a significant role to play in this changing equation. The United States has begun withdrawing from its long drawn protracted engagement in West Asia. As part of its global re-balancing strategy, the US has decided to re position 60% of its strategic assets to the Asia Pacific theatre.

Within the People's Republic of China (PRC), this move is perceived as a US strategy to encircle China.

China has yet to resolve its issues with countries in the South China Sea, especially Vietnam and the Philippines, and in the East China Sea with Japan. China has staked claims on large swathes of the South China Sea citing historical ties in the region. In the last three years, China has stepped up offensive patrolling in the region and faced off with the Vietnamese and Philippine navy on numerous occasions.

The area has extensive mineral deposits and is also a crucial transit hub for almost $5.3 trillion in annual trade. These factors no doubt make the region critical to China's rise. According to a Council on Foreign Relations (CFR) report, under its treaty obligations, the United States would have to defend Japan in the case of an armed attack and the U.S.-Philippine treaty holds both nations accountable for mutual support in the event of an "armed attack in the Pacific Area on either of the Parties."

Prime Minister Narendra Modi's invitation to Barack Obama for India's Republic Day celebrations has no doubt raised eyebrows in China. Indian media houses were quick to point out the close interpersonal relationship that Obama and Modi shared. Growing defence ties between India and the US, as well as between India and Japan will also be of considerable concern to the PRC.

Another interesting occurrence last month was the surprise result of the Sri Lankan general elections seeing the ouster of Mahinda Rajapaksa and the coming into office of Maithripala Srisena, who has so far come off more pro-India than Rajapaksa ever was. India and China had several issues regarding China's forays into the Indian Ocean.

Under President Mahinda Rajapaksa, Sri Lanka allowed Chinese Submarines and long range deployment patrols to dock at Colombo, despite repeated concerns raised by India. Sri Lankan media houses were quick to allege that India's external intelligence agency, the R&AW, were involved in manipulating election results. The veracity of these claims is yet to be ascertained, however the message to the PRC is loud and clear. It is now dealing with a more proactive and assertive Indian foreign policy. This growing assertiveness has definitely played a significant role in changing the strategic equation between China and India.

This change however, is still manifesting itself, and it is essential that both sides maintain the momentum, in order to avoid losing this evolving relationship to rhetorical excesses. Prime Minister Narendra Modi's visit in May is expected to see many new agreements and MoUs signed as well. The key points of discussion during the visit will include bilateral investments and co-operation on multilateral forums like the BCIM connectivity and ASEAN. However, only once the two nations tackle outstanding issues such as the border demarcation can ties significantly move forward.

INDIAN OCEAN REGION – A ZONE OF STRATEGIC COMPETITION

Indian Ocean Region (IOR) has been described as a "Centre Stage for Twenty-First Century" which never lost its strategic sheen since ancient times. During Cold War the Indian Ocean had been a zone of intense rivalry between super-powers sailing with their nuclear-armed flotilla. The super-powers were seen as interlopers by the Indian Ocean states and the efforts were pursued to declare it a 'Zone of Peace' through Sri Lankan efforts. By the end of Cold War the confrontations and competitions in IOR seem to be eluded but to the utter dismay the power dynamics of the region were completely altered given the rise of India and China as major naval powers.

China's ambitions of controlling IOR to fulfil the growing demand for raw materials, energy resources and finished goods at home prioritize the discourse on regional maritime security. The regional maritime security envisages the freedom of Sea Lines of Communication (SLOCs); strategic importance of the Straits of Malacca, Homruz and Bab-el-Mandeb as vital choke-points and growing naval competition has raised the stakes in IOR. India sees itself traditionally connected to Indian Ocean being its strategic backyard whereas China has major strategic interests connected to its economic rise. Given this background of engagements in IOR both the countries remain at loggerheads.

SINO-INDIAN EQUATIONS: BETWEEN AMITY AND ENMITY

India and China emerged as powerful economies with ample of human resources being world's most populous countries. The Sino-Indian relations were initiated through the principle of peaceful co-existence and entered a bitter phase of rivalry on border issues which culminated into Sino-Indian War of 1962. The Asian giants massively expanded their militaries with an added nuclear factor thus claiming regional as well as the global supremacy. With the expansion of their economies and geopolitical sphere, the bilateral relationship between both the countries could well be characterised more of a competition than cooperation.

Both the countries have shown some rapprochement in past few years to stabilise the relationships based on economic progress and growing sensitivity on bilateral security. The initiatives are backed by high-level visits but seem to be lacking the spirit of cooperation. From time and again the Chinese policy of rapprochement is being negated by confrontation in the disputed territories. The recent face-off between People Liberation Army's (PLA) troops with Indian Army in Chumar sector of Ladakh region just ahead of President Xi Jinping's India visit raises concern on the intentions and motivations of China. Though the visit claimed to be highly successful it is debatable whether this act of *détente will ever lead to entente cordiale. There are some external factors hampering the constructive Sino-Indian engagements.*

The Pakistan Factor

China maintains a 'special relationship' with Pakistan to counter India's growing dominance in the region and to maintain a regional equilibrium through politico-military alliances. The Sino-Pakistan nexus also points out their trust-deficit against India. Further, Pakistan's geostrategic location creates a corridor for China to pursue economic alliances with West Asia and the Gulf region to protect its SLOCs in the Indian Ocean to ensure uninterrupted supply of energy resources. It is also important to counter strategically placed India which can retaliate in Indian Ocean to compensate the setbacks in case of any mainland border conflicts with China. China is also looking for bases in the Persian Gulf region as a palisade against United States.

Myanmar – China's gateway to Bay of Bengal

Bay of Bengal is gaining importance in Chinese strategic thinking as a gateway to Indian Ocean and so is Myanmar – a key transit zone in Bay of Bengal. Bay of Bengal is emerging as a new locus of strategic competition in Asia. China is investing heavily in Myanmar to achieve its strategic aim. Most notable is the construction of large scale oil terminal and a gas terminal on Ma Dan Island adjacent to Rakhine and Shwe offshore gas fields where oil and gas is to be pumped to Kunming in China through a high capacity dual pipeline across Myanmar into Southern China. It will significantly reduce its dependence on Straits of Malacca. The activities of Peoples' Liberation Army-Navy (PLAN) is also expected to increase on the pretext of providing security to newly created hubs and SLOCs in Bay of Bengal which includes possible military air bases at Mingalodon, Shante, Nampong and Namsang creating further suspicions.

Geo-strategic interests of United States

IOR is also preeminent in United States' national security policies. It is an important theatre for United States owing to incessant conflict in the Middle East and Global War on Terror (GWOT). Moreover it is an imperative for United States to maintain its influence in the IOR fulfilling its energy requirements from the Middle East as well as to safeguard its trade routes. Ashley Tellis' notion of Indian Ocean as a commercial highway for the United States is upended by China's continuous efforts to control and turn Indian Ocean as its freeway to energy hubs. Indian Ocean is no more a unipolar domain and U.S. sees India as a major stakeholder in the Indian Ocean. The 2010 Quadrennial Defense Review (QDR) of U.S. Department of Defence asserts India as the largest power in the IOR and net exporter of the security in the future. India's bilateral security engagements with United States have started very recently and India does not see itself under U.S. security umbrella but as a strategic partner with mutually beneficial relationship – much to the annoyance of China.

UNDERSTANDING CHINA'S STRATEGIES AND INDIA'S SECURITY CONCERNS

India's major concern is China's growing ambitions and its power-projection capabilities in IOR through the visible presence of its military assets and supporting infrastructure in the region. China's notion of 'String of Pearls' coined by the Booze-Allen-Hamilton in 2003 might be considered frivolous by some experts but holds significant strategic importance for the need of overseas bases in the IOR under the pretext of 'cutting of supply cost through overseas military bases' and to 'promote regional and global stability'. In this direction, China's new strategic discourse emphasizes control of its periphery through 'Silk Road' strategy and to augment its naval influence through the strategy of 'Far Sea Defence' enhancing its naval capabilities.

The Silk Road Strategy

China's strategic discourse emphasizes its rise and harmonious growth through control and influence over China's internal and external periphery. The Chinese leadership sensible to this strategic thinking held the first ever conference on 'periphery diplomacy' just prior to its*Third Plenum* in the last week of October 2013. Apart from the members of Central Committee, the meeting was attended by a small group of leading members responsible for foreign affairs along with Chinese ambassadors to important countries. At the meeting China's need for stable external environment conducive for its domestic economic reforms was emphasized by President Xi Jinping. The underlying objectives revolve around China's policy to exercise an influence along its periphery and to counter the U.S. rebalancing towards Asia.

The Chinese proposal of continental or maritime silk routes is a grand strategy of extending peripheral influence and regional integration to enhance Chinese political and economic influence. From Indian perspective the entire proposal is viewed in context of broader geo-strategic implications, particularly the IOR. Though the initiative will bring economic integration and benefit the region at large but the strategic pitfalls cannot be neglected. The major concerns emanate from the architecture of land silk routes which straddle India from west to east highlighting 'String of Pearls' strategy. In the West is the proposed China-Pakistan corridor connecting restive Xinjiang province in China and Gwadar port in Pakistan passing through Pakistan occupied Kashmir (PoK) – a disputed territory which is against international norms. In the East is the Bangladesh, China, Myanmar and India (also referred to as BCIM) corridor connecting India's north-eastern region with Kunming province of China. It is an acceptable idea for the economic development of India's north-eastern region and its connectivity with Southeast Asia but the strategic concerns hover around the security of Bay of Bengal. Bangladesh and Myanmar being major energy transhipment hubs for China may create a strategic challenge on India's eastern seaboard given the obvious presence of PLAN (People Liberation Army-Navy).

China's Strategy of 'Far Sea Defence'

Chinese military strategy and capabilities evolved alongside its power aspirations over a period of time. The consolidation of its naval power is highly desirable to accomplish the task to control the SLOC in the Indian Ocean region. The Chinese naval strategy went through major changes over a period of time – from 'near-coast defence' (*jin'an fangyu*) strategy designed for coastal defence to the 'near-sea active defence' (*jinhai jiji fangyu*) to counter United States in Pacific have been extended to 'far-seas defence' (*yuanhai zuozhan*) strategy which may create implications in IOR with respect to PLAN's future development and deployment (Li 2011).

The Chinese Strategy of 'far-seas defence" gained prominence during Jiang Zemin's regime who advocated enhancing far-seas defence and operational capabilities to preserve China's maritime security and protection of its maritime interests vital for its economic rise in the territories away from Chinese mainland. The far-seas naval strategy is aimed at control over IOR for the security of its transport routes as all its energy requirements are catered through here. The far-flung naval operations also require continuous logistical support; therefore, the notion of 'String of Pearls' seems to be closely related to 'far-seas defence' strategy given the Chinese infrastructure investments in Pakistan, Sri Lanka, Bangladesh and Myanmar. Construction of these facilities may have economic and commercial motivations but military connotations are also attached to it. Incidentally, the bases around India appear to be 'String of Pearls' but as a matter of fact the locations are most ideal to control China's SLOCs extending from Straits of Homruz to Malacca entering into Pacific Ocean. Strategically, Indian Ocean also serves as China's backdoor in event of any confrontation with United States or Japan in the Pacific, thus, extending its theatre for naval operations.

China reportedly built Yulin (Sanya) Naval Base – an underground nuclear submarine base at Hainan Islands around 1200 NM from Malacca Straits for expeditionary and defensive operations.

Détente or Entente?

The Sino-Indian relations can be characterised as détente with an undertone of strategic competition. A desire is reflected in the relations to reduce tensions through negotiations but at the same time countering each other's influence in the region negates it. The missing element of trust along with a viable solution to amicably resolve the land border issue is a major stumble block in building partnerships and cooperation.

Both the countries are engaged in diplomatic manoeuvres to cease opportunities with Indian Ocean littoral states. Though China has frictions in South-East Asia but it remained successful to consolidate the region through its booming economy and trade partnership with ASEAN. India is responding to the China's strategic initiatives in the Indian Ocean through its engagements with Vietnam and rest of ASEAN nations with its naval presence in the South China Sea. Further India has modified its "Look-East Policy" to "Act East" under Prime Minister Narendra Modi's regime to deepen its economic and strategic links in the South-East Asian region. Indian has several interests in the South China Sea which includes joint oil exploration with Vietnam. At the same time China has embarked upon its "Look-West Policy" which seems to be giving primacy to Sino-Indian relations but tilted more towards countering American influence in Pakistan and involves geopolitics of energy.

The friction between both the countries is more on strategic front but at economic front the Sino-India relations are highly successful with estimation of bilateral trade reaching $100 billion by 2015. Combining their population, the Sino-India bilateral relations will impact the international order to address the transnational threats of pandemics, climate change and global terrorism. Both the countries came forward to establish BRICS Development Bank on the lines of World Bank and Asian Development Bank.

India's engagements in IOR are more like an act of balancing China than to contest it. The usage of the phrase 'strategic rivalry' seems less appropriate here as both India and China are still restraining themselves from a fully fledged contest. It seems that both the countries are following the principle of peaceful co-existence, which holds the foundation of their relationship from the very outset but have virtually turned into co-existence in belligerence. Jeff M. Smith has aptly termed the Sino-Indian relations as 'Cold Peace', which seems to be turning warm after fresh initiatives of both the governments towards cooperation – moving in the direction of entente.

INDIA IN AFRICA: THE ELEPHANT AND THE DRAGON

Independent India's first prime minister, Jawaharlal Nehru, regarded Africa as a sister continent to his own, united by a shared history of colonialism and independence struggle. In a world that was dividing itself along ideological lines, he saw solidarity among the emerging nations that were at last gaining the ability to determine their own futures and work towards mutual peace and development.

His spirit is often invoked today, but behind a modern continuation of Nehru's politics of non-alignment and 'positive neutralism' is a complex mix of geopolitics and strategic realities with commercially driven pragmatism. India's desire to engage with Africa is undimmed, but domestic pres-sures, and an apparent confusion in the formulation of its strategy, has led to it falling behind its largest regional rival, China.

After the end of the Cold War, and as the influence of the Soviet Union began to wane in India's politics, the economy began to liberalise and the country began to look for new ways to express itself on the world stage. In the mid-to-late 1990s, that meant looking towards Africa, in particular to fulfil the burgeoning energy needs of a growing, urbanising population.

"I wouldn't say it was a coherent Africa strategy," says Sanusha Naidu, research di-rector at the South African Foreign Policy Initiative. "I would say it was more driven by the private sector. Subsequently, who is driving the engagement between India and Africa? It's the Indian private sector that comes together under platforms like the Confederation of Indian Industry or the Federation of Indian Chambers of Commerce and Industry."

While there is no doubt that the private sector is the most visible manifestation of the Indian presence in Africa, the past few years have seen a dramatic change of approach by the Indian state, with the lead taken by the prime minister, Dr Manmohan Singh, himself. He has visited Africa seven times over the past seven years.

The most significant visit was in May 2011, when Dr Singh, accompanied by a large entourage of ministers and businessmen, attended the second Africa-India Summit in Addis Ababa, Ethiopia, the headquarters of the African Union. This was the largest ever gathering of Indian and African leaders on African soil. Dr Singh pledged $5 billion worth of soft loans over three years, and $1 billion support for education, training and railways.

Stating that Africa was emerging as the new growth pole of the world, Dr Singh added, "The current international economic and political situation is far from favour-able, particularly for developing countries. Even as the global economy is recovering from the economic crisis, fresh political up-heavals are taking place. The world faces new challenges in assuring food and energy security. Global institutions of governance are outmoded and under stress.

"We therefore need a new spirit of solidarity among developing countries. We must recognise that in this globalised age we all live interconnected lives in a small and fragile planet. We must work together to uplift the lives of our people in a manner that preserves the sustainability of our common air, land and water."

This sentiment, implying genuine partnership with Africa, has gone down well, particularly in East Africa with its long historical connections with the subcontinent. A series of bilateral projects in education, ICT, food processing, textiles, agriculture and transport infrastructure, announced during the summit, has been equally welcomed.

While critics have complained that India's direct political engagement in recent years – composed of smaller-scale, seemingly disparate initiatives that trail in the wake of the huge infrastructure projects and grand gestures coming from Beijing – appears to lack an overarching strategy, it does offer a friendlier alternative to China's more muscular approach.

This, in part, Naidu says, is due to the necessity to layer on the strategy ex post facto, a strategic element to their engagement, taking in economic development and energy – and national security.

This is not easy to do, and comes with considerable risks. While Indian companies – particularly those in the health care, pharmaceutical, agriculture and transport sec-tors – can offer considerable developmental benefits to their host countries, the potential for corporate missteps reflecting badly on the government is high.

Its diaspora has also given the private sector at least strong links into the East African community. However, it is diversifying, looking to the hydrocarbon economies of West Africa and deepening ties with Ethiopia, where it is both a diplomatic partner and a major investor. It was telling, Naidu notes, how quick New Delhi was to offer condolences on the death of the Ethiopian prime minister, Meles Zenawi, earlier this year.

India's attempts to widen its diplomatic presence will inevitably be compared to that of its Asian rival, China, which since the turn of the millennium has embarked on a massive, coordinated programme of commercial, economic and diplomatic engagement. This in turn has precipitated considerable hand-wringing in Western capitals, and also in New Delhi.

"It has always been the context of India's emergence in Africa, that it seems to be following in China's footprint," Naidu believes. "Analysts have said that China's resource strategy is being emulated by the Indians. China set up the Forum on China- Africa Cooperation, the Indians set up the Africa-India Forum Summit in 2008. There seems to be an interesting dynamic of, perhaps, the elephant chasing the dragon's tail."

In some areas, India's interest is nakedly for the acquisition of strategic minerals, such as uranium, to be used in its civilian nuclear programme. Indian companies have also invested heavily in coal and iron ore.

"What is interesting is that they moved into Namibia, Niger. But what we don't re-ally get out of the relationship between India and Africa is the backlash, as is the case in China," Naidu adds.

"In a way, I think India likes to play in the shadows, because as long as China is in the spotlight, China is getting all the attention, China is getting all the criticisms."

As the country's interests in the natural re-sources sector in Africa increase, and as its companies take a greater role in agriculture, including the politically sensitive issues of land rights which that entails, the chance of the focus shifting on to India grows.

Sometimes the rivalry between the two is very much in the open. When Chinese President Hu Jintao visited the Seychelles in 2007, beginning a pattern of overtures to the Indian Ocean islands that New Delhi has long considered its backyard, it caused considerable introspection in India.

The Indian Ocean remains the transit route for the majority of the country's energy resources. Somali piracy has spread across the region, causing concerns for the safety of shipping, while China's explicit strategy of building a chain of military outposts – the so-called 'string of pearls' – stretching all the way to Africa has placed it in direct competition with India.

"Hu Jintao was really putting himself about when he was visiting the Seychelles and Mauritius. China was building airports, setting up special economic zones off the Seychelles, and that impelled India to buck up its ideas," says Gerard McCann, a lecturer in modern history at the University of York and an expert in India's engagement with the developing world.

"I remember this memorable quote from a general I met in Delhi, who said that the Indian Ocean used to be India's Ocean," he continues. "It was assumed that this was India's backyard. But this competitiveness has developed. In 2004 or so, they came up with a new maritime doctrine, bucked up their ideas and became more interventionist."

As a result, India ramped up its rhetoric of cooperation in the region, working with both the US and South African navies. "Two years ago, China made a contribution of a few hundred thousand dollars into the Indian Ocean Rim Association [for Regional Cooperation] and wanted to become an observer member, and suddenly you had this flurry of activity around an association that had for a long time been pretty much moribund," says Elizabeth Sidiropoulos, director of the South African Institute of International Affairs.

"China recognised the Indian Ocean as being absolutely critical to its own energy security... India has been in a bit of a responsive, reactive mode, and they've realised that if they don't do something, they're going to have the Chinese with bases a couple of hundred nautical miles from their borders."

India's engagement with East Africa will, by necessity, increasingly take on a component of naval security, Sidiropoulos believes. However, the issue of it reacting to China, rather than proactively formulating and articulating an Africa strategy, means that India risks falling further behind.

Where China has succeeded and India has struggled is in the creation of a narrative. Chinese investment and trade offered African nations what many were looking for in a seemingly unipolar world – an alternative. In other words, financing with few strings attached and a clear developmental example.

"[China's] narrative was a unified and coherent one. It was about mutual benefit, it was about China as a developing country working together with other developing countries to realise developmental objectives," Sidiropoulos explains. "African states certainly believed that they could learn from the Chinese experience... and what they've achieved over 30 years, clearly that's a very compelling narrative. It is a compelling narrative not only in terms of the economics, but also because of the ideological and anti-colonial factors.

"You don't hear the narrative around Africa of how India is changing the way that development is happening in the way that you would about China."

However, that narrative may be starting to fray, as concerns grow over the role of Chinese trade in the de-industrialisation of African economies, she adds.

However, India has also been less successful in injecting itself into a leadership position in global debates. Whereas China has laboured to position itself at the fore-front of a developing markets bloc, India's role has been more muted, even in smaller groupings, such as the newly formalised BRICS (Brazil, Russia, India, China and South Africa) association of leading emerging countries.

Financial clout may have some part in it, but the Nehru-era rhetoric of solidarity among the 'Global South', which India pursued in a large part through the Non- Aligned Movement, seems to be less seductive than China's more forceful, almost confrontational approach to South-South partnerships.

"I would see it in the context of how the appreciation of India's national interests have changed, largely also brought on after the end of the Cold War," Sidiropoulos says. In light of developments within its subcontinent, and of a nuclear rapprochement with the USA, India is less interested in taking on an antagonistic role to counter US and European influences, she suggests.

India's democracy, too, slows down its decision-making process, which means that despite the smaller scale of its engagement, it is unable to deploy its resources as quickly. Those resources are also constrained. China's current account balance in 2011 was more than $200 billion – India's was in deficit by $47 billion. India's engagement is, by necessity, more sensitive to price. Local interests could also have a lot to do with the loss of focus on Africa. With instability in Afghanistan and Pakistan still weighing heavily on the domestic agenda, more long-term, strategic issues tend to fall by the wayside. "India's focus over the last couple of years has been its northwest – to Afghanistan and Pakistan," Sidiropoulos says. "I think there are some very domestic issues which have created stasis in regards to foreign relations, particularly vis-à-vis Africa, and I think there are issues in its immediate region that have become, from a national security perspective, far more important. But, of course, it focuses on those at its peril, because it then loses out on strategic opportunities outside."

MODI IN ASIA: STARING DOWN THE DRAGON WHILE EMBRACING IT

With the conclusion of his three-nation tour of China, Mongolia and South Korea last month, Prime Minister Narendra Modi capped a frenetic first year of diplomacy. It is becoming apparent that the emphasis on the Asian region will continue to be an imperative for the rest of his term. In this past year alone, the Indian Prime Minister has invested about twice as many days visiting the 'east' — Asia, the Indian Ocean Region and the Pacific — as against his 'westward' travels.

Is this a reinvigoration of India's Look East policy? Does it mean relatively less importance to the West? And, what are the drivers of this policy? Barring the notable absence of West Asia from his travel schedule, it is clear that 'Engage Asia' has been the predominant mantra of Modi's early days in office.

This Asian focus is decidedly different from previous efforts by Indian leaders to integrate with the neighbourhood. Those efforts were driven by the idea of demonstrating Indian leadership in a particular geography, or they were manifestations of south-south solidarity, or they were necessitated by security concerns emanating from across the border.

The current effort is something more. It is primarily aimed at completing two specific national projects, while at the same time positioning India at the helm of global affairs.

The first national project is to complete '20th century India': future-proofing Indian infrastructure; installing enough energy to power the nation; connecting the country with its periphery and beyond via roads, rail, ports and airports; developing manufacturing bases to employ the millions entering the job market each year; and investing in housing, agrarian and other social infrastructure that most developed economies take for granted.

Modi's Asian thrust is designed to find partnerships, technology and funds to complete this 20th century project. The Atlantic countries do not have the financial capacity to invest in large infrastructure and energy projects. They do not have the political room to commit to carbon-intensive industrialisation. And they no longer have the wherewithal to offer 20th century inputs (equipment, energy and technology) for an insatiable India.

All of these are readily available to the east of India. Consider this: China, Japan and Korea between them have close to US$5.5 trillion in foreign exchange reserves, funds desperately needed for this 20th century project.

There is a coincidence of needs as well. Each of these economies needs to invest in new geographies. They need to generate wealth out of what are now stagnant reserves. These are countries that have successfully completed their industrialisation projects and need to find outlets for investment in the industrialisation of others. That's why China has become the biggest provider of energy-generation equipment to India and wants to build high-speed trains here. It is why South Korea wants to build nuclear reactors and ports in India. And it is why the Japanese want to set up industrial corridors in India. Asia is also the source of most of the energy needs that are indispensable to this national project. Be it gas, uranium, coal variously sourced from Australia, Mongolia, Central Asia and the Middle East, this region offers India plenty of energy opportunities.

When Modi travels to these countries, it is tacit recognition that the response to Indian requirements carried forward from the last century reside there.

Then there is India's '21st century project', driven by innovation, based on new technologies, located within digital economies and fuelled by enhanced human capacity. This is the service-sector paradigm that India is already experiencing, and for which India needs high end solutions at rock bottom prices. For example, most of the 6 million new internet users India adds each month operate on handheld devices priced around the US$50-100 range on connections priced at a fraction of a dollar. Here too it is Asian countries — China, Taiwan and South Korea — that dominate the market. The expansion of this market, which will happen in tandem with the Digital India, Make in India, Skilling India and Smart Cities initiatives, will only see the market dominance of these Asian countries increase.

However, here is the poser: can India manage this Asian engagement while balancing an increasingly expansive China? This is the second element of the 'Engage Asia' mantra that Prime Minister Modi seeks to address.

Most Asian economies have their largest partnership with China and will always be looking over their shoulder as they define new partnerships with others. China's soft expansionism is being driven by its economic weight and through its pursuit of creating new political and economic governance institutions, like the AIIB, that will offer it a new dimension of power. Its One Belt, One Road project seeks to redefine and recreate Asia's geography.

In India's sense of its own role and position in global affairs, such Chinese dominance is unacceptable. New Delhi's running dispute over the 4000km border with China also complicates the bilateral relationship. India's existential dilemma for the 21st century, then, is to 'stare down the dragon while embracing it'.

This is where the US, a predominant Asian power, comes into play. It offers India two playing cards. First, it encourages others in Asia, such as South Korea and Japan, to participate in the India story in all sectors without the fear of China. In fact, this US gambit of midwifing Asian middle-power cooperation from arm's length is a seminal arrangement for the 'congagement' of China. Second, the unassailable US lead in security, defence and other high technology segments gives India a qualitative edge in its bilateral negotiations with China.

When Prime Minister Modi landed in Mongolia and South Korea on his way back from China, he was signaling that he intends to challenge the narrative of the Asian century as being a Chinese century. He was signaling that he intends to break the Chinese stranglehold in the Asian imagination of its future. He was signaling that here is an India willing to live up to expectations and take its rightful place as a major Asian power. Put simply, he was embracing the dragon while staring it down at the same time.

CROUCHING DRAGON, AMBLING ELEPHANT, AND THE HAWKISH EAGLE

Brief Significance of Indo-US and Sino-Indian Relations

Since 2001, there has been an upswing in US-India relations, greatly facilitated by the Bush Administration's reversal of the decades-long US policy of indifference towards India. The signing of the Next Steps in Strategic Partnership (NSSP) between the Bush Administration and the Manmohan Singh government heralded a new beginning to Indo-US relations and cemented India's growing rising power status. The 2005 civilian nuclear deal, which facilitated US technology assistance to India's civilian nuclear program and allowed the Nuclear Suppliers Group (NSG) to trade with India, a non-signatory to the NPT treaty, was unprecedented in the lengths to which the US and Indian governments co-operated to ensure the successful completion of the deal. Indo-US relations since the 2000s have been built largely on public harping on shared values of both states, such as democracy, but more importantly, on the unspoken shared threat, i.e. the rise of China. In 2008, the Obama Administration's "Pivot toward Asia" policy, as described by the then Secretary of State Hillary Clinton, included India as an important part of its strategy. Although the Indo-US relationship cannot be described as ultra-smooth, it can be argued that it has dramatically changed compared to the Cold War era.

The rise of China has been touted by many scholars as one of the defining events of the 20th century. The explosive and sustained economic growth by China for the past 25 years has resulted in the lifting of millions of its citizens from poverty and established the country as a major global power. However, unlike the Indo-US ties, which have progressively improved since the end of the Cold War despite minor hiccups, the Sino-Indian relations have been weighed down by a history of conflict and mutual suspicion over the border issue, with frequent "incursions" reported by both sides across the Line of Actual Control (LAC); China's close relationship with Pakistan; the 1998 Indian nuclear tests; and the recent India-US strategic relationship and the resulting civilian nuclear deal. While the Sino-Indian relations have witnessed rapid strides in the economic realm, with burgeoning trade between the two countries, the advantage is on China's side, as India has a huge trade deficit *vis-à-vis* China. China's attempts to form a "string of pearls" (which India perceives more as a choker necklace) in the Indian Ocean Region by forming close economic ties with Sri Lanka, Bangladesh, Mauritius, Maldives and Pakistan have been ignored by India. In this context of deepening but lopsided economic partnership on one hand, and unresolved strategic issues on the other, the Sino-Indian relations have been made more complex by the US strategic pivot toward India. India needs US' strategic partnership, which promises to "assist India in becoming a major world power," by strengthening the Indian military through arms sales, transfer of advanced technology, joint military exercises and intelligence sharing. At the same time, Indo-US strategic proximity could have the potential to stoke deep insecurity in the Chinese establishment over fears of containment and lead to a security dilemma, which could upset the fragile geopolitical stability in the Asia-Pacific region.

US-India-China Sandwich: A Palatable Option?

This chapter places the US-India and Sino-Indian relations in the context of international relations theories, namely, "balance of power" and "hegemon-rising power" theory. It also touches upon India's reaction to US overtures for strategic alliance.

US overtures toward India in the last decade are classic examples of a balancing act aimed at deterring a newly assertive China that is buoyed by its economic success and wants to expand its influence in the Asia-Pacific region, where the US has cemented its status as a non-resident great power for over half a century.

Both India and the US are wary of China's future hegemonic ambitions, and thus the strategic partnership can be seen as a natural act of external balancing by the two states directed at China.

Moreover, some scholars have stated that US hegemony is on the decline while China's power and influence is on the rise, and offensive realists like John Mearsheimer do not buy the view that China's rise will be peaceful and will resemble the 20th century Great Britain-US peaceful transfer of hegemony. India views China as an aggressive neighboring power with territorial ambitions while the US perceives China to be the only potential challenger to its unipolar status. China, on the other hand, views the ultimate goal of the US-India pairing up as the containment of its influence and power.

The Obama Administration has termed India as the "lynchpin" for the Asia pivot, thereby cementing its importance. However, India has reiterated that the US-India strategic partnership was not and never will be an "alliance" and has allegedly dismissed US offers of a strategic alliance. The reasons behind the steadfastness of Indian foreign policy makers in rejecting alliance formation with the US may range from post-colonial reservations and adherence to a non-aligned foreign policy to simply not wanting to fall into entrapment or upset its hostile neighbors and create an accidental crisis.

The US is frustrated by the perceived lack of proactive interest from India's side in taking forward the bilateral relationship. India wants to hold hands (with reservations, of course) with the US in order to steady its strategic position but is absolutely averse to embracing the US.

While the US views India's aloofness to be exasperating, India has wisely adopted a pragmatic approach in conducting its foreign policy. After all, it was only a few decades back that the US embraced China, and now, it wants India to side *against* China? India would rather be an ambling elephant and take its time to evaluate and, if necessary, pace its relationships with the superpower and the potential challenger, rather than trample upon the fragile stability that prevails in its neighbourhood.

Does the Eagle Bring Forth Instability?

Now that the dynamics of India-US strategic partnership and India-China relations have been laid out, this paper's central question arises: is the former a source of stability or instability to the latter? There have been a number of arguments on how the US strategic pivot to India is a source of instability to India-China relationship. The main argument is that the Indo-US strategic partnership may increase Chinese fears of a containment strategy and, thereby, fuel a security dilemma. This could result in a potential arms race between India and China, and induce China to partner with Pakistan to form a counter-containment alliance against India. Another argument is that India-US strategic relationship formed to "contain" China could lead to a self-fulfilling prophecy: i.e. China could use the containment argument in order to bolster its own military forces and engage in provocative behavior against India, especially with regard to the border issue. Or, the US partnership could embolden India to behave in a more hawkish manner in dealing with China. A third argument could be that US does not really matter in the overall Sino-Indian equations, i.e. the strategic "pivot" toward India that was championed by the Bush Administration has cooled considerably, especially in the present Obama Administration. After all, one can argue that the US strategic partnership did not serve as a deterrent for the Chinese from occupying disputed Indian Territory at the Daulat Beg Oldi/ Tiannan River Valley sector in April 2013.

However, considering the measured way in which India has responded to the US strategic pivot, showing neither extreme disinclination nor an overt lean toward the US, it has managed to assuage, if not dispel, Chinese fears of containment. India's conduct of its bilateral relationship with regard to the US has been tempered and pragmatic, mindful of China's sensitiveness about the relationship. For example, India cancelled a joint naval exercise with US and Japan in the Indian Ocean in May 2013, after the Chinese expressed their reservations. Thus, both China and India are highly sensitive and attuned to each other's views in order to prevent accidental escalation of tensions or an arms race scenario in the region. The Dempsang incursion has been termed by both sides as a "localised" and an "isolated" incident and was resolved through frantic working of the diplomatic channels on both sides. It can also be argued that the alleged Chinese incursion into Indian territory was a trigger for the signing of the comprehensive Border Defence Cooperation Agreement by the two sides in Beijing in October 2013, which stipulated that both states would never use force to resolve the border issue, a confidence-building measure that has stabilized the India-China relations to some extent. Critics who argue that US-India relations have cooled since 2009 are, however, partially correct. It is obvious that Obama has chosen to make Afghanistan and the Middle East as his priorities and is not as ecstatic as Bush was about India. However, the US-India strategic partnership is still "hot", as evidenced by the fact that US is now the largest arms supplier to India, overtaking Russia. In September 2012, India bought six C-130J Super Hercules multi-purpose aircraft from the US and is poised to obtain more long-range maritime patrol aircraft and other combat vehicles in deals worth billions of dollars. Therefore, while the political relations between India and the US may have hit a speed breaker according to some scholars, the strategic aspect is still moving forward at a rapid pace. And it is this strategic aspect that apparently worries the Chinese.

Why the Dragon Need Not Crouch

This chapter argues why the US strategic pivot toward India and Sino-Indian relations is not necessarily a zero-sum game. India can walk the proverbial tightrope between US and China while simultaneously furthering its own interests. This chapter bases its arguments on economic cooperation and capability-versus-intent arguments.

Sino-Indian relations have been beset with feelings of mutual suspicion and distrust, lingering after-effects of the 1962 border war in which India was comprehensively defeated. As a result, any and every foreign policy initiative taken by both sides would obviously be taken apart and scrutinized minutely to check if either side was indulging in an one-upmanship game. Thus, it was only logical, according to advocates of instability, that the India-US relations would adversely affect the Sino-Indian relationship.

However, this need not be the case, i.e. a zero-sum game might not necessarily be the accurate analogy to describe the complex relationships that India pursues with both US and China. Sino-Indian economic trade ($59.24 billion as of November 2013) is eclipsed by that between US and China (which totaled $421.3 billion as of December 2013), and China is the largest trading partner of both countries. Therefore, the US strategic pivot to India and the latter's response would always take cognizance of the China factor. An intimate strategic partnership between India and the US cannot be at the expense of alienating the Chinese, and it is important here to note that both India and the US run huge trade deficits with China. To put it more bluntly, US and India need China more than China needs them. Thus, it is in the interests of both US and India to have cordial and stable relations with the Chinese and not embark on a foreign policy adventures that antagonizes or alienates China.

Another evidence for a US strategic pivot to India facilitating stable Sino-Indian relations can be put forth by the "intent versus capability" argument. India buying arms from the US and deploying it in the Sino-Indian border does not necessarily translate into using them against China in the first instance it can. The same can be said of China, which has always stressed on peaceful co-existence with India and a distaste for the use of force to resolve any Sino-Indian disputes, as detailed by Premier of China, Le Keqiang during his visit to India in 2013. Thus, both India and China are clear on where they stand: they do not want to use force to resolve outstanding disputes and are eager to use the diplomatic route. Moreover, India and China are joining hands in many international forums such as climate change talks in resisting the US-led West's attempts to impose curbs on greenhouse gas emissions unilaterally on all countries. Thus China and India, as developing nations with billion-plus populations much in common between them than with the US in many policy aspects.

A Compgagement Approach

This chapter proposes that India should use the US strategic pivot to embark on competitive engagement ("compgagement") with China, as opposed to containment-engagement (i.e.

"congagement") which IR scholars use to describe the hawkish US strategy toward China. The congagement approach could work for the US as it is does not share borders with China. However, India cannot follow the US strategy because (1) it does not possess the means to contain China, and (2) even if it did, the "containment" part of the congagement strategy would prove detrimental to peace building in the region. Compgagement would, however, stabilize the Sino-Indian relationship because India's goal in this case would not be to contain China by modernizing the Indian military forces with technologies sourced from the US. Rather, India should signal to China that it could now equal the latter's strategic capability but *chooses* instead to focus on economic cooperation while continuing to compete with China in securing its economic and national interests (such as energy security) through peaceful means. The "compgagement" policy strategy would serve the double purpose of alleviating China's fears of containment (thereby significantly weakening the China-Pakistan relationship directed against India) while at the same time strengthening India's strategic position in the Asia-Pacific. This would also result in a better bargaining position for India in future diplomatic talks with China.

US would also benefit from the compgagement strategy pursued by India, as it would result in more arms sales to India, lesser threat perception from China, and greater stability in the Asia-Pacific region. Future stability in Sino-Indian relations would also dependent on whether China intends to be a status-quo or revisionist state. This essay tends to believe in the former. China is obviously not looking at world dominance, at least not until it addresses pressing domestic issues such as the income inequality. Thus, the US can be confident that China would not want to usurp its status, at least in the near future. India can be a valuable and mutually beneficial economic partner, with yet-untapped natural resources that it can export to fuel Chinese economy and having a huge market with purchasing power for Chinese manufactured goods. However, it is to be noted here that compgagement should also be supported by increased diplomatic interactions between India and China. India should also be wary that too much competitiveness (e.g. extreme build-up of arms sourced from the

US) supported by little constructive engagement would definitely destabilize the Sino-Indian relationship.

Conclusion: The Elephant in the Region

This chapter concludes that the US strategic pivot toward India need not necessarily destabilize Sino-Indian relations. India should use the newfound US interest in pursuing a strong bilateral strategic partnership to refine and upgrade its defense systems and military strategies while simultaneously pursuing a policy of compgagement with China. Therefore, the onus is on India to: (1) strengthen its strategic position *vis-à-vis* China while intensifying high-level diplomatic interactions; (2) resist US attempts in jointly pursuing a containment policy against China and continue to pursue an autonomous foreign policy that places India's interests first; and (3) continue to pursue mutually beneficial economic interactions with both US and China. If China perceives India as overtly leaning toward the US in the future, this might exacerbate Chinese fears of ganging up by US and India to prevent its rise. Meanwhile, China should come to terms with the fact that the US-India relationship is here to stay. The main tussle India would face in the future is increased US pressure to contain China in the Indian Ocean Region. India should resist US charm (which it has abundant past experience in doing) and recalibrate its autonomous foreign policy toward achieving greater efficiency in furthering its national interests. The first step to do so is to try and reduce the huge trade deficits that it runs up with China. A stronger India, a more secure China, and a confident US would be the best bet to ensure that Sino-Indian and Indo-US relations continue to progress from strength to strength and lead to overall peace and stability in the region.

5

The Real Roots of China-Japan Tensions

China and Japan, the world's second and third largest economies, do not get along. Increasingly noisy nationalist movements in both countries seem to consider the other country their ancient enemy, with citizens leading sometimes violent anti-Japanese or anti-Chinese protests and national leaders, including the heads of state, promoting confrontation over diplomacy.

The two most recent conflict points are a string of tiny, disputed islands, called the Senkaku in Japan and Diaoyu in China, to which both countries have sent increasingly belligerent naval patrols, and Japanese Prime Minister Shinzo Abe's hints that he might partially retract Japan's official apologies for its World War II-era abuses in Asia.

These conflicts can often look like just the most recent manifestations of an ancient and sometimes vicious rivalry. And this is often the view in those countries themselves. As Japanese Deputy Prime Minister Taro Aso said during a recent visit to India, "For the past 1,500 years and more, there has never been a history when our relations with China went extremely smoothly." In this telling, the ancient, ingrained tensions are being worsened by present-day factors: China's rise, Japan's decline, the unaddressed legacy of World War II. But what if it's the other way around? What if its those contemporary (and temporary) issues that are driving the war-of-words, with past conflict little more than an excuse?

That's what Ian Buruma, a highly respected historian who focuses on Asia (and who wrote "Inventing Japan: 1853-1964," a great book about modern Japan), argues in an essay for the Wall Street Journal. "On the surface, the dispute is about history," Buruma writes. "In fact, it is more about politics, domestic and international, revealing the tangled relations in a region where history is frequently manipulated for political ends."

It turns out that even China's communist-era founder, Mao Zedong, had pretty smooth relations with Japan. The conflict, in other words, is much, much more recent than you might think. Here's Buruma with a surprising story from Mao's era, when things seemed downright jovial:

When Prime Minister Kakuei Tanaka visited Beijing in 1972 to restore Japan's relations with China, a country that had been devastated by Japanese military aggression in the 1930s and '40s, his host Mao Zedong allowed himself a moment of levity. Responding to Tanaka's apology for what Japan had done during the war, Mao answered that there was absolutely no need to apologize. After all, he said, without the Japanese invasion, the Communist revolution would never have succeeded.

Secure in his nationalist credentials, as the leader who unified China, Mao could afford this little joke, which also happened to be the truth. Such a remark would be unimaginable for any of the technocrats who rule China today. Maoism can no longer justify the Communist Party's monopoly on power, since few Chinese believe in any kind of Communism. Nationalism is now the dominant ideology, and the rulers have to prove their mettle, especially toward Japan. This need is particularly acute when a new leader takes power. The latest party boss, Xi Jinping, needs to show people, not least the military brass, that he is in charge.

In other words, because Chinese isn't really Maoist or Marxist anymore, the country had to find a new ideology, a new way to legitimate the Communist Party's rule. That ideology is nationalism, but nationalism requires an "other," a foreign country to galvanize patriotism and against which to define national identity.

And the United States has played a role in all of this, using its post-war influence in Japan (we still have tens of thousands of troops there, and the U.S.-backed pacifist constitution leaves the country conveniently reliant on U.S. support) to "contain" China. Buruma writes, "Even when Japanese businessmen pressed for closer relations with China in 1970, the Japanese prime minister, Eisaku Sato, staved them off out of deference to the U.S. policy of containing China."

And Japan has still not fully recovered its own national identity, which was once sternly nationalist but was outright destroyed when the country lost World War II. The country's struggle to reinvent itself, ongoing for 60 years now, includes a major dilemma about whether or not Japan gets to be a real world power again.

This internal tension between "the need to act like a major power while still being deferential to American interests," as Buruma puts it, has sometimes led the country's leaders to embrace nationalism as a way to compensate for the embarrassing reliance on the United States. Buruma argues that the only way to return stability to East Asia is for the United States to withdraw from Japan and allow the country greater independence.

Maybe he's right, but if the United States really leaves Japan on its own at a time when the country's power is declining and China's is rising, that will force Tokyo to make a very difficult choice:

Japan could rearm, maybe even develop nuclear weapons so that it will be strong enough to balance against China. Members of the foreign policy "realist" school warn that this could lead to a potentially dangerous China-Japan arms race.

Or Japan could choose to "bandwagon" with China rather than competing with it, thus turning it back against the United States. This would potentially transform the balance of power in East Asia, making China rather the United States the dominant power, something that could have enormous knock-on effects in the region, for example on the Korean peninsula, with South Korea suddenly isolated among its neighbors.

That's a worst-case hypothetical, but it's exactly the sort of scenario that the Obama administration is seeking to avoid with its "pivot to Asia."

A SINO-JAPANESE CLASH IN THE EAST CHINA SEA

Tensions have risen to dangerous levels between Japan and China over a small group of uninhabited islands in the East China Sea, called the Senkaku by the Japanese and the Diaoyu by the Chinese. These islands were once controlled by the United States as part of its post–World War II occupation of Japan and only returned to Japanese administrative control with the reversion of Okinawa in 1971. As Washington prepared to return these islands to Japan, the People's Republic of China (PRC) and Taiwan contested Japan's sovereignty. Two years earlier, a United Nations (UN) geological survey of the East China Sea revealed the potential of significant hydrocarbon resources. Contending sovereignty claims over the islands thus have both historical and resource-related dimensions.

Until recently, this territorial dispute was little more than a minor irritant in Sino-Japanese relations. However, against the backdrop of China's growing military power, the island dispute has increased concerns in Tokyo about Beijing's regional intentions and the adequacy of Japan's security, while stoking nationalistic politics in both capitals. Political miscalculation in Tokyo or Beijing, or unintended military interactions in and around the disputed islands, could escalate further, leading to an armed clash between Asia's two largest powers. The United States, as a treaty ally of Japan but with vital strategic interests in fostering peaceful relations with China, has a major stake in averting such a clash and resolving the dispute, if possible.

The Contingencies

Sino-Japanese tensions in the East China Sea have been building steadily since 2010, when a Chinese fishing trawler rammed two Japan Coast Guard (JCG) vessels in waters near the Senkaku/ Diaoyu Islands and Japan detained the captain. Although the crisis was eventually defused, the territorial dispute came to a head again in September 2012, when Japanese prime minister Yoshihiko Noda announced his government's decision to purchase three of the five islands. The islands were privately owned, but a new wave of activism, including Chinese attempts to land on the islands and a public campaign by the Tokyo governor to purchase them himself, prompted Noda to attempt to neutralize nationalist pressures. The decision triggered widespread anti-Japanese demonstrations in China, resulting in extensive damage to Japanese companies operating there. Eventually China dampened the popular response, but it has since repeatedly stated its intent to assert its own administrative control over the disputed islands. China's Marine Surveillance agency intensified its patrols of the waters in and around the islands, and China's Bureau of Fisheries patrols followed suit. The JCG in turn increased its patrols and put them on 24/7 alert.

The danger of escalation to armed conflict increased when the two militaries became directly involved. On December 13, 2012, a small Chinese reconnaissance aircraft entered undetected into Japanese airspace above the islands. The JCG alerted Japan's Air Self-Defense Force (ASDF), which scrambled fighter jets based in Naha, Okinawa; however, they were too late to intercept. In January, China sent its reconnaissance aircraft back toward the islands accompanied by fighter jets, but stopped short of entering Japan's airspace, and no direct aerial confrontation occurred. Japan's Maritime Self-Defense Force (MSDF) reported that a Chinese frigate locked its firing radar on the Japanese destroyer *Yudachi* on January 30, 2013. Chinese authorities instigated an investigation into the incident in response to Japan's protest, leading to speculation that Beijing was unaware of the ship captain's actions. Although China's Ministry of Defense later denied that the incident took place, it did acknowledge the danger such an act posed. Given current circumstances in the East China Sea, three contingencies are conceivable: first, an accidental or unintended incident in and around the disputed islands could trigger a military escalation of the crisis; second, either country could make a serious political miscalculation in an effort to demonstrate sovereign control; and third, either country could attempt to forcibly control the islands.

Accidental/Unintended Military Incident

Although recent incidents have sensitized China and Japan to the risk of accidental and unintended military interactions, the danger will persist while emotions run high and their forces operate in close proximity. In stressful and ambiguous times, when decision-making is compressed by the speed of modern weapons systems, the risk of human error is higher. The 2001 collision between a U.S. reconnaissance aircraft and a Chinese fighter jet near Hainan Island is a case in point, as was the intrusion of a Chinese Han submarine in Japanese territorial waters in 2004. So-called rules of engagement (ROEs), intended to guide and control the behaviour of local actors, are typically general in scope and leave room for personal interpretation that may lead to actions that escalate a crisis situation. Compounding the risk of unintended escalation between Chinese and Japanese air and naval units is the unpredictable involvement of third parties such as fishermen or civilian activists who may attempt to land on the islands. Their actions could precipitate an armed response by either side.

Political Miscalculation in an Effort to Demonstrate Sovereign Control

Political miscalculation of either country's intent or resolve, as well as miscalculation of the U.S. position, could lead to armed conflict. First, Japan and China are already finding it difficult to read each other's actions. Past Japanese government leasing of the Senkaku/Diaoyu Islands effectively kept nationalist activists—Japanese as well as Chinese and Taiwanese—at bay. In mid-2012, however, rising nationalist sentiments during leadership transitions inflamed the dispute. This stimulated heated debate in Tokyo over how to consolidate Japanese sovereignty and was a factor in the December 2012 election of conservative prime minister Shinzo Abe, who advocated inhabiting the islands. This escalation in asserting sovereignty claims through the use of patrols, populating the islands, and perhaps even military defense of the territory could lead to heightened tensions between the two countries and whip up nationalist sentiments, potentially limiting the capacity of leaders to peacefully manage the dispute.

Second, China could miscalculate U.S. interests and intentions. Since last year, U.S. policymakers have sought to lessen tensions but have also taken steps to clarify the U.S. role in deterring any coercive action by China. U.S. and Japanese forces have conducted regular exercises to strengthen defense of Japan's southwestern islands and maritime surveillance capabilities.

Both former secretary of state Hillary Clinton and former secretary of defense Leon Panetta clearly stated that the United States will defend Japan against any aggression, and on November 29, 2012, the U.S. Senate passed a resolution accompanying the 2013 National Defense Authorization Act to demonstrate congressional support for the Obama administration's commitment to Japan's defense. As tensions escalated late last year, Washington increased its deployments in and around Japan. Early this year, as military interactions raised the potential for conflict, Clinton restated the U.S. position that it would not accept any unilateral attempt to wrest control of the islands. Still, Beijing could miscalculate Washington's commitment to defend Japan and/or seek to test that commitment. Finally, U.S. assurances could lead Tokyo to overestimate Washington's response and to act in a manner that would increase the chance for confrontation. To date, however, Tokyo has tended to err on the side of caution in planning and exercises with U.S. forces, and it is unlikely Japan would act without evidence of U.S. assistance.

Deliberate Action to Forcibly Establish Control Over Islands

Although this seems highly unlikely today, either party could take military action to assert sovereignty over the disputed islands. Rising domestic pressures or an unexpected opportunity for a fait accompli could lead to a decision by either government to establish military control over the territory.

CHINA AND JAPAN'S SIMMERING RIVALRY

China and Japan, the giants of Asia, account for nearly three-quarters of the region's economic activity and more than half of the region's military spending. Despite their deep economic ties and a doubling of their bilateral trade in the past five years, their relationship is increasingly strained, with dangerous implications for the United States and the world at large.

Historically, relations between Japan and China were clearly structured. One country was always more prosperous or powerful than the other. Before the nineteenth century, China was usually dominant; since the Meiji Restoration, in 1868, Japan has generally been preeminent. The prospect that China and Japan could both be powerful and affluent at the same time has only recently emerged, largely because while China's economy and influence have grown rapidly, Japan's have remained stagnant. China has nuclear weapons and intercontinental ballistic missiles, and its military budget has grown by double-digit rates for 17 consecutive years. Although Japan has a relatively low military profile, with its "no-war" constitution and strong alliance with the United States, its defense-relevant technology is sophisticated and it has recently become more proactive. The stage is now set for a struggle between a mature power and a rising one.

Some liken current Sino-Japanese relations to the Anglo-German rivalry prior to World War I. As with the United Kingdom and Germany a century ago, the contest for regional leadership between China and Japan today is creating new security dilemmas, prompting concerns over Chinese ambitions in Japan and fears of renewed Japanese militarism in China. Both states are adopting confrontational stances, partly because of rising popular involvement in politics and resurgent nationalism exacerbated by revived memories of World War II; mutually beneficial economic dealings alone are not effectively soothing these tensions. Fluid perceptions of power and fear, Thucydides observed, are the classic causes of war. And they are increasingly present in Northeast Asia today.

Pair of Rivals

Many contentious issues confront China and Japan. Among the most pressing is their thirst for energy. Japan depends on imports for 99 percent of its oil and natural gas; coastal China is similarly bereft of resources. Thus, the offshore oil and gas fields under the East China Sea are attractive "domestic" sources of energy for both Beijing and Tokyo — and both have laid claim to them. China argues that the entire East China Sea continental shelf, extending eastward nearly all the way to Okinawa, is a "natural prolongation" of the Chinese mainland. Japan has declared its boundary to be a median line between its undisputed territory and China — a line that runs roughly 100 miles west of the Okinawa Trough, which lies undersea just west of Okinawa and is where the richest petroleum deposits in the area are believed to be concentrated.

The conflict began escalating in May 2004 when China started serious exploratory operations in the Chunxiao gas fields, only four kilometers from the median line. Actions by both parties have since raised tensions. In November 2004, a Chinese nuclear-powered attack submarine intruded into Japanese waters near Okinawa for more than two hours, ostensibly by accident. Since the spring of 2005, the number of flights into disputed airspace by Chinese military surveillance aircraft has risen to record levels. In May 2005, Japan's Ministry of Economy, Trade, and Industry (METI) authorized Japanese companies to explore contested areas for natural gas. On the eve of the Japanese elections in September 2005, Chinese warships patrolled near the now-active Chunxiao fields. In response, both Japan's ruling coalition, led by the Liberal Democratic Party (LDP), and the opposition Democratic Party of Japan (DPJ) have prepared bills proposing to protect the operations of Japanese drillers and fishermen in disputed waters — by force, if necessary.

The Korean Peninsula and the Taiwan Strait also present challenges for the Sino-Japanese relationship and for regional stability. Since the Pyongyang summit in June 2000, trade between South Korea and North Korea has grown by 150 percent, cross-border tourism has boomed, railway lines across the demilitarized zone have been reconnected, and a special economic zone in the peninsula's ancient capital of Kaesong, now in North Korea, has begun to flourish with South Korea's backing. As the likelihood of inter-Korean conflict declines, the long-term rivalry between China and Japan for influence on the peninsula may be rekindled — a rivalry that helped spark the first Sino-Japanese War, of 1894-95. Unification or reconciliation could also deepen the sense Japan has that its position in Northeast Asia is under siege. Were the military forces of North Korea and South Korea to be combined, they would number close to ten times those in Japan's Self-Defense Forces (SDF).

Like the Koreas, Taiwan and China have grown more intertwined economically. According to most estimates, investment across the Taiwan Strait now totals over $100 billion. More than 70 percent of Taiwan's foreign investment went to the mainland in 2004, 10 percent of Taiwan's labour force works in China, and four Taiwanese-owned firms are among the mainland's top ten exporters. (Taiwan now trades substantially more with China than it does with the United States.) There have also been signs of an emerging political détente between Beijing and Taiwan's opposition parties: Lien Chan, chair of the Kuomintang Party (KMT) that Chiang Kai-shek led to Taiwan at the end of 1949, went to the mainland in April 2005, where he visited his ancestors' graves and the former KMT capital of Nanjing and met with China's president, Hu Jintao. Meanwhile, both countries' military capabilities have increased. China has deployed dozens of submarines and frigates, 800 short-range missiles, over 1,200 fighter aircraft, and tens of thousands of troops along the Taiwan Strait. Taiwan has countered by deploying its own missiles and nearly 300 top-of-the-line fighter planes, mainly U.S.-built F-16s.

Beijing's military buildup has implications for Tokyo: the missiles China has aimed at Taiwan could easily reach Japan's main islands as well as Okinawa, where 70 percent of U.S. defense facilities in Japan, including the indispensable Kadena Air Force Base, are located. Both U.S. and Japanese defense specialists thus view neutralizing this potential threat as a vital goal.

The United States and Japan will conduct missile tests in Hawaii during the spring of 2006 to establish the efficacy of ballistic missile defenses. If a missile defense system were deployed, the U.S.-Japanese alliance's capabilities would be enhanced — and Beijing would be alarmed by the weakening of its relative position. The issue is therefore emerging as yet another area of controversy in Sino-Japanese relations.

As Sino-Japanese tensions increase, it is becoming more and more likely that Japan will revise its constitution in ways that will allow the SDF greater freedom of action, even as other nonmilitary reforms are achieved as well. (The constitution, written in 1947, limits the SDF to a narrowly defensive role.) Beyond the regional tensions themselves, important long-term structural changes in Japanese politics are at work: the combined socialist and communist representation in the Diet has fallen from 14 to 3 percent over the past decade, leaving the conservative LDP and its coalition partner with the two-thirds majority needed to begin amendment of the constitution and leaving the left with only 16 of 480 seats in the Diet's dominant lower house. The recent ascendancy of defense hawks in the DPJ has also amplified the left's collapse.

The current LDP draft amendment, published in October 2005, would retain the historic Article 9, which states that "the Japanese people forever renounce war as a sovereign right of the nation." But the proposal would also clearly legitimate the SDF (an institution whose role has been constitutionally ambiguous); clarify Japan's prerogative to participate in collective self-defense, the linchpin of the security cooperation between Japan and the United States; and simplify procedures for amending the constitution in the future. This procedural change could further exacerbate Sino-Japanese tensions by increasing uncertainty regarding Japan's future rearmament.

THE 'CHINA THREAT DEBATE' REVISITED

China is the biggest and fastest-growing rising power (Garret, 2010:29). Its rapid and profoundly steady economic growth increasingly facilitates the simultaneous expansion of its military power. Beijing's gravitas as an actor in the international system was considerable even before the last 30 years of impressive growth. In 1970 China already held a permanent seat in the UNSC and had 20 nuclear-tipped ICBMs (Burr, 2000). This essay analyzes whether China's 30-year-long economic development and its far-reaching implications pose a genuine threat to the United States. It does the same with China's military development. But before outlining how we are approaching these central questions in this chapter, we need to clarify what we understand as a 'genuine threat'. Succinctly, we interpret here a 'genuine threat' to be an eminent danger or direct challenge to another actor's existence or his vital interests. We first tackle the question of China's economic development, examining the potential challenges this may pose to the US, to demonstrate, that the challenges posed are mostly outnumbered by the opportunities at hand. The argument of growing interdependence and the enmeshment of China in the structures of global economic governance will be evaluated, to examine its potential significance for Sino-American relations. Subsequently, an analysis of the military dimension of China's rise will follow, examining the challenges posed by Beijing's ascension in Asia and beyond, with the aim of identifying the space for conflict, accommodation and understanding with America and its regional interests. Throughout the essay, we refer to the 'China Threat' theory, developing their arguments and testing them against evidence at hand. We agree with Ramo (2004:7), that of the most interesting aspects of the 'China Threat' debate is that the 'louder...it becomes, the less sense it makes'. Our findings suggest that attempts to present China as an existential, pressing and genuine threat to the US, are, at this stage at least, exceedingly exaggerated.

Chinese Economic Development: Threat, Challenge, or Opportunity?

Nicholas Kristof, predicted in 1993 that, 'if continued, China's rise will be the most important trend in the world'. Well China has in fact continued to rise rather steadily for 17 years since that prediction, and it seems China will continue to rise in the proximate future. As Bijian points out, the main driver of China's rise, the motor behind its expanding influence, is its profound economic growth. In the last 32 years, China has averaged GDP annual growth rates 'of more than 10%' annually. This trend accounts for China being the 'fastest-growing' economy in the world (Makiel, 2008:24). Since 2010, China has emerged as the world's second largest economy after the US. Overtaking its regional competitor, Japan, China emerged as the most powerful economic actor in Asia.

Despite these impressive economic achievements, this chapter will argue that China's emergence as an economic superpower, is certainly not a threat, and though it does pose some challenges, they clearly are of less magnitude than the great opportunities it presents. To begin with, it is important to remember that America remains by far the most technologically advanced economy and still possesses roughly four times China's share of the global wealth - China is not pushing America in the sidelines of the global economic order just yet. Moreover, China is still a developing country, still ranking 97th in terms of GDP p.c. (IMF, 2010). One may rush to say this is irrelevant. Well, this is not true in the case of China. China's priority is economic development and modernization. For as long as China lags behind in terms of economic development and living standards, China's leaders will concentrate on thriving in this arena (Bijian, 2005:18). It is critical for the progress of China as a nation, the survival of the CCP and its leadership, as well as for social cohesion and national unity.

Economic Interdependence

'[China] has come to rely on international markets, global institutions and free trade to achieve economic growth'. Moreover, as Waldron points out, there are several reasons to believe that though possible, it will certainly not be easy for China to continue to rise at that pace. It will indeed require the prioritization of the economy over all other issues, and also the minimization of any tensions in its foreign relations, as China is dependent 'to an unhealthy degree on exports'. There are many additional factors why Chinese economic progress largely depends on the country's (evident) commitment to 'heping juegi'. Notions of 'codependance' and interdependence are central to understanding, why Beijing and Washington genuinely need each other for their mutual economic advancement.

Importantly, it is true that China's Central Bank holds the world's largest foreign currency reserves, including the largest share of US dollars. Some like Miller (2010) see a danger in this, stressing that China's dollar reserves equip it with leverage over the US. Such analysis neglects the fact that if China does attempt to speculate against the dollar, this means China will lose billions because of the dollar value it holds. Hence, it has become partially China's interest for the dollar to be stable and thriving as opposed to unstable and collapsing. Furthermore, it is important at this stage to reiterate that China needs to devote a larger effort to remain a reliable economic partner, as potential repercussions are graver. Reversely, US's long held position at the peak of the global economic pyramid enables it to turn more easily to other rich economies to secure increased partnership (even at a higher cost).

Additionally, China has been buying American debt in IOU's and bonds. This chapter agrees with Garrett (2010:29-31) that the format-'China buys American debt and Americans buy Chinese goods will endure'. This is the case because both benefit through this model, addressing their imbalances to strike a mutually beneficial equilibrium. 'China Threat' proponents might again be alarmed by this 'erosion of America's economic sovereignty'. They again seem to be missing the whole picture. Instead of interpreting this development as a danger, they should be welcoming it as a positive step. Chinese purchases of US debt integrate China further into the world economy, but also tie China to the flourishing of the American economy. Based on the analysis conducted above, it should also become clear that if US fails/stops for some reason to continue repaying its debt, this would first and foremost damage Chinese economic interests, leaving the CCP leadership with very restricted room for manoeuvre.

CHINA THREAT PROPELS A NEW DEFENCE THINKING IN JAPAN

Concerned with Chinese military assertions and increased surveillance around its southern islands, Japan has unveiled its will in its new National Defense Program Guidelines1 (NDPG) to fill the "defence vacuum" by deploying permanent troops to these "outlaying islands". The approval of the new defence guidelines by the Japanese government comes at the backdrop of Japan and China's diplomatic spat following Chinese fishing trawler's collision with a Japanese coast guard's patrolling vessel off the southern Senkaku Islands. The uninhibited Senkaku Islands are under effective administration of Japan since 1895, but its sovereignty is contested by its two other neigbours-Taiwan and China.

Japanese new defence thinking of deploying troops to secure its southern Islands reflects the fact that Japan gears itself to counter any assertion by China over its territory and therefore the guideline has identified Nansei Islands, Ishigaki Islands and Yonaguni Islands - all in the geographical proximity of China and Taiwan - where it would double the presence of its Self Defense Force (SDF) and will also reinforce the presence of the Air and the Maritime Self-Defense Force.

Japan is also considering deploying troops to the west of Okinawa's Miyako Island an area the defence ministry recently described as a "defence vacuum" or "defence void" as no SDF units are permanently deployed there. "With the anticipated participation of more SDF troops in the area, Japan hopes to keep tabs on China, which has continued to increase naval activities in waters surrounding Japan," a Japanese newspaper quoted an unnamed source in Japanese defence ministry as saying.

For the first time in its defence planning, Japan has introduced the concept of "dynamic defence capability" which emphasises on mobility of its defence troops to secure its outlaying islands from an invasion rather than uniform deployment of troops on Japanese archipelago. As part of this concept, Japan will reduce deployment of its troops from its northern Island Hokkaido and move these troops to southern islands, identified in the new defence guidelines. Japan had deployed heavy troops on northern Hokkaido Island (closer to present Russia) during the Cold War amid the perceived threat from the Soviet Union. Considered from this aspect, it is a major shift in Japan's Cold War security policy as China has officially replaced Soviet Union as a major threat to country's security.

China is becoming prime security concern for Japanese security planners, also stems from the fact that the Japanese administration took the bold step of an envisioned downsizing its troop from northern Hokkaido Island despite Russia's renewed assertion over the Northern Island chains – a disputed territory between Russia and Japan under Russian effective administration since the end of the World War II off Hokkaido. Last month Russian President Medvedev visited Kunashiri Island (one of the four disputed Islands). He was the first ever Russian leader who stepped on the island, ignoring the Japanese warning. Though Russia had aborted similar efforts of former Japanese Prime Minister Junichiro

Koizumi's bid to land on the disputed territory. This month Russian first Deputy Prime Minister Igor Shuvalov visited the disputed island which further irked Tokyo and the diplomatic standoff between the two neighbouring countries continues. Therefore the Japanese strategic planners' southern shift amidst Russian assertion over its northern territory suggests the fact that Japanese are taking Chinese assertion more seriously than the Russian one. And certainly they are considering their southern islands more vulnerable than the northern one.

The new defence guidelines which is Japan's fourth defence guidelines since 1976, has raised concerns over Chinese navy's increased presence and surveillance in its water around Japan. The new NDPG has described Chinese activities a "matter of concern for the regional and international security." This is also considered a departure in Japanese defence thinking vis-a-vis China as previous guidelines has merely stressed the "need to focus on the trends of China in future." As regards North Korea it says that the reclusive state's "military movements are a major element of instability."

How to meet the challenges of rising Chinese threat amid 1% GDP cap on its defence spending put in place by the Japanese Diet since 1976 and the recession hit economy has been biggest puzzle for Japanese strategic planners. To achieve the task of improving mobility in order to deploy SDF to Nansei Island, Japan needs more vessel and high speed aircraft carriers. So in order not to exceed the defence spending from the present level, the Japanese defence planners have envisioned a cut in its SDF personnel as well as fighter tanks. An appendix in the present guidelines shows that Japan will downsize its troops by 1,000 personnel. With that the total number of the Japanese Ground Self Defence Force (GSDF) will come down to 154,000 the lowest ever maintained by Japan. Under the first Defence guidelines in 1976 Japan had maintained 180,000 GSDF troops. So the Japanese defence trend suggests that it is the GSDF which faces the axe to meet the challenge of maintaining 1% GDP cap on defence spending. The appendix in the NDPG also shows that Japan will reduce the number of fighterr tanks used by its GSDF from about nearly 600 to 390 over the next few years. But to achieve the target of mobility, the Guideline foresees increasing the number of submarines in its naval fleet from the current 16 to 22. Japanese defence planners have added appendix for the first time in its new NDPG showing its defence strength and requirement of future procurement in order to bring transparency in its defence policy. The move is yet again targeted against China from which Japan has been demanding to bring transparency on its defence spending.

But too much China centric defence planning is also likely to cause alarm and suspicion and could give China an excuse to expand its military including the naval capability. Sensing the possibility the *Asahi Shimbun* has cautioned the Japanese government from going too close to China. In one of its editorial the daily has questioned Japanese new defence policy asking that "it may be necessary to prepare for contingencies, but isn't it wiser to enhance readiness to enable vessels and aircraft to be deployed from a distance? Showing off armor alone does not serve as a deterrent." A week before endorsement of the new defence guidelines, the daily has suggested the Japanese and the Chinese governments to "create a mechanism for communications and establish rules for avoiding dangerous situations."

A harsh reaction was expected from China on the adoption of China centric defence planning by Tokyo. China was quick to react to the endorsement of new defence guidelines and slammed Japanese view as "irresponsible". Chinese Foreign Ministry's spokesperson Jiang Yu commenting on Japanese defence guidelines said that "individual countries have no right to represent the international community and make irresponsible remarks on China's development."

However, in a bid to calm the international and domestic reaction, the Japanese Prime Minister after the adoption of the guidelines said that "Challenges and uncertainties to Japan's national security are becoming more complex and multilayered... we need to shift our defence policy to deal such situations."

The Japanese Cabinets decision to approve the defence guidelines, which was due for an year since the previous guidelines expired in December 2009, comes at the backdrop of operation

"Keen Sword" jointly conducted by the US and Japanese troops aimed at achieving twin task of checking North Korea's military provocations and China's assertion in East China Sea. In the past, such moves were fiercely opposed by Japanese pacifist groups which saw these steps as moving back to prewar militarism. The same was expected this time around. But the DPJ government, it seems, waited for an opportune time to avert public opposition towards its defence policies. Since these decisions coincide with the volatile security situation in the region following North Korean shelling on South Korea's Yeonpyeong incident, the Japanese government has been able to avert a possible protest by opposition parties as well as the peace groups. The DPJ government this time has been able to drive the point to its public of a Korea and China threat, who in the past had not bought these arguments.

CHINA-JAPAN-ASEAN RELATIONS AND EASTERN ASIA'S INTEGRATION

In the context of globalization, cooperation as well as competition is becoming intensified among different countries, and more and more countries have realized that regionalization is a wise choice. Therefore, in order to survive from fierce competition, countries adjoining to each other choose to cooperate and build up communities and compete with other regions as a whole, as a result, some economic blocs have been set up in the Americas and Europe such as the North American Free Trade Area (NAFTA) and the European Union (EU).

Among all the regional organizations, the most successful case of regional integration is the European Union. After the World War a!, Western Europe suffered from disastrous economic recession. Facing the descendent of international status and challenge of US rise, two leading countries of Western Europe, Germany and France, decided to stop fighting and cooperate with each other, which was started from <Schumann Agreement>. Nowadays, EU, which has already become the world's largest political and economic integration organization, keeps expanding and its remarkable development and influence have been recognized around the world. Politically, under most circumstances,

EU member countries share consistent stances and act as a whole. Economically, EU members have eliminated tariff barrier and realized free trade within the region; besides, in order to protect regional economic development, EU members made common tariff policy when trading with countries outside the region. As a result, it is comparatively difficult for countries from other regions such as Eastern Asia to keep competitive when trading with EU, which is harmful to their development. Therefore, given that Eastern Asia takes up 1/3 of the world's population, 2/5 of the world's foreign reserves, and approximate 1/4 of the world's GNP, it is a wise choice for Eastern Asia to build up economic bloc and trade with countries outside the region as a whole.

When it comes to the conditions necessary for regional integration, Eastern Asia has many similarities with Western Europe. More specifically, firstly, the idea of unification of Western Europe was originated from promoting economic development and regional secure environment, represented by the European Coal and Steel Community (ECSC), the European Economic Community (EEC) and the European Atomic Energy Community (Euratom). In Eastern Asia, some economic organizations such as ASEAN, "ASEAN+1" and "ASEAN+3" have already gained great achievements. Secondly, the integration of Western Europe is premised upon the agreement reached by Germany and France which realized that cooperation was a win-win choice. Similarly, the two great powers in Eastern Asia, China and Japan, also express their supports for regional integration and declare to make contribution to the integration process. Thirdly, the recession of Western Europe and the rise of US propelled Germany and France to cooperate. Eastern Asia remains comparatively the least unified region compared with other regions. Undoubtedly, it is difficult for Eastern Asia to maintain competitive when trading with other regional organizations. Thereof, the increasing pressure from international competition also forces Eastern Asia to promote regional integration.

In spite of these similarities, several forces in Eastern Asia are driving the proliferation of free trade areas as well. Firstly, the 1997 Asian financial crisis ended the so-called "economic miracle" and caused Eastern Asia to enter into a period featured by economic recession. Furthermore, the Asian financial crisis made Eastern Asian countries realize the importance of economic and financial interdependence and interconnectivity among them. Besides, some Eastern Asian countries tend to see the financial crisis as the failure of the "Washington consensus" and their resentment over the "Washington consensus" also gave a push to regional integration. In this context, regional integration has become increasingly attractive for Eastern Asia to deal with both external and internal challenges, especially Southeast Asian countries, after the financial crisis, they have become much eager to pursue regional integration.

Secondly, some Eastern Asian countries, on the one hand, realized that cooperation and integration could enhance their competitiveness in the global market. On the other hand, they believed that Eastern Asia's forming a large community could boost the regional economic development and gain more effective voice in international affairs dominated by western countries.

Thirdly, the rise of China promotes the Eastern Asian integration to some extent. During recent decades, China is known as rapid economic growth. After China entered WTO in 2001, it has shown growing interest in regional economic integration such as offering economic cooperation agreements to ASEAN, which also helps Eastern Asia to promote regional integration.

In recent decades, remarkable changes have happened in Eastern Asia, for example, the outward-looking trade strategies and capital liberalization in Newly Industrialized Economies (NIEs), and the market-oriented economic reforms and opening-up policy in China. Since the mid-1980s, Eastern Asia has been undergoing rapid regionalization. After the commencement of Asia Pacific Economic Cooperation (APEC), almost all the Eastern Asian countries have been committing themselves to regional integration.

However, the integration of Eastern Asia has not achieved much as expected, for example, most cooperation were realized in the framework of "ASEAN+1" and "ASEAN+3"; besides, regional conflicts such as the Diaoyu Island disputes between China and

Japan, the South China Sea issue between China and Southeast Asian countries and the historical issue between Japan and Southeast Asian countries, have been kept escalating in recent years. It seems that Eastern Asia has little possibility to achieve regional integration.

Problem Formulation

The regional integration in Eastern Asia and here comes the question:

Why is it difficult for Eastern Asia to achieve regional integration? In order to answer the main question, this chapter will focus on the relations of great powers in Eastern Asia such as China, Japan and ASEAN. First, China and Japan, as two leading countries in this region, play significant roles in promoting regional integration. It can be said that the complicated China-Japan relationship largely accounts for the difficulty of Eastern Asian integration. Second, as the biggest governmental organization in Eastern Asia, ASEAN maintains close relationships with both inside and outside great powers and it has been trying to keep balance among those powers and fight for voice of regional integration. Last but not least, both China and Japan hope to gain the support of ASEAN in the competition of regional leadership; as a result, the triangle relations among China, Japan and ASEAN also exert significant influence on the integration of Eastern Asia. Therefore, this chapter will try to analyse from three perspectives: China-Japan relations, China-ASEAN relations and Japan-ASEAN relations.

In addition, two theories, namely, constructivism and the strategic triangle, will be applied in the chapter. Constructivism will be used to demonstrate the bilateral relations respectively, and make definitions (enemy, rival or friends) on bilateral relations. The triangle theory will be used to describe the pattern of trilateral relations among China, Japan and ASEAN.

Methodology

In order to carry out this chapter with the goal of achieving its aims and objectives and to be able to answer the problem statement, methodology must be implemented. Methodology implies the way researchers investigate, approach problems and seek answers to pre-defined research issues. Against this background, this part is devoted to methodological approaches, namely the research approach, the methodological implications and the use of data. Besides, in order to clearly answer the main question, important definitions on regional integration and Eastern Asia will be given.

Research Approach

Adopting an approach is buying into a set of choices with far-reaching implications. Therefore, approaches need to be given careful consideration. However, approaches can never provide solutions and all the approaches involve assumptions as well as deficiencies.

The strategic triangle will be used as the research approach. First, as the three biggest entities in Eastern Asia, China, Japan and ASEAN could have important influence on regional issues and their relations also affect the process of regional integration. Second, due to the complex interdependency of international system, it is not enough to analyse policies and bilateral relations regardless of the consequence to other countries. Last but not least, identities divided by constructivism, involving friend, rival and enemy, can be illustrated as plus (+), minus (-) and minus (-) respectively. Different relations will lead to different triangular patterns which help explain the current situation in Eastern Asia.

There are four patterns of strategic triangle: 1) "ménage à trois", featured by triple amicable; 2) "romantic triangle", referring to the amity between the pivot and two wings with enmity between two wings; 3) "stable marriage", meaning the amity between two wings with enmity between pivot and two enmities; and "unit-veto," characterized by triple enmities. It is noted that these four patterns could shift into each other under certain circumstances. Therefore, the strategic triangle can not only demonstrate the current situation but also present the possible changes.

However, the strategic triangle still has shortcomings. More precisely, the pattern presented in Eastern Asia according to the strategic triangle may not result from triangle relations. In other words, the third party may also have influence on the relations of the other two. Sometimes two countries make alliances not because they build up high level of mutual trust, but the third party is too powerful.

Methodological Implications

The methods would be used in locating, explaining and predicting social regularities and patterns. Thus, both quantitative and qualitative techniques are applied to analyse data collected and to answer the main question.

Use of Empirical Data

In order to gather as much relevant and recent literature on the issue as possible and answer the main question, books, journals, research reports and information from government websites are used in this chapter. The main sources in this chapter are the website of United Nations, the East Asia Study Group, the website of Ministry of Foreign Affairs of People's Republic of China, the Contemporary Southeast Asia and Japan Export Trade Organization. Firstly, the website of United Nations is applied to define regional integration in Eastern Asia. Secondly, the East Asia Study Group and the website of Ministry of Foreign Affairs of China are used to illustrate the competition on economic and regional leadership between China and Japan respectively. Thirdly, Contemporary Southeast Asia is used to present the views and policies of ASEAN countries, especially its relations with China and Japan. Last, the data from Japan Export Trade Organization will be applied to illustrate Japan's policies to China and ASEAN.

The data will be mainly adapted in analytical part. Firstly, the intentions of integration and national sentiments of both China and Japan are expected to be described separately, and their rivalry on regional and economic leadership will also be illustrated. Secondly, specific terms such as "Sino-centric system" and "tianxia" concept will be introduced in order to present historical order and one of existing thoughts of China's think-tank. "China threat" and the exclusion of Taiwan from international affairs will also be illustrated to demonstrate the rival relations between China and

ASEAN. Thirdly, the unfavourable views between Japan and ASEAN as well as different objectives will be used to support that Japan-ASEAN relations are featured by rivalry. Last but not least, according to the first three analytical parts, the current triangular pattern will be concluded, which helps explain the difficulty of achieving regional integration in Eastern Asia.

"CHINA THREAT" TO ASEAN

"China threat" consists six parts: economy, diplomacy, military, resources, cyberwar and education. In this chapter, the first three aspects which have close relations with ASEAN countries will be analysed.

In economic aspect, the threat level is "high". Although social instability may affect China's growth, this is still China's century. According to Goldman Sachs, China will become the world's largest economy by 2027. However, based on purchasing power parity, the Conference Board predicts it could happen much earlier. China's remarkable economic performance presents not only opportunities but also challenges for ASEAN countries; in addition, the economic fluctuation of China may have dramatic impact on the domestic stability and the economic prospects of the rest of Eastern Asia due to the high degree of interdependency. In order not to be dominated, ASEAN countries collaborate and integrate with China economically while compete politically. Thus, given that China's significant status in regional economy, ASEAN adopted "hedging" policy to prevent China from being political leader.

In diplomacy aspect, the threat level is also considered as "high". In 2011, Chinese leaders circled the globe: signing oil and gas deals in Central Asia, buying up farmland in sub-Saharan Africa, and building up Confucius Institutes all over the world. Besides, China set up bilateral relationships with many neighbors such as Vietnam in Southeast Asia, and its "Five Principles of Peaceful Coexistence" makes it attractive. In order to maximize interests, Southeast Asian countries choose to collaborate on South China Sea issue; however, China keeps seeking for bilateral solutions by using its economic advantages, which intends to differentiate Southeast Asian countries.

In military aspect, the level is "medium". China has been training military forces on the western Pacific, especially Taiwan, increasing military budget, applying high-tech weapons such as anti-ship ballistic missile and "carrier killer", and changing into a more assertive stance when it comes to its marine interests. When it comes to China-ASEAN relations, due to the South China Sea issue, ASEAN seems quite sensitive to China's military behaviour. Especially after China declared South China Sea as its "core interest", ASEAN tends to consider China's military exercises, huge amount of military budget and high-techs as the preparation for violence.

Thereof, it can be concluded that ASEAN views China as rival due to its economic, diplomatic and military threats.

Conflicts on Taiwan Issue

Moreover, for most of ASEAN countries, Taiwan issue remains a major security threat. China declares Taiwan issue as "core interest", and one of its most important foreign policy is to oppose the independence of Taiwan. To achieve this, China keeps exerting influence on international framework, aiming to minimize Taiwan's status in international society, and China insists blocking Taiwan from joining in international or regional organizations such as World Health Organization and ASEAN+4. Besides, China has been carrying on military exercises around the Taiwan Strait irregularly.

However, as Taiwan is an important economy in the world in terms of GDP and has close investment and production network with other countries in Eastern Asia, ASEAN countries show enthusiasm to the involvement of Taiwan during the process of regional integration. As a result, China's actions may hurt the interests of those countries. From other countries' perspective, such actions, on the one hand, shows China's determination to safeguard its national interests regardless of potential cost to regional instability and prosperity; on the other hand, these postures make China considered as "uncertainty" which may prevent China from being regional leader. Considering the fear of being dominated again, the prevalence of "China threat theory" among ASEAN countries and the conflicts on Taiwan issue, ASEAN is unlikely to trust China. Therefore, it is not likely for China to play as a leader in regional integration, either.

Conclusion

The conflicts between China and ASEAN started to emerge in recent decades, which is mainly because China's rise in recent years triggers ASEAN's fear of China's domination. Although China insists declaring "peaceful development", ASEAN cannot truly believe it. Besides, with China's getting powerful, it also becomes increasingly aggressive in protecting its national interests, which aggravates ASEAN's doubt about "peaceful development". Therefore, there is little possibility that ASEAN will believe in "peaceful development", and ASEAN is unlikely to trust China out of the fear of "China threat". In turn, due to the Taiwan issue and disputed islands issue, China cannot really get along with ASEAN, either.

From constructivism's perspective, the acception of "China threat" refers to ASEAN's view towards China in macro-structure aspect, while the fear of Sino-centric tributary system and the refuse of "tianxia" concept, which are mainly from ordinary people, indeed are the feelings in micro-structure aspect. Apart from these feelings, China's actions on Taiwan issue also make ASEAN feel insecure. Besides, conflicts on disputed islands keep intensifying recently which undoubtedly deteriorates the bilateral relations. China-ASEAN relations belong to Lockean culture and the identity both sides tend to treat each other is rival.

A SINO-JAPANESE CLASH IN THE EAST CHINA SEA

Tensions have risen to dangerous levels between Japan and China over a small group of uninhabited islands in the East China Sea, called the Senkaku by the Japanese and the Diaoyu by the Chinese. These islands were once controlled by the United States as part of its post–World War II occupation of Japan and only returned to Japanese administrative control with the reversion of Okinawa in 1971. As Washington prepared to return these islands to Japan, the People's Republic of China (PRC) and Taiwan contested Japan's sovereignty. Two years earlier, a United Nations (UN) geological survey of the East China Sea revealed the potential of significant hydrocarbon resources. Contending sovereignty claims over the islands thus have both historical and resource-related dimensions.

Until recently, this territorial dispute was little more than a minor irritant in Sino-Japanese relations. However, against the backdrop of China's growing military power, the island dispute has increased concerns in Tokyo about Beijing's regional intentions and the adequacy of Japan's security, while stoking nationalistic politics in both capitals. Political miscalculation in Tokyo or Beijing, or unintended military interactions in and around the disputed islands, could escalate further, leading to an armed clash between Asia's two largest powers. The United States, as a treaty ally of Japan but with vital strategic interests in fostering peaceful relations with China, has a major stake in averting such a clash and resolving the dispute, if possible.

The Contingencies

Sino-Japanese tensions in the East China Sea have been building steadily since 2010, when a Chinese fishing trawler rammed two Japan Coast Guard (JCG) vessels in waters near the Senkaku/Diaoyu Islands and Japan detained the captain. Although the crisis was eventually defused, the territorial dispute came to a head again in September 2012, when Japanese prime minister Yoshihiko Noda announced his government's decision to purchase three of the five islands. The islands were privately owned, but a new wave of activism, including Chinese attempts to land on the islands and a public campaign by the Tokyo governor to purchase them himself, prompted Noda to attempt to neutralize nationalist pressures. The decision triggered widespread anti-Japanese demonstrations in China, resulting in extensive damage to Japanese companies operating there. Eventually China dampened the popular response, but it has since repeatedly stated its intent to assert its own administrative control over the disputed islands. China's Marine Surveillance agency intensified its patrols of the waters in and around the islands, and China's Bureau of Fisheries patrols followed suit. The JCG in turn increased its patrols and put them on 24/7 alert.

The danger of escalation to armed conflict increased when the two militaries became directly involved. On December 13, 2012, a small Chinese reconnaissance aircraft entered undetected into Japanese airspace above the islands. The JCG alerted Japan's Air Self-Defense Force (ASDF), which scrambled fighter jets based in Naha, Okinawa; however, they were too late to intercept. In January, China sent its reconnaissance aircraft back toward the islands accompanied by fighter jets, but stopped short of entering Japan's airspace, and no direct aerial confrontation occurred. Japan's Maritime Self-Defense Force (MSDF) reported that a Chinese frigate locked its firing radar on the Japanese destroyer *Yudachi* on January 30, 2013. Chinese authorities instigated an investigation into the incident in response to Japan's protest, leading to speculation that Beijing was unaware of the ship captain's actions. Although China's Ministry of Defense later denied that the incident took place, it did acknowledge the danger such an act posed.

Given current circumstances in the East China Sea, three contingencies are conceivable: first, an accidental or unintended incident in and around the disputed islands could trigger a military escalation of the crisis; second, either country could make a serious political miscalculation in an effort to demonstrate sovereign control; and third, either country could attempt to forcibly control the islands.

ACCIDENTAL/UNINTENDED MILITARY INCIDENT

Although recent incidents have sensitized China and Japan to the risk of accidental and unintended military interactions, the danger will persist while emotions run high and their forces operate in close proximity. In stressful and ambiguous times, when decision-making is compressed by the speed of modern weapons systems, the risk of human error is higher. The 2001 collision between a U.S. reconnaissance aircraft and a Chinese fighter jet near Hainan Island is a case in point, as was the intrusion of a Chinese Han submarine in Japanese territorial waters in 2004. So-called rules of engagement (ROEs), intended to guide and control the behavior of local actors, are typically general in scope and leave room for personal interpretation that may lead to actions that escalate a crisis situation.

Compounding the risk of unintended escalation between Chinese and Japanese air and naval units is the unpredictable involvement of third parties such as fishermen or civilian activists who may attempt to land on the islands. Their actions could precipitate an armed response by either side.

Political Miscalculation in an Effort to Demonstrate Sovereign Control

Political miscalculation of either country's intent or resolve, as well as miscalculation of the U.S. position, could lead to armed conflict. First, Japan and China are already finding it difficult to read each other's actions. Past Japanese government leasing of the Senkaku/Diaoyu Islands effectively kept nationalist activists—Japanese as well as Chinese and Taiwanese—at bay. In mid-2012, however, rising nationalist sentiments during leadership transitions inflamed the dispute. This stimulated heated debate in Tokyo over how to consolidate Japanese sovereignty and was a factor in the December 2012 election of conservative prime minister Shinzo Abe, who advocated inhabiting the islands. This escalation in asserting sovereignty claims through the use of patrols, populating the islands, and perhaps even military defense of the territory could lead to heightened tensions between the two countries and whip up nationalist sentiments, potentially limiting the capacity of leaders to peacefully manage the dispute.

Second, China could miscalculate U.S. interests and intentions. Since last year, U.S. policymakers have sought to lessen tensions but have also taken steps to clarify the U.S. role in deterring any coercive action by China. U.S. and Japanese forces have conducted regular exercises to strengthen defense of Japan's southwestern islands and maritime surveillance capabilities. Both former secretary of state Hillary Clinton and former secretary of defense Leon Panetta clearly stated that the United States will defend Japan against any aggression, and on November 29, 2012, the U.S. Senate passed a resolution accompanying the 2013 National Defense Authorization Act to demonstrate congressional support for the Obama administration's commitment to Japan's defense. As tensions escalated late last year, Washington increased its deployments in and around Japan. Early this year, as military interactions raised the potential for conflict, Clinton restated the U.S. position that it would not accept any unilateral attempt to wrest control of the islands. Still, Beijing could miscalculate Washington's commitment to defend Japan and/or seek to test that commitment. Finally, U.S. assurances could lead Tokyo to overestimate Washington's response and to act in a manner that would increase the chance for confrontation. To date, however, Tokyo has tended to err on the side of caution in planning and exercises with U.S. forces, and it is unlikely Japan would act without evidence of U.S. assistance.

DELIBERATE ACTION TO FORCIBLY ESTABLISH CONTROL OVER ISLANDS

Although this seems highly unlikely today, either party could take military action to assert sovereignty over the disputed islands. Rising domestic pressures or an unexpected opportunity for a fait accompli could lead to a decision by either government to establish military control over the territory.

Warning Indicators

Although it seems that neither Tokyo nor Beijing wants to use force to pursue its interests in the territorial dispute, it is possible that either government could choose to do so in the future. Indicators of a strategic decision by either country to escalate tensions include:

- *Introduction of Japanese or Chinese military forces on or in the vicinity of the islands to claim or defend sovereignty.* Japan and China have kept their militaries distant from the disputed islands; a military presence would intensify the dispute and raise the probability of armed conflict.
- *Deliberate use of economic sanctions.* China's informal embargo on rare-earth exports to Japan during the 2010 crisis and the setback to Japanese investment in the latter half of 2012 suggest a new role for economic instruments of pressure in this dispute. The imposition of sanctions (i.e., embargos, boycotts, or blockades) to harm economic performance would signal a desire to escalate conflict. Government action to reduce conspicuously economic dependence

would be a lesser but equally important indicator of a strategic shift.

- *Government-sponsored nationalist activism.* Nationalist activism has until now come from a host of social actors, including fishermen, local politicians, and advocacy groups. A deliberate effort by either government to stimulate popular nationalism against the other nation would signal a shift in intentions away from resolving the territorial dispute peacefully. Government calls to mobilize popular support for the defense of the islands, lift regulatory controls over access to the islands, or elect leaders who advocate sustained confrontation over the sovereignty dispute would be indicators of a strategic shift in the conflict.

Short of a deliberate effort to exert physical control over the Senkaku/Diaoyu Islands, several specific indicators raise the likelihood of an inadvertent clash between Japan and China:

- *Incident involving the loss of life in the waters off the disputed islands.* No lives have been lost over the disputed islands, but should these interactions result in the loss of life, crisis management would be a serious challenge for both governments. China's Bureau of Fisheries and its Marine Surveillance patrols have increased the tempo of operations near the disputed islands. JCG ROEs give ship commanders the authority to respond; the ROEs for Chinese paramilitary agencies are less clear. In addition, fishing boats from Taiwan accompanied by their coast guard have periodically complicated the standoff.
- *A protracted airborne standoff between Japanese and Chinese forces in the East China Sea.*China's intrusion into Japan's airspace prompted Prime Minister Abe's cabinet to review its air defenses. Heightened Japanese sensitivity over the territorial dispute with China could raise the stakes for Japan's air force if Chinese forces test their readiness in the vicinity of the islands.
- *Loss of national command control over local commanders.* Local commanders could act independently in ways that are

interpreted as presaging hostile intent (such as the Chinese radar lock on Japanese forces), which could trigger a defensive response that escalates the crisis. Local commanders will be hard-pressed to remain calm should interactions increase near the islands, especially if miscalculations continue. Postwar constitutional constraints on Japan's military have produced well-articulated principles and procedures for civilian control over the SDF, with clearly established ROEs and careful central government oversight over local forces. Civil-military command structures in China are less clear and not well described. Moreover, the degree of oversight of local commanders by Beijing is also unknown. Strong central government command over local forces will be absolutely essential to avoid unintended incidents from escalating.

Implications for U.S. Interests

The United States has major interests at stake in the growing tension between Japan and China. Three risks in particular stand out:

- *Risk of armed hostilities with China.* U.S. forward-deployed forces are deeply integrated with Japan's SDF and assist with intelligence, surveillance, and reconnaissance (ISR) support, as well as exercises designed to enhance Japan's defense capabilities. U.S. forces may be asked to assist Japan's SDF in the case of a broader military conflict, and would likely provide logistical support as well as continued ISR collaboration. Direct armed conflict with China would harm a broad array of vital U.S. economic, political, and strategic interests.
- *Risk to U.S.-Japan alliance.* The U.S. response to a Japan-China conflict would determine the future of the U.S.-Japan alliance, as well as other alliances in the Asia Pacific. Tokyo remains concerned that Washington might not fulfill its treaty obligations if Beijing escalates the conflict, and U.S. government statements of its intentions notwithstanding, domestic perceptions in Japan of U.S.

hesitancy in the case of Chinese coercion will shape Japan's future security choices. Japan's postwar policy of military self-restraint and reliance on the United States for strategic protection, including its continued abnegation of nuclear weapons, would likely come to an end if the United States chose not to defend Japan against Chinese aggression.

- *Risk to regional stability.* China's dispute with the Philippines over the Scarborough Reef in the South China Sea has set a particularly dangerous precedent. Many leaders in the Asia-Pacific region are beginning to see China's maritime behavior as unpredictable and will be watching to see if Washington ultimately resists or accommodates Chinese military pressure on its periphery. The Japanese case will be decisive not only for Japan's future choices but for many other allies and friends in the region adjusting to the rise of China.

Preventive Options

The United States has considerable interest in doing all that it can to prevent armed conflict between Japan and China. The policies for preventing such a conflict include the following steps.

Deter and Dissuade Unilateral Actions to Contest Japan's Administrative Control of the Islands

Washington can regularly and consistently communicate its interest in, and position on, the island dispute to avoid ambiguity in the U.S. security commitment to Japan. Privately, Washington could also communicate to both capitals the need to avoid statements and assertions that would incite popular sentiments on the dispute and encourage peaceful dispute resolution.

To deter potential Chinese assertiveness, the United States can consult closely with Japan on its response to Chinese activities near the disputed islands, and can ensure seamless U.S.-Japan defense cooperation. To counter any impulse toward Japanese assertiveness, Washington and Tokyo should confirm the conditions under which U.S. defense assistance would be rendered. Japan's leaders remain committed to limiting their use of military force to defensive missions. Should that change, U.S. policymakers should revisit the terms of defense assistance.

U.S. forces can also assist Japanese agencies in a maritime emergency, should an incident involving the Japanese and Chinese militaries occur. For example, Washington can urge Tokyo to update communications and exercises between the JCG and MSDF, providing assistance if needed. To date, there has been little need for Japan to integrate its civilian maritime policing with its defense operations. As Chinese maritime forces in the East China Sea expand and the distinction between civil and military maritime forces becomes less clear, Japan can develop its planning and capabilities for sharing maritime missions. A special JCG task force at the eleventh regional headquarters in Okinawa has responsibility for the Senkaku/Diaoyu area, and a U.S. liaison team could be assigned there as well as onboard JCG vessels. Data links and other communications upgrades could be added, along with real-time exercises between the JCG and MSDF, which could include consultations with relevant U.S. forces.

Risk-Reduction Measures for the East China Sea

Crisis management protocols are needed for Chinese and Japanese maritime and aerial forces in the East China Sea. The United States can encourage a bilateral agreement between Japan and China along the lines of the U.S.-China Military Maritime Consultative Agreement. In May 2012, the first Japan-China High-Level Consultation on Maritime Affairs was held in Hangzhou, China, and in June, Tokyo and Beijing concluded an agreement to establish crisis communications, including a hotline. Japan and China can be encouraged to restart this initiative and push forward with consultations on a search-and-rescue agreement. A multilateral code of conduct in the East China Sea, modeled on the Association of Southeast Asian Nations (ASEAN) code of conduct in the South China Sea, could also be considered. This would require participation by South Korea, in addition to Japan and China, and could be pursued in trilateral China-South Korea-Japan talks or in a new forum with Chinese, Japanese, South Korean, and U.S. participation.

Military interactions between Japanese and Chinese forces can also be more predictable if regular bilateral military-to-military consultations are held. Recent tensions with China have increased worries in Tokyo about China's long-term intentions. To ease these heightened concerns, the United States could encourage Beijing to be more transparent about its maritime strategy and strategic goals.

DIPLOMATIC EFFORTS TO MANAGE (OR RESOLVE) THE TERRITORIAL DISPUTE

Preventing armed conflict between Japan and China over the Senkaku/Diaoyu Islands dispute ultimately depends on Beijing and Tokyo finding a mutually acceptable framework for managing their differences. An active diplomatic effort to embed the island dispute in a stronger and more constructive Japan-China relationship will be needed and could be encouraged by Washington. Several options exist for managing the dispute. The first, and most preferable, is a bilateral diplomatic effort. Since 1978, both governments have sought to control their citizens from seeking access to the islands. The Japanese government's decision to preempt activist purchase of the islands does not preclude a return to the status quo ante.

Second, Washington could encourage Beijing and Tokyo to explore new collaborative formulas for managing their island dispute. Developing proposals for transforming the islands into a nature preserve or some other entity that would restrict human access could also offer a way to demilitarize the dispute. However, this approach seems unlikely to attract attention in either Beijing or Tokyo at the moment.

Third, if the dispute cannot be managed peacefully through bilateral negotiations, Japan and China could be encouraged to seek international adjudication. The International Court of Justice (ICJ) could be asked to open a hearing. Beijing, having challenged Japan's sovereignty claim in 1971, should initiate the ICJ adjudication process. Washington should not expect Tokyo to take the first step, but should encourage Tokyo to respond if Beijing were to submit the dispute for international mediation.

Finally, Japan and China could be encouraged to develop cooperation in the management of their East China Sea maritime boundary. The East China Sea is 360 nautical miles wide, falling short of the 400 nautical miles that would be required to enforce the UN Convention on the Law of the Sea (UNCLOS), which defined 200-mile exclusive economic zones. While Japan argues for the establishment of a median line halfway between the two coastlines, China argues for an exclusive economic zone based on its extended continental shelf. This contested maritime boundary exacerbates the unpredictability of interactions between Japanese and Chinese forces across the East China Sea. Japan and China should be urged to implement their 2008 joint development agreement for exploring hydrocarbon resources in the East China Sea to build trust and cooperation in maritime management.

Mitigating Options

Should a military conflict erupt between China and Japan, the United States can react in several ways to contain and minimize the threat to its interests. The U.S. response would depend on the scale of the armed clash. Options for U.S. policymakers include:

- *Urge Tokyo to stand down.* Withholding U.S. military support could change Japan's strategic calculus in the context of a conflict. This option would create a severe backlash against the United States in Japan and fatally undermine the bilateral alliance. Appeasing Beijing would also embolden China to use force against other U.S. allies in the region.
- *Contain any inadvertent incident involving the use of force.* In the event of an incident between Japanese and Chinese forces, Washington could immediately use all means at its disposal to communicate to both Tokyo and Beijing its interest in preventing an armed clash from escalating. The U.S. military could offer search-and-rescue assistance for any vessel and crew involved in an armed clash. Communications with Beijing may prove difficult, but all means, including the hotline and crisis communication mechanisms outlined in the U.S.-China Military Maritime Consultative Agreement, could be used to encourage a

stand-down of forces. Real-time communication between Japan's chief of joint staff and the commander of U.S. Forces–Japan will make local military coordination with Tokyo easier, but immediate attention should be given to communication between the U.S. president and the Japanese prime minister on how to control the situation.

- *Plan for southwestern island contingency in U.S.-Japan defense cooperation.* Washington and Tokyo could continue regular exercises and planning to deter, and, if necessary, defend Japan against an armed attack. Japan may ask the United States to assist should China unilaterally opt to take military action to occupy the disputed islands. The scale and timing of that assistance will depend on the scale of attack. If the conflict were to expand beyond the disputed islands to become an all-out military clash between Japan and China, the United States should be prepared for integrated defense operations ranging from maritime and air defenses to ballistic missile defense as requested by Japan.
- *Call for an emergency session of the UN Security Council.* This option would engage the UN in the effort to de-escalate the crisis, although China's seat on the Security Council could limit the effectiveness of UN action. Nonetheless, the UN could facilitate a ceasefire and a negotiated end to hostilities.
- *Impose economic sanctions on Beijing.* Washington could impose sanctions on financial transactions, the movement of goods and services, and travel between China and the United States. However, China can retaliate in kind by barring U.S. exports, curtailing or ending purchases of U.S. treasuries, and limiting investment flows.
- *Threaten China with a U.S. military response to any use of force against Japan.* Washington could adopt a strategy of escalating any use of force to gain control over the Senkaku/ Diaoyu Islands into a U.S.-Japan coordinated response designed to repel Chinese forces and establish Japanese military control over the disputed islands. This could severely damage the United States' relations with China.

Recommendations

The United States should pursue three policy goals: promote de-escalation of the dispute, initiate crisis management consultations with Japan, and intensify efforts to create multilateral maritime risk reduction mechanisms in the Asia-Pacific region. More specifically:

- *The United States should consistently and clearly reiterate its treaty obligation to assist in Japan's defense if China uses force to resolve the dispute over the islands.* Until the risk of miscalculations subsides between Japan and China, the United States should continue to make clear its long-standing position that the Senkaku/Diaoyu Islands are covered by the U.S.-Japan security treaty.
- *The United States should continue to encourage China and Japan to seek peaceful resolution of the dispute and remind Beijing that the unilateral actions of other powers will not change U.S. recognition of Japan's administrative control over the islands.* Secretary Clinton's January 18, 2013, statement, reiterated by Secretary John Kerry on April 15 in Tokyo, offered a valuable clarification of the U.S. position. Washington should condemn harshly the use of force to settle this dispute.
- *The United States should urge Japan and China to avoid any steps that might escalate tensions in and around the disputed islands.* Washington should encourage Tokyo to continue to avoid populating the islands or deploying military forces to defend its control so long as there are no efforts by Beijing to seize control of the islands. The United States should encourage China to restart High-Level Consultations on Maritime Affairs with Japan and to implement their agreement to establish crisis management communications.
- *The United States should continue to advocate for transparency between maritime forces in the East China Sea and the development of mechanisms for confidence building.* As China's maritime power grows, greater comfort with the procedures and prohibitions on interactions with military

and nonmilitary vessels, including aircraft, across this increasingly crowded sea will be required. Opportunities for Chinese participation must be expanded in existing regional maritime cooperation, such as the annual Rim of the Pacific exercises, regular regional fisheries exercises, and coast guard exercises dedicated to search-and-rescue operations and humanitarian assistance. The United States should also encourage the countries of Northeast Asia to develop Incidents at Sea agreements.

- *Should China initiate the use of force against Japan, the United States should be fully prepared to provide military assistance to Japan.* The United States should maintain the requisite capability and readiness to fulfill its commitment to assist in defending Japan.
- *The United States and Japan should develop clear alliance crisis management procedures for an incident or armed clash in and around the disputed islands.* Washington and Tokyo should design plans to manage a military clash between Japanese and Chinese militaries, including how to control escalation and communicate effectively with Beijing. Past U.S. and Japanese incidents with Chinese forces should be closely examined as the basis of an alliance response. Containing escalation should be the highest priority for alliance crisis management.
- *The United States and Japan should continue to improve defense consultations and exercises designed to enhance Japan's southwestern defenses.* The island dispute exacerbates an increasing trend of interaction between Chinese and Japanese forces in Japan's southwest. As Chinese naval strength grows, these interactions are likely to increase, raising concern that Chinese military presence in and around Japan could impinge on the United States' ability to assist in Japan's defense. Washington and Tokyo should improve ISR and amphibious landing cooperation and strengthen Japan's air defenses.
- *The United States should strongly encourage China to expand consultations with its maritime neighbors on its evolving*

strategy. China's rise is creating deep uncertainty about its longer-term intentions regarding the use of its military power. Washington should continue regular regional security consultations in the ASEAN Regional Forum and encourage annual meetings of regional defense ministers. Open sea lanes, including antipiracy operations, are the lifelines of Asia's growing economy, and the United States should continue to advocate freedom of navigation.

- *Finally, the United States should ratify the UN Convention on the Law of the Sea in order to become a more forceful actor in global deliberations over maritime rights and sovereignty dispute resolution.* In both the East and South China Seas, China's neighbors are seeking the adjudication of maritime disputes in UNCLOS. The United States cannot shape the maritime debate in the Asia Pacific or defend its own maritime interests if it is not a full participant in international maritime deliberations.

ANTI-CHINESE AND ANTI-JAPANESE SENTIMENTS IN EAST ASIA: THE POLITICS OF OPINION, DISTRUST, AND PREJUDICE

Spanning the presidencies of George W. Bush and Barack Obama, anti-Americanism has become somewhat of a growth industry. Its products are avidly consumed not only in the United States but around the world, often for quite different political purposes. It is not surprising that anti-Americanism plays a large role among traditional enemies of the United States in the Middle East. But the same is true of America's allies just across the border, such as Canada and Mexico, and living far apart, such as Australia and New Zealand.

It would be a big mistake, however, to think that these oppositional sentiments—the complex mixture of opinion, distrust and prejudice—are directed only against America. It plays a role in all parts of the world. Secondary or subordinate states in each world region resent the regional top dog. Such resentment can take various political forms. In Europe, latent anti-German feelings linger, sometimes very close to the surface. When Germany takes a stance against its partners in the European Union, as it has at various times in the unfolding financial crisis, historical anti-German sentiments are quick to appear. Small states in Latin America and Africa also harbour resentment against the self-proclaimed leadership roles of Brazil and Nigeria. And in the Middle East, cross currents of nationalism and religion generate different kinds of political resentment.

East Asia is no exception to this generalization. A large literature focuses on the role of history in shaping the region's current political fault lines. Even minor political crises of the day reveal lingering, deep resentments.

In sharp contrast to Europe, however, painful historical memories continue to shape directly, even to provoke, current political crises. This is one important reason why, in a world of regions, East Asia differs from Europe.

The heavy hand of history, however, has not uniformly played out in East Asia. Upon close inspection, one would quickly discover a wide range of oppositional sentiments toward more powerful neighbors. As examined in the analysis below, such sentiments have also evolved, activated and deactivated by various forces, both internal and external. Identifying the mechanisms behind the politics of oppositional sentiments in East Asia—as well as their consequences—is the central objective of this study.

The alternative explanations showing why it is important to distinguish between the different types of oppositional sentiment, and what the existing literature misses by failing to take such variations into account.

The next two sections survey what we know, respectively, about the evolution of anti-Chinese and anti-Japanese sentiment in East Asia. As this is a vast subject, for practical reasons we do not try to include in this article all empirical manifestations of anti-Chinese and anti-Japanese sentiment. Focusing on anti-Chinese sentiment in Japan and Korea, and anti-Japanese sentiment in Korea and Taiwan leaves to future analysis important subjects such as anti-Japanese sentiment in China and anti-Chinese sentiment in Southeast Asia. The article ends with a brief discussion of our findings and possible policy implications.

OPINION, DISTRUST, AND PREJUDICE: THE POLITICS OF OPPOSITIONAL SENTIMENT IN EAST ASIA

Oppositional sentiment in East Asia stems mainly from the 'history problems' that have been contested periodically in the past century. Existing work on the role and politics of historical animosity in East Asian international relations is vast, but its overall consensus is unmistakable: that the region's troubled past has been, and continues to be, one of the defining features of East Asian international relations, with largely negative regional consequences for alliance ties and regional institution-building. Despite the overall consensus on the crucial role history plays in interstate relations in the region, however, scholars differ in their treatments of history as a factor shaping policymaking among East Asian countries.

Pointing to the long-lasting legacy of colonization and foreign occupation, one school of thought highlights the role of history as a regional fixture that has persistently caused deleterious effects on interstate relations in the region. Given regional experiences such as Japanese imperialism and Cold War ideological tensions, what underlies East Asia international relations has been 'the ashes of a century of memories of multiple sorrows'. Thomas Berger cites the history problem between Japan and Korea as the main reason for the 'hostile' relationship between the two, despite 'all the good structural reasons for bilateral cooperation on national security'. Similarly, Nicholas Kristof attributes Japan's continued failure to apologize properly for atrocities committed during its colonial rule to regional tensions between Japan and its neighbours, especially Korea and China. As long as the region's tortured past remains unresolved, in this line of thinking, the prospects for regional cooperation and community building are remote.

Although the 'weight of history' account correctly highlights the continuing salience of the history issue, its main weakness lies in its view of historical animosity as a constant that will remain a latent source of tensions in the region. In other words, it fails to specify the conditions under which the politics of historical memory are activated or deactivated under different contexts. As

Victor Cha's study of alignment behaviour between Japan and South Korea implies, there exist wide variations in the effects of historical animosity between the two US allies. From the high point of friction between the two countries immediately after the end of Japanese colonial rule in Korea, to a period of cooperation in the late 1970s, bilateral relations between the two have been changing despite their deep-seated enmity. Similarly, Jennifer Lind portrays an evolutionary process of historical memory and contrition, in which the aggressor's well-meaning remorse may provoke a domestic political backlash by angering and mobilizing conservatives who reject contrition. This in turn incites oppositional sentiment in the victim country, 'creating a spiral of acrimony that makes reconciliation even more elusive'.

More broadly, many scholars view oppositional sentiment as a variable. For instance, South Korean President Syngman Rhee's strong anti-Japanese stance derived from his political need to consolidate his domestic power base by 'playing on anti-Japanese popular feeling'. From this vantage point, we would expect anti-Japanese sentiment to calm down when leaders face few political challenges. South Korean President Kim Dae-jung's forward-looking foreign policy approach towards Japan in the late 1990s can be seen in this light. Similarly, Cha's structural account treats oppositional sentiment as highly malleable—as something that can be changed with relative ease when a proper mix of material incentives emerge. Sung-hwa Cheong's analysis on the politics of anti-Japanese feeling is particularly convincing in its explanation of the political origins of anti-Japanese sentiment in the Syngman Rhee regime in South Korea, whereas Cha's study is most persuasive in its analysis of variation over time in bilateral cooperation between Japan and South Korea, as shaped by changing structural dynamics in the form of the US military commitment to the region.

What existing accounts neglect to take into account, however, is a complex interplay between internal and external dynamics under which oppositional sentiment is shaped, both internally through domestic political contestation and externally by states' historical experiences with outside powers. The latter is structurally given, as the overall attitude towards the outside power is established by the nature of the historical experience. The former, however, may be more fluid, depending upon the nature of contemporary domestic political dynamics. Rather than a priori assuming deep structural or contingent effects of oppositional sentiment, we investigate whether or not anti-Chinese or anti-Japanese sentiment in East Asia varies according to a spectrum of attitudes that may result from the combination of historical path dependence and more recent politicization.

The structural versus contingent divide in existing studies of anti-foreign nationalism, or the role of historical animosity in East Asian international relations parallels the literature on anti-Americanism (in Asia and elsewhere), which tends to view anti-American sentiment as either irreversible 'prejudice' or malleable 'opinion'. The distinction among opinion, distrust, and prejudice represents a continuum, with distrust lying in the middle. Most opinion reflects a mixture of reasoned assessment based on historical judgment, and is also structured in some ways by schemas that, in the case of anti-Americanism, create negative predispositions. Some of these may be so mild that they still fit within the category of opinion. As the schemas harden, one moves into the range of more or less serious distrust, and, eventually, to prejudice. Generally speaking, though, it seems true to say that attitudes towards the United States are typically best characterized by distrust rather than opinion or prejudice.

It is also true that the United States has not been the only or even most important target of such negative attitudes, which run the gamut from opinion to distrust to prejudice. Oppositional sentiments directed against China and Japan have been similarly politicized and contested at different periods in East Asia as part of elite attempts to bolster their weak or weakening legitimacy or public debates on the role of foreign influence and intervention in the forging of national identity. Just as anti-American movements emerged under changing political contexts, anti-Chinese and anti-Japanese sentiments in East Asia were mobilized as part of evolving region-wide trends, external and domestic, such as the Cold War environment, democratization (in South Korea and Taiwan), and the rise of China.

Our cases of oppositional sentiments vary in strength on two dimensions. They are: (i) the nature of historical experience; and (ii) the degree to which it has been politicized in the postwar period. The first variable—the nature of historical experience—refers to the depth or comprehensiveness of the dependent relationship vis-à-vis the external Great Power (or hegemon) in the past. Anti-Chinese and anti-Japanese sentiment, like anti-American sentiment, exists and is still relevant in East Asian politics today because of the power and influence of these past and present dominant powers. At the same time, Great Power dependence has not been a uniform experience, as Japanese and Korean dependence on China in the 17th to 19th centuries was experienced largely at the level of the ruling elite and confined to political–military rules of engagement. Japan's colonization, in contrast, entailed a deeper form of domination which penetrated all segments of Korean and Taiwanese politics and society. In this way, different historical 'legacies' set up different initial conditions for the politicization of history in post-1945 East Asian politics. That is to say, not all history resonates in the same manner, nor is it equally usable or used.

The second factor determining the intensity of oppositional sentiments is how regularly such historical experiences have been politicized—both in terms of frequency and mobilization structure. For example, anti- and pro-China sentiment has been expressed through party politics in Japan, as a form of conflict between the Left and the Right, especially during the Cold War. In both Japan and Korea, anti-Chinese and anti-Japanese mobilizations respectively occur through established political channels—right-wing organizations and nationalist politicians in the case of Japan and various non-governmental organizations and citizen-activist groups on the Korean side. Leaders, such as Syngman Rhee in South Korea and Ishihara Shintaro in Japan, have regularly utilized memorials and rituals as well as nationalist discourse to bolster their political legitimacy and drum up domestic political support. Not all history, or use of history, however, has been attempted or resonated with success. In Taiwan, colonial rule under Japan has not necessarily led to a salient anti-Japanese movement for most of the postwar period, although it began to surface as a source of 'national identity' mobilization in the 1990s. Similarly, anti-China sentiment in South Korea remains episodic and issue-based.

ANTI-CHINESE SENTIMENT IN POST-WAR JAPAN AND SOUTH KOREA

Japanese and Korean Attitudes towards China during the Cold War

In the postwar period, 'Chinese–Japanese security relations have never been purely bilateral but aspects of larger patterns and developments'. Although Iriye's statement is intended to emphasize the role of the Cold War and Japan's structural dependence on the United States in conditioning bilateral relations, Japanese (and arguably Korean) policy and popular sentiment towards China were also heavily shaped by historical legacies and domestic politics—even at the height of the Cold War. In fact, China played an important symbolic role in domestic political debates in postwar Japan—that of a site for contesting current and future security policies, various ideologically-tinted party platforms, and national identity.

Even with the onset of the Cold War in Asia, and despite American influence in Japan, anticommunism was not as strong in Japan as it was in the United States, and not many Japanese viewed Communist China as a 'Cold War' enemy. According to at least one commentator, the older generation, educated in the decades following the Sino-Japanese War, were accustomed to regarding Japan as the Asian leader in modernization, and China as a very poor second. '*Chankoro*, or pigtailed fellow, was a typical expression of the disdainful way in which Japanese referred to Chinese. It was to them simply inconceivable that the same*chankoro* could now manage the most powerful nation in Asia and pose a genuine threat to Japan'. Another explanation for the lack of Japanese threat perception towards China points to the role of cultural affinity, racial similarity, and geographical proximity in driving the Japanese to be 'overly optimistic about friendship with the Chinese people while viewing China more as part of East Asian civilization than as communist'.

Anti-Chinese sentiment was hence neither widespread nor salient in Japanese politics in the 1950s and 1960s. Throughout the Cold War, the general feeling in Japan was one favouring maintained ties with the People's Republic of China. In 1952, public opinion polls showed that 57% of respondents favoured restoring diplomatic relations with China. In 1960, those in favour of normalization rose to 75%. On the other hand, policy on China in Japan's party politics was used as a political campaigning issue, wherein a pro-China position was staked out by the Left, which supported unarmed neutrality, against the Right, which believed that it was in Japan's national interest to align with the United States for the time being until it could regain its former power and glory. In charting out a course that prioritized economic reconstruction under the US security umbrella over immediate rearmament, the so-called Yoshida doctrine was hence a compromise between the two extremes.

But policy on China was not always a divisive issue; it also united 'nationalists' who sought greater autonomy from the United States. Transcending party and ideological lines, Japan's China policy in the 1950s and 1960s was often a metaphor for Japan's autonomy from the United States. Even more than the Left, it was the 'pro-China' conservatives, led by former Prime Minister Ishibashi Tanzan, who were responsible for advancing trade with China. Progressive intellectuals favoured close ties with Communist China due not only to the belief that Japan was guilty of rising to great power status through Chinese sacrifice, but because they regarded China as a 'fighting friend' against the 'common enemy of American imperialism'. While arguments by the Japan Socialist Party (JSP) and Japan Communist Party (JCP) were couched in Marxist language, their campaigns were actually appeals to Japanese nationalism and attacked the government's subservience to American policies over China.

By the 1970s, Japan's China policy had become less politicized, and popular sentiment about China weaker and less well-informed. Following diplomatic normalization, Sino-Japanese relations entered the phase of what Japanese analysts describe as 'the 1972 system' or 'the 1972 framework', wherein Japan habitually bowed to Chinese demands. Japan's sense of guilt about the past and China's historical 'weight' were important factors that shaped its China policy during this period (1972–1989). According to Reinhard Drifte, Japanese leaders showed restraint or deference to China as a short-term, pragmatic means of compensating for Japan's past aggression, thus avoiding the long-term, humiliating, and painful process of facing up to its past.

As a result, China was mostly used by Japanese scholars, largely limited to academic circles, as a platform for ideological debate, much of it sympathetic to Beijing. On the whole, with the notable exception of the explicitly pro-Taiwan *Sankei Shimbum*, the Japanese media were also uncritical in reports of China. Although postwar Japanese culture was heavily influenced by the United States, a sense of guilt combined with the image of China as an inspiration would remain. Until the late 1980s, there existed in Japan the 'ideal of reentering Asia through cultural affinity as well as economic integration'. Japan, as a 'champion of Asian values' saw itself as a cultural bridge between a backward, authoritarian China and the West's human rights agenda.

While, in Japan, policy on China played some role in debates on foreign policy and national identity, especially during the Cold War, references to the Chinese were rare in postwar South Korean politics. As evident in the sparse literature on postwar Korea–China relations, for most of the period after 1945 and throughout the Cold War, the significance of the erstwhile 'lips and teeth' relationship declined to near non-existence. Owing to the separation of the Korean peninsula into two enemy camps and China's sponsorship of North Korea, China remained a distant and ideologically hostile neighbour to the South Koreans until the late 1980s. Thus, attitudes towards China—either positive or negative—were not politicized in South Korea during the Cold War.

In the immediate postwar period, South Korean politics was dominated by debates on trusteeship and the UN-sponsored general election. Aided by American occupation authorities, conservative parties battled leftist forces, utilizing anti-communism and anti-Japan sentiments to build up their legitimacy. With the early eradication of the Left, and eventual banning of communist parties in Korea, China policy could not be debated nor pro-China sentiments voiced, as was the case in Japan.

Relations with China did not become a salient issue in South Korean politics, even though the two countries fought as enemies during the Korean War (1950–1953). Interestingly, China's military actions against South Korea during the Korean War appear to have been either forgotten or forgiven—or both—by the South Koreans. Although anecdotal, it has been observed that retired South Korean generals do not harbour negative feelings towards China, despite having faced Chinese soldiers as adversaries during the Korean War. In South Korean polls, China still gets listed as one of Koreans' favourite countries. This is in stark contrast to the bitter feelings harboured towards Japan and Japan's 36-year colonial rule over Korea, despite the fact that most of the hundreds of foreign invasions that Korea experienced throughout its history came from the various dynasties and tribal groups of China, seeking to keep Korea within their sphere of influence.

With the onset of the Cold War, bilateral relations were firmly entrenched within the Cold War framework, in which China acted as North Korea's patron against the United States and South Korea. The China–North Korean Friendship Treaty signed in July 1961 was viewed as more of a threat than the North Korea–Soviet Union alliance because the former had been 'sealed in the blood' shed during the Korean War. The intensity of the Cold War and inter-Korean ideological conflict remained high, and both China and Korea had to cater to their Cold War allies, respectively North Korea and Taiwan. China maintained its hostile stance towards South Korea even through the period of détente in 1972–1974. Beijing and Seoul both concealed their indirect trade, conducted through Hong Kong and Singapore since the late 1970s, until normalization in 1992, to avoid provoking respectively Pyongyang and Taipei. Prospects for bilateral relations were further hindered by the implicit link between the Korean peninsula and the Taiwan situation, wherein the PRC's recognition of Seoul would constitute a 'two-Korea' policy, which would go against Beijing's insistence on a 'one-China' policy.

Despite China's continued hostility and persistent anti-Seoul posture at the UN, South Korean president Park Chung Hee made attempts to reconcile with China throughout the 1970s. In January 1971, President Park displayed his willingness to seek rapprochement with 'non-hostile' socialist countries. His Foreign Minister Kim Yong-sik reiterated the Korean government's 'flexible' approach towards the Soviet Union and the PRC. Moreover, even as anti-communism continued to prop up successive authoritarian governments in South Korea, China did not become an obvious object of hatred or blame among Koreans.

Relations between South Korea and China remained distant, if not overtly hostile, until a minor breakthrough following the successful diplomatic resolution of a hijacking incident in May 1983 and subsequent 'sports diplomacy'. In addition, Deng Xiaoping's modernizing reforms of China made the Chinese Communist Party (CCP) more receptive to trade with South Korea. By 1985, China–South Korea trade ($1.16 billion) surpassed that between China and North Korea ($488 million). Government-sanctioned trade through the creation of the Korea Trade Promotion Association (KOTRA) and the Chinese Chamber of Commerce in 1990 further increased bilateral trade relations. Bilateral relations finally thawed with normalization in 1992 as a result of President Roh Tae Woo's*Nordpolitik*, which began as his presidential election campaign in 1987.

Japanese and Korean Responses to the Rise of China since the Early 1990s

The Tiananmen Incident in 1989 is commonly cited as the watershed year in which Sino-Japanese relations began to sour. But the impact of the Tiananmen Incident on Japan's China policy was in fact limited even as Japanese public sentiment towards China worsened. The United States and Japan were more concerned about potential instability in China than human rights violations, and the Houston G7 summit the following year lifted all the important sanctions. The real turning point in bilateral relations—and Japanese perceptions of China—came with the recalibration of the power balance between the two countries caused by China's rapid economic development and the collapse of the bubble economy in Japan. Until the early 1990s, China's stable development was believed to be vital to the interests of Japan and the region. This is evident in China's becoming the sole exception to the rule that prohibits the Japanese government from providing Official Development Assistance (ODA) to countries that produce weapons of mass destruction (WMD) and export arms.

By the mid-1990s, however, bilateral relations spiralled downward into what was commonly regarded as the lowest point since normalization in 1972. Not only did Japan stop deferring to Chinese demands based on feelings of guilt, it began also in the post-Cold War era to compete against China for regional leadership. In the late 1990s, and especially after Jiang Zemin's somewhat disastrous visit to Japan in 1998, Japan's stance towards China visibly hardened. Japan began openly to compete with China by seeking closer relations with the ASEAN countries, and with India, Russia, South Korea, and Central Asia too, to check China's growing regional influence.

The near-inevitability of the problems facing the two competitors is summed up as follows: 'In the past when China was strong, Japan was weak; and when Japan was strong, China was weak. Now China and Japan are both strong'. In other words, the realization of this unexpected power balance was at the root of the sharp deterioration in Japanese images of China during the period 1995–2000. With the structural shift in the East Asian political economy in the 1990s, negative sentiment was brewing among certain Japanese elites, the media, and non-competitive business sectors to the tune that China was emerging as a threat to Japan. Amidst discussions of the 'rise of China' in the mid-1990s and onwards, 'China acquired the image of a strong competitor, a stubborn antagonist determined to gain at Japan's expense, and a growing security problem. It had become a rival rather than a means to Asian regionalism'.

The rise of China poses a challenge to the regional balance of power, and threatens Japan's self-perceived identity as an economic superpower. Due to the colonial legacy and political constraints, economic power more than anything else, 'influences not only Japan's foreign policies, but also its perceptions of the global hierarchy and its identity as a global civilian power in this hierarchy'. China's economic rise thus threatens Japan's prestige as Asia's number-one economic power and feelings of superiority vis-à-vis China in the economic sphere. It is not then surprising that Japanese pride and patriotism were expressed in other spheres, such as the burst of popular 'cultural nationalism' during this period. Since the 1990s, popular monthly journals like *Seiron* and *Shokun*have carried numerous articles and debates related to patriotism and national identity, which often have as their central theme anti-American, anti-Chinese, or anti-Korean sentiment. Although such aggressive expressions of neo-nationalism were sometimes encouraged by the government, they have also caused unwanted difficulties, with spontaneous, grass-roots movements putting bilateral economic exchanges at risk.

Another important change in Japan's China debate is the fragmentation and reshuffling of political parties since 1993. One consequence of the end of the '1955 system' and constant political realignment is that it has weakened the influence of the Japanese Left and strengthened the conservatives. The decline of the JSP in the early 1990s killed off an important pro-China force in Japanese domestic politics. The JSP under Murayama thus gave up its time-honoured principle of supporting unarmed neutrality and staunchly opposing the United States–Japan alliance as an expedient strategy to forge a ruling coalition with the Liberal Democratic Party (LDP). As a result, China lost its traditional ally in Japanese domestic politics. Around the same time, Japanese policy-making on China saw a decline in the influence of the Ministry of Foreign Affairs (MOFA) and its Bureau of Asian Affairs (aka the China School), which adversely affected bilateral relations.

In addition to the reorganization of political actors and the balance of power among them, a key change has also occurred in the identity of the actors that evoke China as a political issue. During the Cold War, China policy became politicized predominantly by the pro-China forces on the Left, but since the mid-1990s, China has become the target of rightwing criticism. Examples of Japanese 'grievances' include: resentment of the CCP's righteous attitude, given its own human rights abuses and aspirations to regional hegemonism; China's lack of appreciation of the massive ODA provided by Japan; and Chinese opposition to Japan's entry as a permanent member of the UNSC. Recently, there has been a backlash in Japan against China's repeated use of the 'history card'. Moreover, the hardening sentiment towards China in the 1990s is 'clearly a reaction to anti-Japanese demonstrations in China, as well as to China's military actions, including the nuclear submarine intrusion into Japanese waters in November 2004'.

Japanese public opinion has thus become increasingly negative towards China in response to the rise of anti-Japan nationalism in China. Surveys taken by the Cabinet Public Information Office reveal that the greatest changes in public opinion in the past decade have occurred vis-à-vis China and South Korea. Most Japanese felt close to China throughout the 1970s and 1980s, but in the 1990s and thereafter the percentage of those who did so declined from about 60–70% to 40–50%.

Anti-Chinese mobilization has been led by nationalist politicians, such as Ishihara Shintaro, who have not shied away from anti-Chinese commentary. This has led to a growing pressure on the Japanese government to reduce or stop Japan's foreign aid to China. The elimination of ODA to China was the most important foreign policy agenda of those favouring a policy of containment in dealing with the Chinese. Containment of China, however, has additional underlying meanings in the context of Japanese domestic politics, different from its standard usage in the United States. Not only is it a defence on the part of the Japanese rightwing of views of past wars and occupations in Asia, but an attack on 'leftist intellectuals' and the Japanese media for their apologetic worldview—quick to criticize their own country while being too soft on China.

In South Korea as well, views of China have changed substantially since normalization in 1992—from viewing China as a revisionist power intent on aiding the North Korean goal of overthrowing the South Korean government to seeing it as a status quo state preferring 'peace maintenance' over 'unification' on the Korean peninsula. The Korean public is generally unconcerned about the rise of China, although there are some concerns at the elite level about the 'uncivil faces' of China, such as maritime piracy and territorial intrusion by Chinese fishing vessels, violation of environmental protection, particularly regarding airborne pollutants, and human rights concerns, such as branding North Korean 'refugees' as 'escapees' and extraditing them to North Korea, and the audacity and imposing attitudes of Chinese diplomats.

For most of the 1990s, the centrality of China in Asian regional affairs has been most felt in the economic realm, and less so in the political, diplomatic, and security spheres. Korea is no exception, as bilateral trade has been expanding at a rapid pace. Although the general attitude of the media and the public has been favourable towards the lure of the 'great Chinese market', glimpses of Sinophobia (*gongjungjeung*, in Korean) have surfaced sporadically in discussions of the rise of China. The 'garlic battle' of 1999–2000 between the two countries also put an end to the 'honeymoon period' during which mutual accommodation dominated the bilateral relationship. According to Jae Ho Chung, the trade dispute between Seoul and Beijing intensified as a result of premature escalation by the Korean government, which appeared to have been relying too heavily on its 'special' relations with China.

As the focal point of the bilateral relationship gradually shifts from the economic to the political realm, the compatibility of relations between China and South Korea across all dimensions also comes under question. Since the heated controversy in 2004 over China's Northeast Project (*dongbuk gongjeong*), the image of the PRC among South Koreans has been significantly damaged, after nearly a decade and a half of very good relations. A poll in April 2005 showed that 57% of South Koreans believed that China's economic growth would have negative impact on Korea. The Northeast Project is perceived by Koreans as an effort to incorporate the historical kingdom of Koguryo as China's 'local history', and Beijing's refusal in 2004 to accede to South Korean requests to amend its decision to erase all references to Korean history before 1948 from its Ministry of Foreign Affairs website enraged Korean nationalists and historians. To the Koreans, Koguryo, a region located in northern China and parts of Korea, and a powerful state that resisted Chinese attempts at annexation, is an essential part of Korean history. Beijing's 'imposing' stance was hence especially regarded with disdain and stirred up negative public sentiment in Korea. The Koguryo incident has revealed some of the possible tensions underlying the bilateral relationship, as China grows ever more powerful, economically and politically.

Discussions of South Korean attitudes towards China have tended towards two extreme positions—that is, either projecting further deterioration of bilateral relations, based on recent events, or assuming a 'natural' alliance, based on shared cultural attributes.

Neither side paints an accurate picture, as South Korean opinion on China has been, and continues to be, politicized. At the same time, politicization has been less institutionalized compared to Japan, and more issue-based and contingent on shifting political contexts.

For example, Korean policies and attitudes towards China have been heavily influenced by developments in inter-Korean relations. President Roh Tae Woo's *Nordpolitik* can be viewed as an attempt at autonomous diplomacy to engage Chinese help in making progress on relations with Pyongyang.

Significantly, it is only with the deterioration of relations between Seoul and Washington amid disagreement over their respective North Korea policies that China has emerged as a serious subject in domestic debates on foreign policy, and more broadly in Korean national identity politics.

Mistakenly or not, many Koreans suspect that the United States and Japan are opposed to Korean unification, while believing China to be more supportive of inter-Korean reconciliation, as evidenced in the Six Party Talks. In other words, South Koreans' 'China fever', closely monitored by Washington for its possible connection to the recent upsurge in anti-Americanism, could be a function of their disenchantment with the United States, their long-time ally and supporter, rather than an innate pro-China tendency.

ANTI-JAPANESE SENTIMENT IN SOUTH KOREA AND TAIWAN

Getting Out of the Colonial Empire

The Japanese colonial empire came to an abrupt end on August 15, 1945, several days after the detonation of two nuclear bombs in Hiroshima and Nagasaki. What replaced this sudden political vacuum in Korea and Taiwan, however, was neither the immediate restoration of political independence nor autonomy. Two months after the Japanese surrender, the Nationalist mainlanders under the administrative leadership of General Chen Yi arrived in Taiwan, effectively bringing it back into the Chinese fold. In Korea, the delayed Japanese surrender led on August 8, 1945 to the Soviets' entry into the Pacific War, and they soon came to occupy the northern half of the Korean Peninsula. With the arrival of the US military command in Seoul, the division of Korea was finalized, setting up different paths out of the colonial experiences in the two Koreas and in Taiwan.

In the immediate postwar years, Kim Il Sung, a charismatic guerrilla leader during the Manchurian struggle, emerged in the northern half of the Korean Peninsula as a central political figure. There were several nationalist and communist contenders in the North at the time of Japanese surrender, but Kim's 'unblemished reputation as an anti-Japanese fighter' put him in an excellent position to dominate politics over his 'more established communist rivals who had stayed in Korea throughout the colonial period'. Rather than mere Soviet manipulation, it was the anti-colonial struggle that shaped the contours of postwar North Korea politics. With the effective backing of the Soviets, Kim II Sung was able to capitalize on his anti-Japanese struggles to buttress his political legitimacy.

Such politicization of anti-Japanese struggles made North Korea's anti-Japanese sentiment approximate deeply held prejudices against the Japanese. This unique trait of 'sovereign-nationalist' anti-Japanese sentiment shaped in the early postwar years often resurfaced in North Korean negotiators' later emphasis on 'the principle of non-interference with a state's internal affairs'.

In contrast to the North Korean case, the political use of anti-Japanese sentiment in South Korea and Taiwan during the early postwar years was somewhat minimized due to the role of the United States and the emergence of the Cold War structure in the region. For instance, upon his arrival in Seoul, John Hodge, US commander of the South Korean occupation, effectively neutralized indigenous political parties, such as the Korea People's Republic and the local People's Committee headed by leftist and centrist Korean nationalists, due to their assumed procommunist credentials. Moreover, the US occupational authorities temporarily used Japanese police and officials to maintain law and order, and let many Koreans who had worked for the Japanese take key positions in the South Korean government. When the National Assembly passed the National Traitors Law to punish Japanese collaborators, even the first President Syngman Rhee, known for his strong anti-Japanese view, had to modify the law, simply to maintain political order and to expel a communist uprising in South Korea.

Similar patterns emerged in Taiwan during the immediate postwar years. Here, the mainland Nationalists (*Kuomintang*, or KMT) were determined to eradicate the Japanese colonial legacy from the island and to retrocede it into the Chinese nation. Compared with Japanese colonial rule, however, the inability of the KMT officials in maintaining law and order soon became fodder for public outcry against the Nationalists' misrule and rampant corruption, which further exacerbated the worsening economic and social conditions in Taiwan. The stage was thus set for 'the clash between the collective memory of the Japanese era and the reality of Nationalist rule', resulting in a massive uprising followed in March 1947 by the Nationalist regime's massacre of Taiwanese islanders.

The incident, later known as the February 28 Incident, was significant because of the huge number of casualties, ranging from 10,000 to 50,000, but also due to its impact on postwar Taiwanese society. The decolonization process forced by outsiders 'at gunpoint' and the island-wide anti-communist campaign known as 'the White Terror' silenced the Taiwanese discourse on political reform and colonial legacy. As a result, many Taiwanese came to harbour strong aversion against another 'occupier' of their island, which had the effect of pushing to the background existing antagonistic memories of Japanese colonial rule. Following the Nationalist defeat in 1949 in the Chinese Civil War, and the subsequent emergence of the confrontation across the Taiwan Straits, the Chiang Kaishek regime had to transform 'the image of Taiwan from a province tainted by Japanese influence to the last redoubt preserving the essence of China' in the struggle against the communists on the mainland.

Aside from the salience of the anti-communist campaign in both South Korea and Taiwan, the Korean War also dramatically increased the United States' role in both maintaining security in the region and helping to mend South Korean and Taiwanese ties with their former colonial ruler, Japan. In fact, even before the outbreak of the Korean War, American officials were determined to develop 'political cohesion among non-Communist groups'. To this end, the US Commander of the military occupation in Japan General MacArthur invited President Rhee of South Korea to meet with Japanese officials in Tokyo in October 1948, and also received in January 1949 a South Korean diplomatic mission to the SCAP General Headquarters in Tokyo. It was the outbreak of the Korean War, however, that prompted the United States to 'reverse its assumption that Korea was not vital to Japan's defence and affirmed the interdependence of Japanese and South Korean security interests'.

In Taiwan as well, the impact of the Korean War was immediate. In fact, until January 1950 President Truman let it be known that 'The United States will not involve in the dispute of the Taiwan Strait'. Once the war broke out, however, President Truman both declared 'neutralization of the Straits of Formosa (now the Taiwan Strait)' and sent the Seventh Fleet to the Taiwan Strait. With the Cold War structure fully in shape, American aid through the medium of the Mutual Security Act poured into Taiwan, reaching $1.5 billion by 1965. As with the South Korean case, the United States was eager to push for an early reconciliation between Taiwan and Japan. When Japanese Prime Minister Yoshida Shigeru was reluctant to do so due to his 'preference for a "two-China" approach in Japan's diplomatic and economic policies', the US government put intense pressure on the Japanese government by linking Japan's pro-Taiwan commitments to the Senate ratification of the San Francisco Peace Treaties.

POSTWAR POLITICS OF HISTORICAL MEMORY AND RECONCILIATION

Despite the common presence of anti-communist campaigns and the United States role in the early years of the Cold War, decolonization in South Korea and Taiwan took different forms. Owing to different colonial experiences in South Korea (e.g. a more deeply-held negative predisposition towards Japan, memories of nation-wide independent movements, reinforced national consciousness), South Korean's path towards reconciliation with Japan in the postwar period proved exceedingly difficult. Nothing is more indicative of this trend than the contrast between the South Korean and Taiwanese governments' efforts to normalize diplomatic relations with Japan. In Taiwan, with some US push, the Nationalist and Japanese governments signed the ROC-Japan Peace Treaty on the same day in 1952 that the San Francisco treaties came into force, and their diplomatic relations were soon restored. In South Korea, however, it took 14 years to finalize the normalization process. Unlike the Taiwan case, repeated US calls for speedy normalization got nowhere until June 22, 1965, when the Park regime made its own decision to finalize the treaty.

As a possible cause of the lengthy process, some link South Korean president Syngman Rhee's strong revulsion for Japan to South Korea's difficulty in normalizing its diplomatic relations with Japan. As a long-time leader of the exile independence movement, Rhee's anti-Japanese sentiment was such that he warned the US government that he 'would rather surrender to the much-hated North Korean communists invading from the north than accept a Japanese role in the US-led defence of the peninsula'. Rhee also managed to form the short-lived Asian People's Anti-Communist League, a loose multilateral Asian grouping comprising South Korea, Taiwan, Hong Kong, and the Philippines. He refused inclusion of Japan as a member and used the league mainly 'to alert his fellow Asians against the menace of resurgent Japan'.

One of the biggest stumbling blocks in the lengthy negotiation process was the two sides' different understanding of the Japanese colonial role. Whereas the Koreans emphasized 'human sufferings and indignities', their Japanese counterparts stressed 'material benefits they had brought to the Koreans'. Given the Korean colonial experiences in which a Korean national consciousness was constructed primarily against the Japanese, the gap in their respective understandings of colonial rule was too big to reconcile. It was only after the dwindling of US aid in the 1960s, during which the United States was growingly preoccupied with the war in Indochina, that the South Korean military government gave serious thought to speeding up the process of mending ties with Japan. Due in large part to the lack of political legitimacy and the worsening economic situation in South Korea, the Park regime was determined to push for rapid economic development. In this context, the prospect of Japanese investment and technology transfer after the normalization treaty was difficult to ignore. Put simply, it was the economic factor that drove the signing of the treaty in 1965. This also marked the beginnings of the bilateral relations later described as *yuchak* (in Korean) or *yuchaku* (in Japanese), which literally means the collusion between the two governments by which the Park regime formulated its policies based on economic opportunities given by Japanese corporations.

What was missing in the normalization process was a sincere apology from the Japanese for their colonial rule and also a reparation clause in the treaty. Although Japanese Foreign Minister Shiina Etsusaburo mentioned in a brief statement his 'deep reflection on the unfortunate past', the treaties themselves made no reference to a Japanese apology. With no genuine efforts at reconciliation, the treaty was hence largely 'a marriage of convenience' between the two governments. Japanese provision of $800 million over 10 years was also included not as reparation for Japan's past wrongdoings, but merely as 'an economic cooperation agreement'. Far from reconciling their differences, therefore, the hasty normalization in 1965 left room for future political exploitations by subsequent governments. With South Korea's rapid economic development and the growing business ties between the two countries in the late 1960s and 1970s, South Korean attitudes towards Japanese became a 'latent anti-Japanese-ism', somewhat weakened but ready to be ignited by political events. During the early 1980s, the Chun Doo Hwan government exploited a loophole in the 1965 normalization treaty. In requesting massive economic aid from the Japanese government, President Chun talked openly of giving Japan an opportunity for a 'second diplomatic restoration'. After the successful loan agreement between South Korea and Japan in 1984, almost four decades after the end of Japanese colonial rule, President Chun made history by becoming the first South Korean president to visit Japan. He also called his Tokyo visit the start of a 'new era of partnership' between the two nations.

In contrast, such a lengthy and arduous path to reconciliation was simply nonexistent in Taiwan, where Japanese colonial legacy was quickly pushed aside in the struggle for political legitimacy between the two political entities across the Taiwan Straits. In fact, the Nationalist government was quite eager to work with Japan over economic and diplomatic aspects. After a brief campaign against colonial legacy, especially in the wake of the February 28 Incident, the Nationalist regime found it useful to maintain 'the Japanese system of military and police, which had proven quite successful on Taiwan and the mainland at exterminating Communists'. They even set up a secret military advisory group known the White Group, headed by an ex-Japanese military officer, to equip and train the KMT armed forces.

Different meanings attached to the Japanese colonial legacy can also be found in the public ritual of commemorating national holidays. South Koreans have two separate national holidays directly related to Japanese colonial rule—March First Day (*samiljeol*) celebrating the nation-wide independence movement on March 1, 1919, and National Liberation Day (*kwangbokjeol*) on August 15, 1945, commemorating Korea's liberation from Japanese rule. But no such holidays exist in Taiwan. Instead of remembering the demise of Japanese rule, the Taiwanese under the KMT rule celebrated the retrocession of Taiwan into the Chinese nation (*wangfujie*, or retrocession day of October 25). When the Democratic Progressive Party led by President Chen Shui-bian ruled Taiwan, however, retrocession day rapidly became a low-key event in light of the greater prominence given to commemoration of 2–28 Peace Memorial Day, signifying the Taiwanese struggle against the KMT's iron rule on February 28, 1947.

DEMOCRATIZATION AND CONTEMPORARY ANTI-JAPANESE POLITICS

Democratization in South Korea and Taiwan, which began in the late 1980s, shows additional evidence of the different politics surrounding the legacy of colonialism under Japan. Given the suppressive nature of authoritarian rule in both polities during the Cold War period, it is natural to expect that the process of democratization would open up public debates about their past. What is striking is the different impact democratization made on domestic debates in South Korea and Taiwan. South Korea's debate about the past is often focused on Japanese colonialism, but the key debate in Taiwan is on something else; that of political movement towards Taiwan's independence, while downplaying the Japanese colonial legacy.

In South Korea, democratic regimes since the early 1990s have shown the tendency to use anti-Japanese sentiment. Japanese colonial legacy was the key target of the Kim Young Sam (1993–1997) government's *Yoksa-baro seuki* (placing Korean history in the rightful place) campaign. Similarly, President Roh Moo Hyun also put emphasis in his two Liberation Day speeches on his election platform of 'cleansing history'.

In contrast, successive Taiwanese governments have since the beginning of the democratization process in the late 1980s exercised considerable restraint in criticizing Japan. For instance, while both the Kim Dae-jung and Roh Moo Hyun governments protested strongly on the issue of Prime Minister Koizumi's visit to Yasukuni Shrine, the Taiwanese Ministry of Foreign Affairs called for restraint, stating that 'Although we cannot forget history, we must face it with a spirit of tolerance and a forward-looking vision'. Former Taiwan President Lee Teng-hui even went so far as to state that

'It is natural for a premier of a country to commemorate the souls of people who lost their lives for their country'. As to territorial disputes, South Korean protests over Tokdo/Takeshima contrast with the relative decline of disputes in Taiwan over the Diaoyutai/ Senkaku islands.

South Korea and Taiwan also display opposite viewpoints on the expanded Japanese security role in the region. Along with the Chinese government in Beijing, the South Korean government attaches particular importance to the US alliance in its assumed role of preventing Japan from rearming. This concern is widely shared by the general public, many of whom select Japan as one of their most disliked countries. According to a South Korean survey, less than 40% of South Korean respondents chose Japan as the country most disliked in 1984, but close to 70% did so in 1995. There is, however, an opposite trend in Taiwan in the newfound push for independence and the attendant threat from mainland China. For instance, the Chen Shui-bian government publicly endorsed Japan's enhanced security role in the region. In a recent interview, Chen even remarked, 'I'm convinced that China would respect Japan more if Japan sticks to its guns more firmly'. Similarly, former President Lee Teng-hui called for Japan's more assertive security and economic role in the region. The Taiwanese government hence welcomed the 2005 joint statement by the United States and Japan that considers Taiwan as their 'mutual security concern'.

What is interesting in Taiwan's contemporary political debate is the reemergence of ambiguous nationalist and oppositional sentiments. In the new political discourse prevalent after democratization and the emergence of the DPP in 2000, Nationalist/ KMT rule is described as 'colonial, little different from the rule of the Dutch, Manchus, and Japanese before them'. As such, so-called *Taidu*, or Taiwanese independence, advocates mounting the offensive against the KMT, rather than Japan, and denigrates the Nationalists 'as an undemocratic clique of outsiders'. In contrast, before assuming his presidency, current President Ma Ying-jeou paid tribute in the commemoration of the 60th anniversary of the end of Japanese rule to anti-Japanese heroes. He also put stress on October 25, 1945 as 'the day when Taiwan was recovered by the Chinese government', criticizing the DPP government for downplaying the significance of that day. The end result is hence a clash between contending visions of the nation between nascent Taiwanese and Chinese nationalism.

In sum, owing in large part to the different postwar politics concerning their colonial experiences, South Koreans often show strong distrust of Japan, while Taiwan's view remains largely situational. In the final analysis, how to interpret the colonial past is a matter of political decision.

Nearly half a century after the demise of the Japanese colonial empire, such a decision is still in the making, as vividly demonstrated by respective different treatments of the central building that housed the Japanese colonial authorities. Whereas in Taiwan the building is still used as the Presidential Palace, South Korea's first civilian government decided to demolish this edifice in the heart of Seoul. It is through this process of remembering and forgetting the past that Japanese colonial legacies continue to hold sway in contemporary South Korea and Taiwan.

Conclusion

What the preceding analysis demonstrates is the extent to which negative sentiment towards great powers has been activated and deactivated at different times by different polities under different regional contexts.

Far from being etched in the public psyche, such oppositional sentiment in East Asia has been more fluid than commonly believed. It has varied in intensity from low to medium to high levels of politicization, deployed by different political forces at different political junctures. Empirically, it is possible to discern a 'rank order' in the hierarchy of oppositional sentiment in East Asia, from opinion (such as anti-Chinese sentiment in postwar South Korea and Japan or anti-Japanese sentiment in Taiwan) to distrust (such as anti-Japanese sentiment in postwar Korea and anti-Chinese sentiment in post-Cold War Japan) to prejudice (such as anti-Japanese sentiment in North Korea). Anti-Japanese sentiment in different polities in East Asia illustrates this point. Owing to the different nature of domestic politicization processes, South Korean and Taiwanese attitudes towards their former colonial master have been less rigid than is the case in North Korea. Far from demonstrating a systematic bias against Japanese colonial rule, postwar governments in both South Korea and Taiwan have often used anti-Japanese sentiment for various political purposes.

The wide variety of oppositional sentiment also suggests that its impact on policy may vary substantially as well. A case in point is South Korea's Kim Dae-jung government (1998–2003), which was initially viewed as willing to chart a new course of diplomatic relations with Japan. In a joint communiqué with Japanese Prime Minister Keizo Obuchi in 1998, the Kim government lifted earlier bans on Japanese cultural products and also addressed more than 40 issues, ranging from security and economy to the environment. Yet despite this new approach, once the issue of Japanese history textbooks became politicized in 2001, President Kim recalled the South Korean ambassador to Japan and also decided to halt the process of opening more South Korean markets to Japanese cultural products. Any remnants of anti-Chinese sentiment in Korea are, in comparison, overshadowed by anti-Japanese and anti-American sentiment. Japan was the referent for Korean national identity during the colonial period, and to this day the collective memory of Japan as colonial oppressor is stronger than centuries of suzerainty under China. Moreover, due to limited politicization of the Chinese historical rule in South Korea, the impact of anti-Chinese sentiment on South Korea's policy towards China has been marginal at best, a dynamic echoed in Taiwan's policy towards Japan. In contrast, during the postwar period, the United States has been the object of both emulation and resentment. American power and influence in the region since 1945 have made it a focal point for opposition.

Although many analysts tend to attribute Korean accommodation of China in recent years to a 'natural' cultural affinity and history of 'brotherly' relations, the possibility nevertheless exists that distaste among Koreans for heavy-handed Great Power intervention could ignite latent anti-Chinese sentiment. China's handling of North Korea's provocations in 2010 and its aggressive approach to the disputed islands in the South and East China Seas could indeed increase anti-Chinese sentiment in both South Korea and Japan. It is not clear at this writing how the latest Chinese diplomatic overtures will affect oppositional sentiment in Japan and South Korea, and their respective policies towards China. What is clear from this analysis, however, is that opinion, distrust, and prejudice will remain part and parcel of East Asia's regional politics.

6

China's Rise: Opportunity or Threat for Northeast Asia

The consequences of China's economic development for the West, and the United States in particular, are being closely watched. But the impact of China's growth for its neighbors is no less important. Over the past decade, North Asian economies that are higher on the economic value chain like Japan, Taiwan, and South Korea have benefited from China's low-end-manufacturing strengths. Meanwhile, Southeast Asian economies, more closely resembling China and offering similar comparative advantages, have often found themselves outmuscled more recently by their much larger neighbor.

Looking to the future, both China and Southeast Asia will seek to climb the economic value ladder—indeed, China is doing so even now. In the process, Beijing and Southeast Asia will increasingly challenge both the North Asian economies and those of the West.

A Mixed Bag for Asia

A decade ago, as East Asia emerged from financial crisis, China's rise was viewed by many neighbors as a potential threat rather than an opportunity. But when economies from South Korea to Thailand revived and the regional production-sharing network matured, everyone seemed to benefit from China's demand for specialized components and primary products. Processing trade—that is, importing raw materials or components for mainland assembly and processing then exporting the finished products—drove China's trade growth, accounting for its entire balance of trade surplus, while "normal trade" usually generated a net deficit.

Yet over the next decade, a split emerged in how China's growth affected North Asian and Southeast Asian economies. Bilateral trade figures illustrate the emerging differences. Between 2000 and 2010, the North Asian trio of Japan, Taiwan, and South Korea saw its collective trade surplus with China (mirrored in China's trade deficits with these countries) soar from $30 billion to $210 billion. This growth came from exporting technology-intensive components to China, which provided an assembly base for the finished products ultimately destined for the West.

In doing so, the North Asian economies avoided American-led criticism of unfair Chinese competition, even as they in fact contributed to a large share of China's contentious bilateral trade surpluses with the United States and the European Union. Australia, another major beneficiary, saw its trade surplus jump from almost nothing in the early part of the last decade to $35 billion in 2010, reflecting China's voracious appetite for raw materials.

The story for ASEAN countries is more complex, given that their resource endowments are similar to China's. Immediately after the Asian financial crisis, the region benefited across the board. Its overall trade balance with China shifted from a deficit in the late 1990s to a surplus of nearly $20 billion by 2004.

But by 2009 this surplus had slowly evaporated as Vietnam and Singapore moved to significant deficits and the surpluses of other countries moderated as their imports of finished products and construction-related equipment from China accelerated. More recently, there has been some bounce-back largely due to Malaysia's unique mix of exports, including both commodities and electronics components, as demand rebounded in the West.

TRYING TO KEEP UP WITH A GIANT

Evolving regional production patterns have, moreover, affected capital flows, investment rates, and wage trends in ways that have benefited some East Asian countries more than others. China's industrialization process will likely still be an opportunity for the more developed North Asian economies, which have managed to strengthen their position at the high end of the consumer electronics and IT product lines. But it is affecting investment and labour markets in Southeast Asia in ways that are complicating the subregion's efforts to moderate widening income disparities, increase productivity, and possibly escape the middle-income trap.

Real wages have stagnated in the Southeast Asian economies as a result of relatively low productivity growth and pressure to stay competitive with China's labour costs. The ASEAN countries have also struggled to boost private investment rates closer to pre-Asian crisis levels in order to sustain long-term growth. For these two indicators, China is in a class by itself.

Starting in the mid-1990s, real wages in China surged by over 12 percent annually. Breaking this down by sector, growth ranged from around 8 to 10 percent annually in manufacturing to 15 percent in financial services. By contrast, real wage growth for the middle-income economies of Thailand, the Philippines, and Malaysia was in line with GDP growth for much of the 1990s but then fell off sharply and either declined or stagnated over most of the past decade.

Growth in Real Wages
(% annual increase)

	2000-2005	*2006-2009*
China	12.6	12.7
Malaysia	3.5	1.1
Philippines	-1.1	-0.7
Thailand	-1.0	1.2

Source: International Labour Organization

China's share of investment to GDP, meanwhile, rose steadily from 35 to more than 45 percent over the past decade and a half. By contrast, investment rates never fully recovered in Southeast Asian economies after the Asian financial crisis, remaining about one-third lower than in the late 1990s at around 20 to 25 percent of GDP compared with as high as 35 to 40 percent earlier. Some of this decline was desirable given elevated pre-crisis levels, but the pendulum has swung too far in the opposite direction. Stagnant real wage growth and relatively low investment rates have been viewed as largely the result of country-specific conditions. But the region's production network has played a significant role in enabling China to pull away from its Southeast Asian neighbors. With multinational firms managing decisions about where components are produced, location is influenced by the relative productivity of labour and wage costs along with the logistical advantages that China's size offers. That means China both attracts the lion's share of investment and sets the bar for labour costs.

China's exceptional investment rates have contributed to industrial labour productivity's estimated 10 to 20 percent annual increases since the mid-1990s—much higher growth than its neighbors have experienced and exceeding manufacturing wage increases. High labour productivity growth added to the advantages China could provide for labour-intensive assembly lines after its WTO accession in 2001. And there was also ample room for importing medium-tech components from Southeast Asia, which was supported by investments from multinational firms that were driving production-sharing arrangements.

Over time, however, China's declining unit labour costs have put pressure on countries like Malaysia to limit wage increases in order to maintain competitiveness within the production chain. Failing to do so would mean that these product lines would likely migrate to lower-cost centers in Vietnam, South Asia, or back to China.

MOVING UP THE LADDER

Meanwhile, China has been aggressively upgrading its technological capacity while its infrastructure base has solidified. Thus even with rapid wage growth, China has been able to strengthen its position in more skill-intensive production lines, though its competitive advantages in more labour-intensive products such as footwear have declined with more recent wage escalation. And in a few cases, production has moved to countries where costs are lower. Location considerations within China are also coming into play. With the rising cost of production along its coast and an expanded interior transport network, firms like Honeywell and Acer have been moving inland, though some are considering locations abroad in order to target external markets or take advantage of cheap labour.

Surging energy prices, which increase transportation costs, and the complexities of a dispersed supply chain are also encouraging some firms that previously outsourced components to Southeast Asia to relocate their operations and associated R&D activities within China to places like Chongqing or Henan. Intel and Dell are two examples. Moreover, as Chinese technology-intensive companies like Huawei expand, local linkages have deepened.

Thus, processing-related imports have fallen from over 40 percent of China's total imports to 30 percent over the past decade. And as a share of its exports, they have declined from 55 percent to about 40 percent as production has become more integrated within China. As its economy matures, more and more parts of the production network are consolidating within or moving to China.

Ultimately, both China and the middle-income Southeast Asian countries face the same challenge: becoming more innovative to achieve high-income status. They all realize that they have no alternative but to move up the value chain—with all the requirements that this will entail, from reoriented education systems to globally linked research networks and open innovation systems. If they are successful, they will eventually encroach on the domain of the North Asian trio and heighten competitive pressures in East Asia more generally.

THE RISE OF CHINA

In 1999 the People's Republic of China celebrated the 50th anniversary of its founding, marking the end of a period corresponding almost exactly to the second half of the 20th century, in which China was restored to its role as a major player in international politics. Given that for the first 50 years of the 20th century China served simply as an arena in which the imperialist powers fought for spheres of influence, this transformation is of significance not only for China but also for international politics in East Asia. However, it was not until the 1960s that China stepped onto the international political stage as a more independent power. In the 1950s China had officially - though not always actually - adhered to a policy of "leaning towards the Soviet Union," and promoted a "China-Soviet Union monolith" during the Cold War as part of the Eastern bloc. The end of the 1950s saw this stance change to one of Sino-Soviet rivalry, and China's first successful nuclear test in 1964 introduced into the bipolar Cold War structure a new orientation towards "multi-polarity."

China's independence grew more prominent in the 1970s, as rapprochement with the US in 1971 brought considerable changes to the international political framework of East Asia. From that time until the early part of the 1980s, China adopted a policy of "a single line" to align with the US and Japan to oppose the Soviet Union's drive for domination. The increasing independence of China's foreign policy from the 1960s through the 1970s did not, however, reflect a similar expansion of China's own strength as a nation. China was during this time still suffering the aftereffects of the Great Leap Forward of the 1950s, the subsequent Great Famine, and the widespread chaos stemming from the self-destructive Cultural Revolution that began in the mid-1960s. China under Mao Zedong sought rapprochement with the US for no other reason than a very keen awareness of the threat posed by the Soviet Union in light of the domestic disorder in China. Thus, the Chinese threat perception of the Soviet Union and the US Asian Strategy seeking an "honorable withdrawal" from Vietnam, coincided well, leading to the Sino-US rapprochement in 1971.

Deng Xiaoping, who after the death of Mao Zedong seized the reins of power, sought through a policy of "reform and opening to the outside world" to revolutionize the "self-reliance" economic approach that had been pursued theretofore. Beginning with the introduction of a "production by contract" system, he set out on a bold course to introduce into China elements of a market economy. This marked the country's first earnest attempts in the 20th century to establish the foundations for expanding its national strength. China began seeing the Soviet Union as somewhat less of a threat in the 1980s. Although the Soviet invasion of Afghanistan did cause considerable alarm, reinforcing the view of the Soviets as a danger to Chinese security, it was apparent thereafter that the USSR had become bogged down in Afghanistan. Causing greater unease for the Chinese was the new Reagan administration, and above all its Taiwan policy, amid the building of a strong "new Cold War" structure to counter the Soviet Union. China began around 1982 unilaterally to revise its policy of rapprochement with the US, aspiring to what it termed "an independent and autonomous foreign policy," and sought to put a certain distance between itself and the US. Another factor behind these changes was that the China-Vietnam War, which had stemmed from an overwhelmingly powerful sense of the Soviet threat, had not gone as China had wished and, in fact, had for all practical purposes been a "defeat." China thus became more convinced that enhancing its own national power had to take precedence over pursuing an active foreign policy.

As China began making adjustments to its foreign policy, the new US-Soviet Cold War posed little direct threat, with China not particularly favoring either side. Over-dependence on the US might be seen as an attempt to intimidate the Soviet Union, and it might also leave China unable to speak out against US policy towards Taiwan. In any case, the success of the "reform and opening to the outside world" policy was Deng Xiaoping's highest priority, as he strove to increase the country's own strength. Apparently, China firmly believed that the "peaceful international environment" needed to achieve this aim could be established without drawing particularly close to the US. From that point on, China assumed a rather passive and reactive attitude towards foreign affairs.

The Tiananmen Square Incident of June 4, 1989, seriously impaired China in its pursuit of a peaceful international environment, as China found itself isolated internationally for about a year thereafter. Another factor setting China apart was its insistence that rule by the Communist Party would be maintained, by force if necessary, following the dramatic end to the Cold War in the latter half of 1989. There were those in the international community who hoped to sweep China into the subsequent wave of democratization, but the Japanese government and the Bush administration in the US feared that this would result in internal chaos, and both instead worked towards normalizing relations with China. As the country began normalizing its international relations, Deng Xiaoping at the beginning of 1992 again issued a dictate on reform and liberalization (during his inspection tour through the southern provinces of China), and the Chinese economy returned once more to rapid growth.

The growth of the Chinese economy in the 1990s allowed China for the first time in the 20th century to wield power as an important member of the international community on the sole basis of its own national power, free from alliances and partnerships with other countries. The Chinese economy began to grow at an annual rate of more than ten percent from 1992, and in that same year, the IMF and the World Bank released estimates of per capita GDP for individual countries calculated using purchasing power parity, the results of which astonished the world. On an exchange rate basis, China's per capita GDP at the time was less than US$500 but, using purchasing power parity, this figure climbs to about US$2000. Thus, the actual per capita GDP of China was more than four times the level calculated through exchange rates; multiplying this new per capita GDP by the population of China, the result is an economy on par with Japan and other major countries. If the present rapid growth continues, the Chinese economy someday might even surpass that of the US in scale.

Besides economic growth, there are other indicators showing China's growing national might, some of which could generate concern in other countries. Publicly released figures reveal a surprising 15% annual increase in defense expenditures. There have also been press reports of China eagerly buying up a vast supply of the weapons that Russia has been selling off since the end of the Cold War. 1992 saw the promulgation of the Law of the People's Republic of China on Its Territorial Seas and Adjacent Zones, and its activities in the Spratly Islands have sparked anxiety among the countries in Southeast Asia. Also noteworthy are the frequent proclamations of PLA naval personnel that their duty is the protection of the "maritime rights and interests" of China.

Given all of these trends, a perception of China as a threat has emerged in the post-Cold War era. Certainly there were those in the 1960s, even in Japan, who considered China a threat. The danger posed by China during this part of the Cold War, however, was an ideological one, which would at most constitute a threat through "indirect invasion." By contrast, the view of China as a threat in the 1990s arises entirely from the power and policies of China itself. Though not allied now with any other country, China's presence has become a concern to other countries, one important consequence of the reform and liberalization policy initiated by Deng Xiaoping.

What is one to make of the emergence of China in this fashion? Since the mid-1990s this question has become a key focus of attention among policymakers in countries such as the US and Japan with ties to East Asia. In the US the debate has centered on whether to opt for engagement with China or for containment of China, with much argument over whether to classify China as a "strategic partner" or a "competitor." The balance of military power between China and other countries, recent patterns of behavior exhibited by China, and other important elements.

CHANGE OF POWER STATUS AND THE SPEED OF CHINA'S RISE

Entering the 21st century, there are more and more predictions about when China will become a superpower. Some guess that China will be as strong as the United States in the coming decade, some bet that in 20 years and some predict its rise in year 2040. In spite of those disagreements among scholars, the forecasts were all based on the speed at which China's total power has been growing in recent years, without any consideration of the influences of the other powers' growth. As we are aware that China's power status is related to that of the other states, when forecasting China's future power status, we should not only take account of the speed of China's power growth but also the growth of the other states' power. To foresee the future change of China's power status, we should clarify the conditions for ascent and descent of international power status.

Conditions for Ascent and Descent of Power Status

As a state's power status is determined by quantitative comparisons of powers among states, the change in power status of a state depends on the difference in power growth rates between two states in a given period of time. Based on the afore-mentioned formula of a state's power status, the expression for the change of a state's power status should be $Sc = A(1 + Ra)/B(1 + Rb) - A/B$. The expression shows that the change of a state's power status depends entirely upon the power growth rates (Ra and Rb) of the two states over a certain period of time. That is, the state with a faster power growth rate will rise, and the other will fall, and the statuses remain unchanged if the growth rates of the two state powers are the same. Over a fixed time period, the difference in power growth rates for the two states may result in three possibilities for change of a side's power status: rising, falling or unchanged. The three scenarios may result from 13 different situations, in which there are five for ascent, five for descent and three for no change.

It will be a political issue if a state is able to rise to a superpower in a few decades, but only an historical issue if a state rises to a hegemon over hundreds of years. As the atrophy of a state's power is a significant factor for the rapid rise of other states' power statuses, it creates an important scenario for a shift of power between two states. Therefore, power atrophy is an important political issue deserving more attention than power growth. A state's power increases in most years, decreases occasionally and very rarely has zero growth. Thus, the probability of the 10 scenarios of power-status change varies. Often both states enjoy positive power growth simultaneously; it is less common for one state to have a positive power growth while the other has a negative one; it is rare for both states to have negative power growth and is even less common that one state incurs zero power growth. When two states simultaneously have positive or negative power growth, it takes a longer time for their power gap to change and their power statuses to shift, and the probability of power-status shift is small. If one of the two states incurs zero power growth, their power gap will change relatively rapidly and there will be a higher probability for their power status to shift. However, the fastest change in the two states' power gap or their power statuses will occur when the two states have opposite power growths, i.e. one state's power increases and the other's decreases ($Ra > 0 > Rb$ or $Ra < 0 < Rb$). Because national power grows in most years and opposite power growths of two states tend to shift power statuses easily, the factors leading to power atrophy are more significant than the factors enhancing national power in terms of changing the power gap and power status between states.

Political turbulence can cause a state's comprehensive power to diminish severely and rapidly, and it alters a state's power status at a faster rate than does economic development. Being defeated in a war, state disintegration, civil war, social turmoil and political movements all work effectively in shifting power status. The shift of power status between China and the Soviet Union after the Cold War serves as a typical example. In 1991, prior to collapse, the Soviet Union was the only competing superpower in the world rivalling the United States, and its power status drastically differed from that of China.

However, as the succeeding state of the former Soviet Union after its collapse, Russia's comprehensive power endured a drastic fall and as a result its geographical area was reduced by about 24%, its population reduced by 48%, its economy decreased by 11%, and the size of its military was cut by 33.7%. At that time Russian comprehensive power was still greater than China's, however, its power status fell into the same class that China belonged to. The power gap between them was only in degree and no longer in character. Thereafter, Russia's economy declined for years, its military capability was severely weakened, and its political power was diminished internationally. Even though it is hard for us to figure out in which specific year the power-status shift occurred, we are quite certain that China's comprehensive power surpassed that of Russia during the 1990s. Up to 1999, sustaining only military superiority over China, Russia fell far behind China in aspects of political power and economic power. In 1999, Russia's GDP accounted for only one-fourth or one-third of China's GDP of $1 trillion.

Economic crisis can cause a nation's power to decrease rapidly and it works as a faster agent than economic development in changing the power gap or power status between two states. The East Asian Financial Crisis during 1997–98 widened the power gap between China and the Southeast Asian countries and meanwhile reduced the disparity of economic power between China and Japan. The East Asian Financial Crisis decreased China's annual economic growth rate to 7% from 9% prior to the crisis while it caused negative and zero economic growth, respectively, for Indonesia and Japan. Indonesian GDP fell to $50 billion in 1998 from $190.3 billion in 1995 (in 1998 its currency exchange rate fell to US$1:IDR7500 from $1:IDR2321 in 1996) and it recovered to $208.3 billion in 2003, with only a 9.5% increase from its GDP in 1995. In that period, Japan's GDP reduced from $5083.1 billion in 1995 to $4326.4 billion in 2003, a total reduction of 15%. During the same period, China's GDP (by currency exchange rate) doubled from $704.1 billion in 1995 to $1409.9 billion in 2003. Therefore, in the eight years from 1995 to 2003, the economic gap between Indonesia and China had been widened from 3.7 times to 6.8 times, while the economic gap between China and Japan narrowed from 7.2 to 3.0 times. In terms of PPP, China's economy even surpassed Japan's, causing a shift in their economic power rankings.

Political Factors Determining the Fluctuation of China's Power Status

According to the principle that opposite power growths among states tend to change power status between states easily, we come to realize that in 10 years (by 2015) whether China can sustain the existing power status will be determined mainly by the likelihood of political crisis that may cause China's power status to descend. Since its foundation in 1949, China's power status has undergone a spell of four rising and three falling periods. During 1950–58 China's power status had been rising. During that period, the Korean War tremendously raised both China's military power status and her domestic and international capabilities of political mobilization. Between 1952 and 1958, China's GDP increased by as much as 1.9 times. During 1959–63 China's comprehensive power atrophied severely. The Anti-Rightwing Movement led the

Chinese government to adopt the policies of 'Great Leap' and 'People's Commune', which resulted in an overall economic crisis. It was not until 1964 that China's economy recovered to the same level of 1960. In 1959, Sino–Soviet relations began to deteriorate and China was facing joint pressures from both the United States and the Soviet Union. During 1964 and 1965, China's national power enjoyed a brief rising period but fell again during 1966–76. In May 1966, the Cultural Revolution occurred and the country was immersed in turbulence and chaos when the government's ability to maintain order was severely hampered, economic activities stagnated, and the military weakened. However, in the same period of time, many Asian states such as Japan, South Korea and Singapore had industrialized their countries and their power status was rising rapidly in relation to China's. From 1978 to 1988 was a period when China restored its social order, increased its domestic mobilization capability and normalized relations with the United States and the Soviet Union. Consequently, China had again enhanced its international political capability, and its economy sustained an average annual growth as high as 10.2%. The political events of 1989–93 slowed China's economic growth, and dramatically reduced its domestic and international political mobilization capabilities. Thus, China's power status fell as her political power diminished in such a drastic manner. From 1993 to 2004 was the third period when China's power status ascended. During this interval, China gradually emerged from the international isolation which had started in 1989 and its capabilities of domestic and international mobilization once again increased. During 1993–2004, China's economy sustained an annual growth of 9.2% and the 1997 East Asian Financial Crisis accelerated the ascendance of China's economic power status. Ever since the founding of the People's Republic of China, each of the three major descents of China's power status was traced back to a political crisis rather than wars or economic difficulties. Therefore, we can believe that as long as there is no future political crisis, China will be able to avoid a fall in its power status.

Based on the principle that national power usually sustains growth in the majority of years, the author argues that the major external elements affecting the speed of rise of China's power status will be: (1) US military commitments and an increase or decrease of its international mobilization capabilities, and (2) the pace of political integration of the European Union (EU). According to the current growth of the comprehensive strengths of major powers, the author assumes that no other single nation, except the United States, could have larger comprehensive power than China in the next 10 years. Although each individual European state has smaller comprehensive power than China, the EU as a unified power will have a superior status to China's. If the political integration of the EU results in an international player with national character in the next 10 years, our references for judging China's future power status should include both the United States and the EU. Some people suppose that China's future power status would fundamentally depend upon China's economic growth. They obviously have neglected the political and military powers of the United States and the EU. China possesses a huge supply of low-paid labour, therefore in the next 10 years China's economic growth will be faster than that of the United States and the EU. It is also quite possible for China to narrow its economic gap with the United States and the EU. Nevertheless, there is uncertainty with regard to the development of the military and political powers of China, the United States and the EU in next 10 years.

In 10 years from now, China may narrow its military gap with the EU but the change of its military gap with the United States will depend on its military containment against Taiwanese secessionists. A favourable security environment will constrain the EU from large military expenditure. Therefore, in the next 10 years, China's military strength will grow faster than that of the EU and will reduce the military gap between the two. Nevertheless, the change of military disparity between China and the Unites States will be determined by the rates of military investment of the two sides. As a result of the pro-independence group introducing a timetable for Taiwan to achieve legitimate independence by 2008, the Chinese government will inevitably enhance its military capability to contain Taiwanese secessionists. If the Chinese government was to launch a military attack against

Taiwan's independence, it would be possible for China to narrow its military gap with the United States. If the United States continues to wage wars against smaller states while China has no need to attack Taiwanese secessionists militarily, the US military budget will increase faster than that of China's, thus the military power gap between China and the United States would be enlarged.

In the coming decade, China will probably reduce the disparity of its political power with that of the United States, but in the meantime her advantageous political power with relevance to the EU may diminish. In the 1990s, global democratization and marketization increased the US international mobilization capability to a historical peak. With little resistance from the UN Security Council, the United States obtained UN authorizations on waging the Gulf War in 1991, the Somali War in 1996, the war in Kosovo in 1999 as well as the war in Afghanistan in 2001. Many countries provided military and economic support to the United States during these wars.

However, the United States current unilateral policy caused its international political mobilizing capability to fall sharply from 2003. Without any UN authorization, the United States waged war in Iraq under the excuse of alleged Iraqi possession of weapons of mass destruction. The US action encountered strenuous objections from many traditional European allies, headed by France and Germany. As no weapons of mass destruction have been discovered in Iraq, US international influence has been seriously weakened. In the next 10 years, hegemonic position will drive the United States to continue its unilateralist foreign policy. Meanwhile, China will maintain its multilateral diplomacy to harmonize relationships with her neighbours, the EU and the developing countries of other regions. Their opposite foreign policies will reduce the political power disparity between China and the United States. Presently, China has greater political power than the EU because China is a single state while the EU is a regional organization with inconsistent foreign policies adopted by its member states. In 1999, the EU introduced the Euro which entered circulation in 2002 and finally established a single currency system on the EU market. In the year 2004, the political leaders of EU member states signed the European Constitution laying a legislative foundation for the EU to become a single state entity. If the EU constitution is approved by its member states, it will establish its own three-in-one entity of administrative institutions including a council, a committee and a foreign ministry. Future political integration of the EU will enhance its character as a large national state, which may help it to narrow its political power disparity with China.

Based on the above analysis, if we assume that both the United States and the EU act as single states, the comprehensive national power gap between either China and the United States or the EU and China will probably be narrowed by the year 2015. China's comprehensive power status may rank third in the world. In 10 years and beyond, it may be possible for China to reduce its economic power disparity with the United States and the EU even though its economic power may still be smaller than theirs. China will narrow its military power gap with the EU but its overall military strength will still be weaker than that of the United States or the EU. In terms of political power, China will narrow the gap but still cannot catch up with the United States. China may maintain her political power superiority over the EU but the disparity between the two may be reduced by further political integration of the EU if all its member states ratify the EU Constitution before 2015.

We have discussed why China enjoys the leading power status among the major powers with the exception of the United States. Based on the principle that a nation's power status ascends in accordance with a faster growth rate, we may presume that China will strengthen its power superiority over Japan, Russia and India within the next 10 years. If the EU becomes a single state entity by 2015, Britain, France and Germany will no longer be regarded as individual international players. Thus, we only assess here the power status between China and three other states: Japan, Russia and India.

With regards to economic power, low-cost labour and a rapidly expanding domestic market will ensure China a faster economic growth than Japan and Russia in the next 10 years. According to

World Bank data based on PPP calculations, Japan, Russia and China have GDP per capita in 2001 of $26,940, $8230 and $4580, respectively. This indicates that China's labour wage level was less than 18% of Japan's and 56% of Russia's. Low-cost labour guarantees foreign investors long-term high profits in China. At the end of 2005, China adopted a floating exchange rate according to World Trade Organization regulations and the Renmenbi (RMB) will appreciate continuously over the next 10 years. The increase in RMB exchange rate will make China's economic growth appear even faster. Although it enjoys the same advantage of low-cost labour as China, India is far behind China in aspects of opening-up to foreign investment as well as other economic reforms. Therefore, the Indian economy will continue to grow at a slower pace than that of China.

In terms of military power, it is anticipated over the next decade none of the three states, namely Japan, Russia and India, will be involved in military conflict with the United States. Therefore, the military spending of these states will increase slower than China's. Even though India and Russia are both faced with the threat of separatism in Kashmir and Chechnya, respectively, they do not face direct military protection of these separatists by the United States. As a result, the threat to Russia and India, from the separatists in these two regions, will not be comparable to that caused by the Taiwanese secessionists. Japan is under US military protection, hence its military investment will not increase as fast as that of China. The Japanese government has decided to reduce its 2005–09 military expenditures to $233 billion, i.e. 3.7% less than its average annual military spending in the previous five years. As a result of the danger of Taiwanese independence, China is faced with potential military clashes with the United States in the Taiwan Straight. China's military spending in the next 10 years will increase much faster than that of Japan, Russia and India. This will in turn reduce the military disparity between China and Russia and at the same time make its military superior to Japan and India.

In terms of political power, China's endeavours in East Asian regionalization will effectively enhance its ability for political mobilization over the next 10 years. China will have the opportunity to further improve its relations with the EU and that will strengthen China's influence on global affairs. India, Russia and Japan, however, will have few chances to further enhance political influence in their own regions. Although India has already been a leading nation in South Asia, the South Asian regionalization has much less momentum than the East Asian. The Eastern expansion of the EU is constraining Russian political influence in East Europe and the former Soviet Republics. To sustain its special relationship with the United States, Japan has adopted a policy undermining the establishment of the East Asian Community. This policy is similar to that adopted by Great Britain with regard to the EU. Japan's policy against East Asian regionalization may ultimately weaken its political influence in East Asia. In terms of global affairs, both India and Japan may have the opportunity to become permanent members of the UN Security Council but they will have little chance of obtaining the power of veto. What they actually obtain may only be a position of permanent/non-permanent membership without substantially increased power. Russian political impact on global affairs will further diminish as it is still trapped in a regressive inertia following the collapse of the Soviet Union.

THE MILITARY BALANCE BETWEEN CHINA AND OTHER COUNTRIES

There is no method of describing or analyzing the balance of military power that will be suitably applicable in all cases. The balance will differ depending on the two countries being weighed against each other, while considerations of the ways in which these countries utilize military force leaves one comparing apples and oranges. Including into the mix comprehensive assessments of war-making capabilities (dynamic balance) makes the issue even more complex. Measuring the balance of military power between China and Vietnam or between China and the Philippines is far different from measuring the balance between China and Taiwan. Furthermore, US involvement on behalf of one side could change these bilateral balances considerably, and much could depend on how the Japan-US and US-South Korea alliances would function in light of such involvement. However, Chinese military capability with regard to Taiwan, the US, Japan, and other countries does not seem to have been enhanced to the degree suggested in the mid-1990s by those observers who view China as a threat. Were China to resort to the use of nuclear weapons, of course, there would clearly be an overwhelming asymmetry in the military balance between China and Taiwan or between China and Japan, but this is not a factor that has only just arisen in the 1990s. In the area of nuclear weapons, though, there is also a tremendous imbalance between the US and China which has not changed for the past several decades.

There have admittedly been some changes in the balance between Taiwan and China. The purchase of Su-27 fighters from the Soviet Union without doubt improved China's air capabilities, but the F-16 and Mirage 2000 fighters introduced by Taiwan are far greater in number and importance. That China has begun extensive deployment of short- and medium-range ballistic missiles is noteworthy, but in cases where the option of employing weapons of mass destruction has been ruled out, the use of ballistic missiles would be of questionable significance and accomplish little.

With regard to capabilities that have not changed, there have been no demonstrable improvements made in China's amphibious assault capabilities. This means that, unless it could achieve overwhelming air superiority, China would find it extremely difficult to execute an amphibious assault across the Taiwan Strait; this fact has not changed.

Any operation designed to land forces on Taiwan would require months of advance preparation, and with such build-ups almost immediately discernible in the modern age, the Taiwanese side would have plenty of time to prepare.

This analysis has thus far only looked at the military balance between China and Taiwan. Were the US to offer its assistance to Taiwan, the inconsequential degree to which the military balance has changed would become even more apparent. US involvement has made, and will continue for some time into the future to make, an amphibious assault on Taiwan by China a practical impossibility. China could still launch a ballistic missile offensive against Taiwan, but the counterstrike capability of the US - in cruise missiles and other weapons - greatly exceeds that of Taiwan.

Given the considerable possibility that the US would indeed stand on the side of Taiwan in a crisis, the military balance in the area of the Taiwan Strait is in no way clearly advantageous for China, i.e., China would have a low probability of achieving its objectives.

PATTERNS OF BEHAVIOR IN CHINESE DIPLOMACY

How should one regard the patterns of behavior in China's diplomacy in the midst of a growing perception of China as a threat? The analysis of military balance given above presumes to a great degree that military rationality would be the determining factor in China's course of action. Should the actual behavior of Chinese leaders diverge from military rationality, however, even a stable military balance would not eliminate the possibility of war. Consequently, analyses of the balance of military power must be combined with analyses of the actual conduct of affairs by China in considering the prospects for the future.

With its attention primarily on domestic policies, China has in the 1990s exhibited a passive and reactionary pattern of behavior in foreign affairs. In actual fact, its preoccupation with domestic matters has been a quite consistent policy since efforts towards reform and liberalization begin in 1978. China has been very cautious, in action if not in rhetoric, about pursuing confrontation with other countries since its failure in the China-Vietnam War. This focus on domestic affairs has become an ingrained part of national policy because of the need for a peaceful international environment in order to implement reform and liberalization measures. It hardly need be said that the success of these measures is hoped for by those Chinese wishing to build a "rich country and a strong military". For Communist Party leaders, though, success has become a matter of life or death in attempting to maintain the legitimacy of one-party rule by the Chinese Communist Party (CCP). To ensure "regime security," Chinese leaders want above all to avoid becoming embroiled in foreign issues that might adversely affect their domestic policies.

Nevertheless, external relations cannot be utterly ignored if the CCP is to retain legitimacy as a governing entity. With Marxism-Leninism having completely lost its appeal, legitimacy requires the CCP to serve as the acknowledged champion of Chinese nationalism, in addition to keeping the economy performing well through reform and liberalization. Any action by an outside party that might adversely affect the unity of China must therefore be met with a swift response. In light of this, the Taiwan issue is likely to become the most acute problem to be addressed. Looking at China's pattern of behavior in the 1990s, though, one can see that even in such nationalist issues as this, China has been passive and reactive. A careful inquiry into the Taiwan Strait crisis of 1996 reveals a reaction against the US visit of President Lee Teng-hui in the summer of 1995 and a reaction against moves towards "independence" within Taiwan. These reactions were tempered, however, as China could not take an overly hard line and still successfully implement its own domestic policies. Calculating the strength sufficient enough to send a message to Taiwan and to the US Congress but not so great as to subject China to condemnation by the international community as a whole, the Chinese opted for military exercises and a missile test.

Those who see China as a threat frequently claim that China is a power seeking to "change the status quo". No doubt it does wish to change the status quo in the Taiwan Strait. It also wants to end the "hegemony" of the US within the international community. Given these wishes, there is some evidence supporting a view of China as a force trying to "change the status quo". It is also true, however, that maintaining a peaceful international environment that will allow its reform and liberalization efforts to succeed is also an important objective of China. Essential in such an environment is ensuring that capital and technology from countries worldwide are able to flow into China and that Chinese goods can be exported to other trading partners around the globe, and especially to the American and Japanese markets. China, in wishing to maintain this international environment, is a force supporting the status quo. The overall pattern of behavior of China in the 1990s, overlooking the rhetoric, shows China acting to maintain the status quo.

The most representative example of this can be found in China's policy towards North Korea. China's behavior indicates that its leaders do not particularly welcome the idea of North Korea either possessing nuclear weapons or developing missiles, nor do they have any desire to witness North Korea collapse as a nation. On the other hand, they do not wish to see North Korea at the mercy of the US. Consequently, in its policy towards North Korea, China has been basically cooperative towards the US, but not so cooperative as to allow US influence to grow overly strong. (Looking at the 1996 Taiwan Strait crisis from the Chinese perspective, a ban on visits by the leaders of Taiwan to major countries was deemed part of the contemporary international status quo. China's forceful reaction was directed against the violation of this "status quo" by the US and Lee Teng-hui; on this matter at least, the PRC was in accord with the US State Department, who also opposed Lee's visit to the US.)

It may be possible to argue that China's aims are extremely long-term in nature, and its present policy of emphasizing domestic affairs itself is a long-term measure for achieving a "rich country and strong military" and that the current reactiveness and orientation of "maintaining the status quo will move to alter the status quo, once China comes to possess an overpowering military capability. However, such an assertion is meaningless as a policy position unless one considers China as a state to be fundamentally "evil." If one's opponent is "evil," then one would certainly not adopt policies that might help him "grow"; it might even be possible to crush him while he is still weak. If such is not the case, however, then as long as the other party does not behave in a manner injurious to one's own interests, one would not take actions against the other party; if the other party is cooperative, then one would be cooperative in return. Normal international relations of this nature are desirable. Maintaining such relations does not, however, preclude the need to keep a close and careful watch on the military capabilities of the other side. Any attempt by China to substantially upgrade its military capabilities as its economy expands can be observed from neighboring countries, at which point the issue can be appropriately addressed.

MILITARY MODERNIZATION

Establishment of a professional military force equipped with modern weapons and doctrine was the last of the Four Modernizations announced by Zhou Enlai and supported by Deng Xiaoping. In keeping with Deng's mandate to reform, the PLA has demobilized millions of men and women since 1978 and has introduced modern methods in such areas as recruitment and manpower, strategy, and education and training.

In 1979, the PLA fought Vietnam in the Sino-Vietnamese War. In the 1980s, the PLA shrunk its military considerably on the theory that freeing up resources for economic development was in its interest.

In June 1989, party hardliners called on PLA to enforce martial law in Beijing and suppress the student-led demonstrations in Tiananmen Square. Over 200,000 troops from a dozen group armies were sent to Beijing in one of the largest mobilizations since the Korean War. Ideological correctness was temporarily revived as the dominant theme in Chinese military affairs. Reform and modernization appear to have since resumed their position as the PLA's priority objectives, although the armed forces' political loyalty to the Communist Party of Chinaremains a leading concern. One other area of concern to the political leadership was the PLA's involvement in civilian economic activities. Concern that these activities were adversely impacting PLA readiness has led the political leadership to attempt to remove the PLA's economic enterprises.

During the 1980s and 1990s, the PLA became extensively involved in creating a business empire including companies in areas not normally associated with the military (i.e., travel and real estate). Much of the motivation for this was to supplement the PLA's normal budget, whose growth was restricted. Mao's belief that people and groups should be self-sufficient also played a role in the PLA's varied business interests.

In the early 1990s, the leadership of the Communist Party and the high command of the PLA became alarmed that these business transactions were in conflict with the PLA's military mission. The business interests of the PLA were eroding military discipline, and there were reports of corruption resulting from the PLA businesses.

As a result, the PLA was ordered to spin off its companies. Typically, the actual management of the companies did not change, but the officers involved were retired from active duty within the PLA and the companies were given private boards of retired PLA officers. Military units were compensated for the loss of profitable businesses with increased state funding.

Beginning in the 1980s, the PLA tried to transform itself from a land-based power, centered on a vast ground force, to a smaller, mobile, high-tech military capable of mounting defensive operations beyond its coastal borders.

In the mid-1980s, Deng Xiaoping began to redefine PLA orientation radically, beginning with a reassessment in 1985 of the overall international security environment that lowered the probability of a major or nuclear war. Instead, Deng asserted that China would be confronted with limited, local wars on its periphery.

The natural consequence of this sweeping reassessment was an equally comprehensive reorientation of the Chinese military. The number of military regions was reduced from 11 to 7, and the 37 field armies were restructured to bring "tank, artillery, anti-aircraft artillery, engineer, and NBC defence units under a combined arms, corps-level headquarters called the Group Army." Between 1985 and 1988, the 37 field armies were reduced to 24 group armies, and thousands of units at the regimental level and above were disbanded. —James C. Mulvernon, 'The PLA Army's Struggle for Identity,' in The PLA and China in Transition, INSS/NDU, 2003, 111. The motivation for these large-scale changes was that a massive land invasion by Russia is no longer seen as a major threat, and the new threats to China are seen to be a declaration of independence by Taiwan, possibly with assistance from the United States, or a confrontation over the Spratly Islands. In addition, the economic centre of gravity of China has shifted from the interior to the coastal regions and China is now more dependent on trade than it has been in the past. Furthermore, the possibility of a militarily resurgent Japan remains a worry to the Chinese military leadership.

The PLA's power projection capability is limited; one Chinese general has characterized China's military as having "short arms and weak legs". There has however been an effort to redress these deficiencies in recent years. The PLA has acquired some advanced weapons systems, including Sovremenny class destroyers, Sukhoi Su-27 and Sukhoi Su-30 aircraft, and Kilo-class diesel submarines from Russia. It is also currently building 4 new destroyers including 2 AAW Type 052C class guided missile destroyers.

However, the mainstay of the air force continues to be the 1960s-vintage J-7 fighter. In addition, the PLA has attempted to build an indigenous aerospace and military industry with its production of the J-10, which currently is in production. It reportedly contains technology supplied by Israel from its Lavifighter program as well as technology reverse-engineered from an F-16 reportedly given to China by Pakistan. The PLA launched a new class of nuclear submarine on December 3, 2004 capable of launching nuclear warheads that could strike targets across the Pacific Ocean.

China's military leadership has also been reacting to the display of American military might during the Gulf War and the 2003 invasion of Iraq.

PERCEPTION OF THREAT

In the late 1980s, China viewed the Soviet Union as its principal military opponent. Simmering border disputes with Vietnam and India were perceived as lesser threats to security. China's burgeoning opening up policy, its claims to the Paracel and Spratly Islands, and the presence of offshore oil deposits made the South China Sea an area in which Beijing saw potential threats to its interests. Finally, although it did not regard Taiwan as a military threat, China nevertheless refused to rule out the use of force as a means of achieving reunification with Taiwan.

Soviet Union

Despite common ideological roots, considerable Soviet assistance in the past, and warming relations since 1982, China in 1987 regarded the Soviet Union's military strength and foreign policy as the major threat to its security. Tensions in relations between the two countries had begun to escalate in the mid-1950s. The 1968 Soviet invasion of Czechoslovakia and the buildup of Soviet forces in the Soviet Far East raised Chinese suspicions of Soviet intentions. Sharp border clashes between Soviet and Chinese troopsoccurred in 1969, roughly a decade after relations between the two countries had begun to deteriorate and some four years after a buildup of Soviet forces along China's northern border had begun. Particularly heated border clashes occurred in the northeast along the Sino-Soviet border formed by the Amur River and the Ussuri River, on which China claimed the right to navigate. Border provocations occasionally recurred in later years—for example, in May 1978 when Soviet troops in boats and a helicopter intruded into Chinese territory—but major armed clashes were averted.

In the late 1970s, China decried what it perceived as a Soviet attempt to encircle it as the military buildup continued in the Soviet Far East and the Soviet Union signed friendship treaties with Vietnam and Afghanistan. In April 1979, Beijing notified Moscow that the thirty-yearTreaty of Friendship, Alliance, and Mutual Assistance—under which the Soviets aided the PLA in its 1950s modernization—would not be renewed. Negotiations on improving Sino-Soviet relations were begun in 1979, but China ended them when the Soviet Union invaded Afghanistan late that year. In 1982, China and the Soviet Union resumed negotiations on normalizing relations. Although agreements on trade, science and technology, and culture were signed, political ties remained frozen because of Chinese insistence that the Soviet Union remove the three obstacles to improved Sino-Soviet relations. Although Chinese leaders publicly professed not to be concerned, the Soviet base at Cam Ranh Bay in Vietnam, Soviet provision of MiG-23 fighters to North Korea, and Soviet acquisition of overflight and port calling rights from North Korea intensified Chinese apprehension about the Soviet threat. Soviet Communist Party General Secretary Mikhail Gorbachev's 1986 offer to withdraw some troops from Afghanistan and the Mongolian People's Republic were seen by Beijing as a cosmetic gesture that did not lessen the threat to China.

In the mid-1980s, the Soviet Union deployed about one-quarter to one-third of its military forces in its Far Eastern theatre. In 1987, Soviet nuclear forces included approximately 171 SS-20 intermediate-range ballistic missiles, which China found particularly threatening, and 85 nuclear-capable long-range Backfire bombers. Approximately 470,000 Soviet ground force troops in 53 divisions were stationed in the Sino-Soviet border region, including Mongolia. Although 65 percent of these ground force divisions were only at 20 percent of full combat strength, they were provided with improved equipment, including T-72 tanks, and were reinforced by 2,200 aircraft, including new generation aircraft such as the MiG-23/27 Flogger fighter. Chinese forces on the Sino-Soviet border were numerically superior—1.5 million troops in 68 divisions—but technologically inferior. Although the PLA units in the Shenyang and Beijing military regions were equipped with some of the PLA's most advanced weaponry, few Chinese divisions were mechanized. The Soviet Union held tactical and strategic nuclear superiority and exceeded China in terms of mobility, firepower, air power, and antiaircraft capability. Chinese leaders reportedly did not consider a Soviet attack to be imminent or even likely in the short term. They believed that if the Soviets did attack, it would be a limited strike against Chinese territory in north or northeast China, rather than a full-scale invasion.

Vietnam

China's relations with Vietnam began to deteriorate seriously in the mid-1970s. After Vietnam joined the Soviet-dominated Council for Mutual Economic Cooperation (Comecon) and signed the Treaty of Friendship and Cooperation with the Soviet Union in 1978, China branded Vietnam the "Cuba of the East" and called the treaty a military alliance. Incidents along the Sino-Vietnamese border increased in frequency and violence. In December 1978, Vietnam invaded Cambodia, quickly ousted the pro-Beijing Pol Pot regime, and overran the country. In February 1979, China attacked along virtually the entire Sino-Vietnamese border in a brief, limited campaign that involved ground forces only. In March, Beijing declared its "lesson" finished and withdrew all its troops.

After the war, both China and Vietnam reorganized their border defences. The border war strengthened Soviet-Vietnamese relations. The Soviet military role in Vietnam increased during the 1980s as the Soviets provided arms to Vietnam; moreover, Soviet ships enjoyed access to the harbors at Da Nang and Cam Ranh Bay, and Soviet reconnaissance aircraft operated out of Vietnamese airfields. Low-level conflict continued along the Sino-Vietnamese border as each side conducted artillery shelling and probed to gain high spots in the mountainous border terrain. Border incidents increased in intensity during the rainy season, when Beijing attempted to ease Vietnamese pressure against Cambodian resistance fighters. In 1986 China deployed twenty-five to twenty-eight divisions and Vietnam thirty-two divisions along their common border.

India

Beijing considered recurring Sino-Indian border clashes a potential threat to its security. Negotiations since the 1962 Sino-Indian border war failed to resolve the conflicting border claims, and each side improved its military and logistics capabilities in the disputed regions. Since the war, China has continued its occupation of the Aksai Chin area, through which it built a strategic highway linking Xizang and Xinjiangautonomous regions. China had a vital military interest in maintaining control over this region, whereas India's primary interest lay in Arunachal Pradesh, its state in the northeast bordering Xizang Autonomous Region. In 1987, although India enjoyed air superiority, rough parity on the ground existed between the two military forces, which had a combined total of nearly 400,000 troops near the border. The Indian Army deployed eleven divisions in the region, backed up by paramilitary forces, whereas the PLA had fifteen divisions available for operations on the border. After a 1986 border clash and India's conversion of Arunachal Pradesh from union territory to state, tensions between China and India escalated. Both sides moved to reinforce their capabilities in the area, but neither ruled out further negotiations of their dispute. Most observers believe that the mountainous terrain, high-altitude climate, and concomitant logistic difficulties and economic trade make it unlikely that a protracted or large-scale conflict would erupt on the Sino-Indian border.

South China Sea

The South China Sea area was strategically important to Beijing because of the discovery of offshore oil in China's 200-nautical-mile (370 km) exclusive economic zone, increased foreign trade in the South China Sea, and China's territorial claims there. The Xisha and Nansha islands also were claimed, and some occupied, by Vietnam, Taiwan, the Philippines, and Malaysia. Beijing's claims to these island groups predated all others except those by the Guomindang authorities. In 1974 the PLA Navy ousted South Vietnamese forces from the Xisha and occupied some of the islands, which were valuable as Chinese fishing bases and guano sites. Although Chinese occupation of the Xisha effectively expanded its exclusive economic zone, the discovery of offshore oil deposits near Hainan Island intensified China's interest in both island groups. With the expansion of Chinese foreign trade, Beijing's interest grew in maintaining a naval presence in theXisha Islands, which sit astride the strategic Hong Kong–Singapore shipping route. Chinese fishermen also used the Nansha Islands, but most of these were occupied by Vietnam, Taiwan, and the Philippines. In the 1980s, the PLA Navy built up the South Sea Fleet, strengthened its naval facilities and deployments in the Xisha Islands, and conducted naval exercises in the South China Sea. To strengthen its military position in the Xisha Islands and protect itself against the Soviet base at Cam Ranh Bay, Beijing also reinforced its claim to the Nansha Islands.

Taiwan

Taiwan does not pose a military threat to China, despite Taipei's previous vow to "recover the mainland." Tensions in the Taiwan Straitdecreased beginning in the late 1970s, when China called for peaceful reunification with Taiwan and reduction of PLA forces in Fujian Province opposite Taiwan. Nevertheless, Beijing refused to rule out the use of force against Taiwan in the event that Taiwan had serious internal disturbances or declared independence. In the late 1980s, a Chinese attack against Taiwan was considered unlikely by most observers. The Navy lacked the amphibious forces necessary to mount a full-scale invasion. The Navy had the capability to mount a blockade of Taiwan, but this measure also was considered unlikely.

CHINA'S POWER STATUS AND ITS IMPLICATIONS

The author believes that in order to study China's power status objectively, we should first understand the true nature of international power and clarify our goal for measuring the differences of national powers. If we fail to do this, then as complexity in these measurements increases, their pragmatic value actually decreases. Therefore, the results of assessment will not benefit us at all in understanding national power status.

Relativity in Assessing China's Power Status

Power status connotes relativity. It refers to ranking the power status of one state with relevance to that of other states in an international sphere. The power status of a state can be understood only through a simultaneous comparative assessment of the power status of other nations. If there is only one nation in the world, then there is no frame of reference with which we can decide if a country's power status is high or low. This means that only when there are two or more countries in the world, that the study of a state's power status and its comprehensive national power has significance. The term 'power status' contains a connotation of both 'the rank of power status' and 'the differences in power status'. Whereas the difference in power status decides the rank of power status, the rank of power status cannot always truly reflect the real nature and degrees of difference in power status. During the Cold War period, the United States and the Soviet Union ranked first and second, respectively, in their power status. However, the difference in power between them remained at a hierarchical level of superpowers. But in the 1990s, while the United States still kept its top ranking (regardless of which major power stayed in second: Russia, Japan or China), the nature of the ranking gap between the first and the second power states changed substantially, because it became a difference in power status between a superpower and a major power.

The power status of a state is based on, but not decided by, its national power. In other words, the increase of a state's power does not necessarily elevate that state's power status. For example, in the late 19th century during the Qing Dynasty, China had enough industrial capacity to arm its military. Its overall national power was far larger than that of the early Qing Dynasty when there was no modern industry. However, internationally, China's power status during the late Qing Dynasty was far behind that of the early Qing Dynasty. Take the current cases of The Netherlands and South Korea. In 1999, GDP in The Netherlands grew from $393.5 billion to $398.1 billion, with an absolute increase of $4.6 billion. However, according to World Bank statistics, the ranking of The Netherlands fell below that of South Korea, whose GDP in the same period increased from $317.1 billion to $406.1 billion.

The rank of a state's power status is decided by the difference between its own power status and that of other states. However, this absolute difference does not indicate the nature and extent of power differences between states. The absolute value of the disparity in power status between two states indicates which state possesses a mightier power status. Therefore, it reflects the rank of the power status of the two states. However, this absolute difference hardly displays the true nature and class difference of a state's power status. For instance, according to the 2003 World Bank GDP statistics, by currency exchange rates, the GDP difference between Japan and Germany was $1.93 trillion while the GDP difference between Germany and Brazil was $1.97 trillion. The absolute values of the two differences vary little, but this by no means indicates that the difference in economic power between Germany and Japan shares any similarity with the difference between Brazil and Germany. Common sense leads us to conclude that Germany and Japan share the same class status, but that Brazil and Germany do not.

The power status of a state depends on how its national power compares with that of other nations. We can clarify this further by looking at GDP comparisons for Japan, Germany and Brazil. In 2003, Japan's GDP amounted to $4.3 trillion, Germany's to $2.4 trillion and Brazil's to $0.5 trillion. Despite the fact that the difference in GDP between Germany and Japan almost equals that between Brazil and Germany, Japan's GDP was only 1.8 times Germany's GDP while Germany's GDP amounted to 4.8 times that of Brazil. This helps us understand that using common knowledge leads us to conclude that Germany and Japan share the same economic class, whereas Brazil and Germany are quite different.

In short, it is the proportional relationship between the power statuses of two states, not the absolute quantity of difference that decides a state's power status. It can be expressed as: $S = A/B$, (where S indicates power status of State A in proportion to that of State B; A refers to the power of State A, and B to the power of State B.) In the reality of international politics, when two states confront each other on a specific issue, the advantages and disadvantages of their powers depend largely on one state's power in proportion to the other. As an example, assume a small military skirmish along a common border between two nations, Side A has three soldiers and Side B only one. Although Side A has only two more soldiers than Side B in absolute number, its power is 200% greater than that of Side B (i.e. the possibility of winning for Side A is three times as much as that for Side B). To cite another example, Side A has 102 soldiers and Side B 100; even if Side A has two more soldiers than Side B, its power strength gains only a 2% advantage. Therefore, the possibility of winning for either side is almost equal. In this analogy, to assess China's power status and its progression, one should focus on China's power status in proportion to the power status of other states, instead of solely on the absolute differences in the power of two states.

Importance of Assessing China's Power Status

Because power status is relative, recognizing China's power status in relation to that of other states is of immediate significance in our study. In order to further understand China's power status we consider the following three aspects. First, by understanding the relativity of power status, we can better understand the major difference in defining the 'Rejuvenation' or 'Rise' of China. In 2003, the Chinese leaders first introduced the term 'Peaceful Rise'. However, in April 2004 at the Boao Asia Forum, it was replaced by 'Peaceful Development'. This was mainly because 'Rise' has a relative meaning in terms of power status. Despite the often heated debates on 'Peaceful Rise', scholars on all sides acknowledge that the word 'Rise' implies attaining superpower status. For the Chinese, 'rejuvenation' bears a similar connotation to 'rise'. Both mean to restore China's power status to the prosperity enjoyed during the prime of the Han, Tang and early Qing Dynasties. It does not simply refer to a regression of China's comprehensive national power down to the ancient level. By early 21st century standards, China's comprehensive national power in the afore-mentioned ancient periods was only equivalent to a state of low power status in the current international system. As power status changes with time and the international environment, China's national rejuvenation will be realized only if its pace of national power growth is faster than that of other countries. Growth at any slower pace will weaken China's power status gradually and thus diminish the hopes of national rejuvenation and rise.

Second, the zero-sum nature of power status helps us understand that there will be no win–win situation in conflicts among international political entities accompanying the rise of China. Power status and international politics share the same zero-sum characteristic.

The rise of a state's power status indicates an expansion of its political power. This in turn causes the fall of other states' power status and political power. Powerful states remain a minority in the world while weaker states remain a majority. Until September 2002, no more than 10 global or regional major powers had been listed among 191 member countries of the UN.

The middle and small powers are represented in greater numbers in this ranking. As the power status of one small state increases, the relative power it gains is drawn from many other middle or small states of similar power status. Thus, an evenly spread decrease in power in every small power is not obvious, and so is unlikely to cause conflict among these states. For instance, the sum of international political power for 100 small states is fixed and stable, and each small state holds 1% of this power sum. When one small state increases its power status to 1.9% of the total power, the share for each of the remaining 99 countries is decreased to 0.99%, i.e. each country loses only 1% of its original power. On the other hand, an increase in power status for a major state usually conveys serious outcomes in this aspect. Great powers are few in number. Therefore, as a major power gains an advantage in its power status, the remainder of the few major powers feel a tremendous loss of their original power. If the dominant world power belongs to a single state, then this hegemony holds 100% of the power. When the power status of another state increases to the same level, there are two states sharing this world dominant power. That means, among those with dominant power, the former hegemony will be diminished to half, or only 50%. Since a change in a major power's power status may result in the restructuring of international relations and a rearrangement of world resources, studies on comprehensive national strength and power status are of the utmost importance only for those few major powers. The zero-sum nature in power status gives us the insight that a majority of political conflicts along China's path to her rise will bear this zero-sum nature as well. In other words, there will be few win–win situations in China's ascent to a superpower.

Third, by recognizing China's current power status, we can better perceive the strategic relationship between China and the other major powers in the post-Cold War era. In a world configured with one superpower against several major powers, the United States is destined to defend its status against any possible challenging states in the future. As one of the major powers after the Cold War, China automatically becomes an opponent of the United States.

None the less, the United States will decide whether to interpret China as its number one rival on the basis of how China's power status changes. Although China and the Western European major powers have been categorized as regional powers, the geographical distances between them cause fewer conflicts of interest. Thus they may even forge a strategic alliance against the United States' hegemonic pressures. However, in East Asia, China and Japan have fundamental conflicts that will cause inevitable confrontations between the two. In the early post-Cold War period, Japan was the world's second economic power after the United States, and the number one economic power in East Asia. If its economic power status decreases due to an increase in power status of other states, both globally and regionally, Japan may take several measures to protect its existing international status by strengthening its political and military power. Thus, if China's economic power status replaces that of Japan, Japan may confront China politically. A better understanding of China's power status enables us to know why structural conflicts exist in China's strategic relationships with the United States and Japan but not with the major European powers.

CHINA'S EMERGENCE AS A GREAT POWER

The preeminent geopolitical factor in Asia for the next several decades would appear to be the emergence of China as a great power. In most discussions of the region's future, this assertion is all but taken for granted, although some observers have dissented. Those who accept this assertion can point to the following realities and trends.

Economic Growth

First and most fundamentally, China has enjoyed rapid and sustained economic growth since 1978, when Deng Xiaoping initiated the current era of economic reform. Indeed, before the Asian economic crisis erupted in 1997, this growth was so rapid that some analysts, using optimistic but not unrealistic assumptions, predicted that China's GNP—evaluated in terms of purchasing-power parity— would surpass that of the United States by 2006.2 Yet while China has escaped the immediate brunt of the region's financial crisis, the Asian economic slump has exposed and highlighted some weaknesses in the Chinese economy as well as in the "Asian model" of economic development in general.

Despite large "pump-priming" efforts by the government over the past several years, the Chinese growth rate has been slowing down. According to some measures, prices have been falling as well, which suggests the existence of excess productive capacity. China also faces serious economic challenges not only with respect to its stateowned enterprises (SOEs), many of which have been losing money as they encounter increased competition from the private sector and from imports, but also with regard to its banking sector, which is burdened with the large nonperforming loans that are required to keep many of the SOEs afloat. Thus, the key question for the immediate future is whether the private sector can grow fast enough to absorb those workers who would inevitably be laid off in the course of restructuring China's SOEs and reforming its banks. This reform process is likely to be accelerated when China is admitted to the WTO, thereby bringing matters to a head more quickly.

China's economic prospects for the next decades thus depend largely on whether its leadership has the political will to back economic reforms that are in the short run likely to lead to the bankruptcy of some SOEs or, alternatively, whether China will opt instead for a Japanese-style policy of putting off hard decisions. In the first two decades of economic reform, the Chinese leadership exhibited a talent for "muddling through"—i.e., for implementing enough reform to keep the economy moving forward while for the most part avoiding major shocks to the political system. However, the urban inflation of the late 1980s, which was closely linked to the public dissatisfaction underlying the 1989 Tiananmen protests, offered one instance in which the leadership's ability to strike this balance was sorely tested and ultimately found lacking. Whether China's leadership will prove capable of juggling these competing economic and social/political requirements remains an open question. This analysis proceeds on the assumption that it will, but it must be recognized that China's economic prognosis may be less optimistic than it now appears.

Technological Modernization

China's economic reform program of the past 20 years has included rapid if selective technological modernization. Nevertheless, China's level of technological sophistication is likely to prove a more significant obstacle to its achievement of great-power status than its overall economic development. Starting as it has from a very low level, China's technological progress—while relatively rapid in some areas— has a long way to go. In eight of nine technologies deemed critical for military purposes, Chinese production capabilities have been found to be significant yet limited. The exception is biotechnology, with respect to which China has good basic research but poor production capability. Although China has access to "all but the most advanced dual-use technologies" and is able to assemble many high-tech products, it remains largely dependent on imported high-tech equipment. Nevertheless, urrent capabilities... reflect a significant improvement over the past two decades. When China's economic reform program began in the late 1970s, Chinese industrial technology was universally obsolescent. Now, while China is hardly a high-tech powerhouse, some sectors are relatively modern.

The key question for the future is the extent to which China will be able to develop a technological base sufficient to support advanced weapon production. Although China purchases some advanced weapon systems on the international market, primarily from Russia, Chinese leaders are unlikely to remain content to base their military power entirely on imported equipment. Indeed, on two occasions— in 1960 and 1989—China suffered an abrupt cutoff of foreign arms transfers from the Soviet Union and the West. Thus, putting aside questions of national prestige, China will not want to remain dependent on foreign suppliers in the future. A RAND assessment of China's future technological capability insofar as it affects the country's military potential asserted that, China's prospects for technological progress are moderate.... By many measures China's potential for technological progress looks comparable to that of South Korea or Taiwan in the 1970s. In terms such as absolute numbers of scientists and engineers or total spending on R&D, however, China already vastly surpasses smaller countries like South Korea or Taiwan. Thus, average technological levels in China in 2020 are likely to be comparable to those of South Korea or Taiwan today, but China's greater size suggests that the number of areas in which China possesses state-of-the-art capabilities will be larger than is currently true in those countries.

It was thus concluded that, while China can expect to make significant technological progress in coming years, it is impossible that China will catch up to, much less "leapfrog," the United States... for the foreseeable future. By many measures, China's prospects ... appear comparable to those of Taiwan or South Korea in the 1970s.... Thus, it seems likely that, by 2020, *average* technological levels in China will be roughly comparable to those in Taiwan and South Korea. There may be a difference, however, due to China's scale.... [South Korea and Taiwan] have become very competitive in particular technological niches.

If China follows a similar development path, its huge size... means that the number of these niches will be far greater. Thus, while China will on average still be significantly behind the United States... technologically, its technological capabilities could be very competitive in a significant number of areas by 2020.

Depending on the strategic insight with which China chooses these niches and the competence with which the relevant R&D is conducted, China could build a technological base sufficient for the development of a military force that could pose some severe challenges to the United States. To be sure, such a military force would not be the equal of that of the United States and might not be designed to defeat U.S. forces in an all-out battle—but by exploiting various asymmetric strategies, it could be used to further Chinese political interests in Asia, even against some U.S. opposition.

Military Modernization

Previous RAND research has dealt with Chinese military modernization in detail and has concluded that by 2015 China could emerge as a *multidimensional, regional competitor* to the United States—i.e., as a military power that, while not a peer of the United States, could nonetheless assert itself in its immediate region so as to thwart U.S. political-military objectives. In particular, it has been asserted that China could credibly:

- exercise sea denial with respect to the seas contiguous to China;
- contest aerospace superiority in a sustained way in areas contiguous to China's borders;

- threaten U.S. operation locations in East Asia with a variety of long-range strike assets;
- challenge U.S. information dominance; and
- pose a strategic nuclear threat to the United States.

Of course it is by no means a foregone conclusion that the Chinese military will reach this level of capability within the second decade of the 21st century. Aside from the caveats expressed in the preceding sections concerning China's economic and technological development, China would probably have to significantly increase its defence spending, continue to trade quantity for quality, and ensure that the PLA opens itself to doctrinal, operational, and tactical innovation in order to do so. Assuming that its economy continues to grow, however, China would not find it difficult to increase defence spending to a sufficient extent to meet this objective; indeed, merely keeping defence spending constant as a percentage of GNP would in all likelihood suffice. In recent years, real defence spending in China has been growing faster than GDP, although it is unclear whether this trend represents a policy shift or a confluence of other factors (e.g., the unexpectedly rapid drop in inflation and "compensation" to the PLA for relinquishing its control of many business enterprises to other governmental entities).

7

Asian Security: Impact of the North East Asia Strategic Quadrilateral

Asian security and stability is nowhere more impacted than by the power- play and balance of power in North East Asian strategic quadrilateral comprising Russia, Japan, China and the United States and this is a strategic reality that has prevailed ever since 1945 when the United States and Russia emerged as superpowers.

The North East Asia Strategic Quadrilateral comprises Russia, Japan and China as the resident powers in North East Asia and the United States as the non-resident power but perceiving North East Asia as strategically crucial for American Homeland security and for its balance of power politics to ensure its continued global predominance.

The power play and the ensuing balance of power in North East Asia is not only confined to this strategic quadrant of Asia but spills over all the way to South East Asia and South Asia or more succinctly put impacts the entire Indo Pacific Asia. It also impacts the entire Asian Heartland.

North East Asia in the last decade stood strategically neglected by both the United States and Russia as the two most dominant powers. United States stood strategically distracted by its military imbroglios in Afghanistan and Iraq. Russia's strategic resurgence had not extended to North East Asia mainly because of its strategic compulsions visa-a-vis the so-called Russia-China strategic nexus which failed to add or complement Russia's strategic weight and postures.

This strategic vacuum in North East Asia facilitated an exponential military rise of China without any checkmating by the United States and Russia as the two dominant powers which could have done so.

The onus of facilitating the emergence of the 'China Threat' which now envelops Indo Pacific Asia lies squarely on the shoulders of the United States as after 1991 disintegration of the Former Soviet Union it had emerged as the sole Superpower and global policeman. The United States had not only contributed handsomely to the economic rise of China fuelling its military rise but also endangered Asian security as a whole by molly-coddling China ignoring the imperatives of facilitating the rise of Japan and India as the other legitimate Asian powers.

North East Asia has been forcefully thrust in the global strategic consciousness as in the run-up to 2014 China has switched over from its much publicised and much trumpeted 'peaceful rise of China' to a robust and unabashed use of China's 'hard power' accumulated in the last decade without any checkmating. Gone are the US think tanks treatises emphasising and glorifying the use of China's 'soft power'.

China after signalling the world in 2009 with its public display of its stupendous military might felt strong enough to indulge in its use of 'hard power' first in the South China Sea against Vietnam and the Philippines and now in the East China Sea against Japan. Both South China Sea and East China Sea conflict escalations by China have now emerged as global 'flash-points'. Concurrently, China also started displaying its use of 'hard power' on the India-Tibet border encouraged by India's timid strategic responses.

The ripostes to China's military rise in North East Asia and its wider strategic impact, and so also its threatening contours, have emerged in the shape of the United States Strategic Pivot to Asia in2009 and Russia's Strategic Pivot to Asia Pacific in 2012. Both implicitly are targeted at checkmating China's unrestrained military adventurism in Asia Pacific.

The strategic landscape in North East Asia today presents a complex and challenging picture as Russia, Japan and the United States are all engaged in reassessing their strategic postures and re-positioning themselves to cope with an overly overbearing China obsessed with a single-point fixation of emerging as a superpower and fashioning a new bi-polar global strategic structure of United States and China which regrettably United States also endorsed spasmodically.

North East Asia in 2014 is visibly in a state of strategic churning resulting from the attempts of Russia, Japan and United States for recreation of a new balance of power to cope with China's switch-over to employment of 'hard power 'strategies.

Russia though still avowing its strategic relationship with China has put China on notice by its declaration in 2012 of the Russian Strategic Pivot to Asia Pacific. The implications stand examined by me in a number of my Papers in 2013. Strategic literature covering North East Asia have started highlighting the Chinese threat to Russian sovereignty where China is said to have subtly but mutely encouraged Russia's Far East provincial administration to secede from Russia. Also highlighted in this direction is the Chinese demographic invasion of Russia's Far East Regions by illegal migration with the end-aim of complete Sinification of Russia's Far East Region.

Seemingly in response to the above developments Russia has embarked on a military build-up in its Far East Regions, expansion and modernisation of the Russian Navy Fleet based in Vladivostok and holding large-scale integrated military exercises in proximity of its borders with China.

In terms of regional power-play with corresponding effects on global power-play, Russia made a significant political and strategic reach-out to Japan as the contending power of China in not only in North East Asia but also in Asia as a whole. This was manifested in the unprecedented Russia-Japan 2+2 Meet in Tokyo last year between the Russian Foreign and Defence Ministers with their Japanese counterparts to discuss strategic and military cooperation.

Japan in recent times has been subjected to intense military brinkmanship, coercion and provocation actions by China using the East China Sea islands territorial disputes as an excuse. The overall underlying reason of China is to effect a strategic diminution of Japan and lower its image as a serious peer competitor of China in North East Asia and in Asia. Japan as it is over the years has been seriously concerned about China's exponential military rise and its effect on Japanese security. Of particular military concern to Japan is the emergence of a powerful Chinese Navy threatening Japan's maritime lifelines. Japan's response to its perceived China Threat has been three- fold. Militarily Japan is currently engaged in a substantial military build-up especially of its Navy and Air Force. Redeployment of Japan's Armed Forces to a Southern alignment has been put into operation. Japan's national security structures have been reinforced and new mechanisms for more integrated functioning have been ordered.

In terms of political and strategic reachout in North East Asia, the significant move by Japan to Russia stands recounted above. The signalling to China of this reachout to Russia by Japan would not be lost on China.

External to the region, what is also visible is Japan's political and strategic reachout to the maritime nations of Asia's littoral located astride the sea-lanes emanating to and from Japan. Particular reference needs to be made to the continuing reinforcement of the Japan-India Strategic and Global Partnership.

Significant for North East Asia strategic power-play is that while Japan continues to swear that its security alliance with the United States is the cornerstone of Japan's security, what is becoming more visible is Japan's thrust of creation of an independent self-reliant Japanese defence capability. This presumably arises from Japan's concerns on the credibility of American support in the event of a Japanese show-down with China.

United States is forecasted as being able to continue with its military global predominance well into the better part of this century. However what has significantly happened are two major developments which affect the credibility of the United States to stand up to the militarily debilitating effects on Asian security of China's bid to achieve superpower status. The first is that of the United States strategic appeasement of China which in Asian capitals appears as American kow-towing to China. The second development is that China is progressively reducing the differentials in its strategic and military might with the military predominance of the United States thereby robbing America of its deterrent power against China even if the United States had the political will to face-off China.

United States Strategic Pivot to Asia is a hostage to the US Congressional moods and its credibility therefore in Asian capitals is that much reduced.

In the strategic quadrilateral of North East Asia, the foregoing analysis would have by now suggested that China is the 'villain of the piece' and that Russia, Japan and the United States are currently involved in reassessing and repositioning of their strategic formulations and policies to cope with the China Threat arising from its switch to use of 'hard power' strategies to achieve strategic superstardom.

Finally, in terms of strategic losses and gains to the powers that comprise the North East Strategic Quadrilateral's ensuing power-play it appears that China and the United States would be the major losers. China is headed towards emerging as the prime loser because its switch to 'hard power' strategies against its Asian neighbours is resulting in an Asian nation's polarisation against China. China today stands strategically alone notwithstanding the United States 'China Hedging Strategy'.

The United States is the second major strategic loser in that it's continued 'China Hedging Strategy' which simply amounts to 'China Appeasement' typecasts it in Asian capitals as a strategically diminished superpower and incapable of providing the required countervailing power against China going 'strategically berserk' in Asia.

In whatever pattern the North East Strategic Quadrilateral power-play emerges in the years to come, what is certain is that the resultant strategic pattern will significantly impact Asian security as a whole. Two impacts are already in evidence, namely, the Asian strategic polarisation against China following the South China Sea conflict escalation by China and the reinforcing of the Japan-India Strategic and Global Partnership.

CHINA'S CURRENT SECURITY POLICY

In response to the attacks in Africa during the last five years, China has confronted the problem of nontraditional security threats in several ways.

The PRC's initial reaction is to work with local governments. "China will cooperate closely with immigration departments of African countries in tackling the problem of illegal migration, improve exchange of immigration control information, and set up an unimpeded and efficient channel for intelligence and information exchange," China's 2006 *Africa Policy* stated.

"In order to enhance the ability of both sides to address nontraditional security threats, it is necessary to increase intelligence exchange, explore more effective ways and means for closer cooperation in combating terrorism, small-arms smuggling, drug trafficking, transnational economic crimes, etc." Beijing has instructed its embassies in Africa to keep a close watch on local security. The swift and successful evacuation of Chinese citizens from Chad also demonstrated that China has developed operational scenarios to deal with these emergencies. The Chinese government has also started issuing travel advisories.

In Sudan and Kenya, state-owned companies receive protection from local armed forces against attacks by rebels. Beijing has signed an agreement with South Africa to prevent the Chinese diaspora from turning into a target for armed gangs. Such measures are designed to help Chinese citizens and companies avoid some of the risks related to operating in Africa, but they do not provide any guarantee for safeguarding China's economic activities if the situation keeps deteriorating. In the case of Sudan, China learned the hard way that prodding instable governments can have drastic consequences. If problems start to occur at the regional level, supporting these emerging states might prove even riskier.

Nor does this narrow security response address China's uncertainty about the military capability of African nations. The dilemma reverts back to the realistic supposition of self-help. Is the PRC trying to safeguard its interests by building up its own military presence in Africa?

Bilateral military exchanges are a first indicator to test whether this assumption holds true. According to the Chinese government, interaction with other armed forces expanded significantly, with 174 high-level visits in 2001 and more than 210 in 2006.

This upward trend was not maintained in Africa, however, where such bilateral exchanges have remained stable at an annual average of 26. Beijing has established a permanent military dialogue only with South Africa. Interviews with European diplomats in ten randomly chosen African countries also reveal that the number of accredited military officers in Chinese embassies, i.e., military attachés and their support staff, has barely or not expanded at all in the last few years. In fact, only in 15 countries are Chinese military attachés assigned on a permanent basis. China's military diplomacy in Africa remains modest, and it has not kept up with the impressive number of Chinese trade officials posted in African nations to strengthen economic ties in the last few years.

Military aid is another indicator. Providing military hardware to partner nations can serve various objectives. In a context of competition, it helps to thwart defence cooperation with other states or to prevent other powers' attempts to alter the regional military balance. Defence aid might help a privileged political partner to safeguard economic interests. Whereas these three objectives are motivated by security issues and long-term economic interests, defence aid may well be the result of more short-sighted aspirations. There is no evidence that China's military aid successfully counterbalances other powers, such as the United States.

Apart from Sudan and Zimbabwe, most countries that have received Chinese military aid in the last few years are also supplied by Washington. In 2007, Beijing temporarily froze the supply of heavy arms to Khartoum after pressure from the West. When Nigeria's Vice President, Atiku Abubakar, announced that his nation would turn to China instead of the United States for arms, Beijing's response was reluctant, and no major supply operations materialized. China's military aid programs should not be considered as support for its forays into the mining industry. For instance, between 2004 and 2008, resource-rich Nigeria received only half as much military aid as Ghana or Uganda. During this period, China provided more military assistance to Angola than to Sudan, even though the security challenges in the latter were much greater.

Although violence in Somalia has threatened China's oil exploration activities in both Ethiopia and Kenya, China only made a commitment to Kenya to help in protecting its border. China has, at times, provided military aid, but such assistance does not seem to be part of any coherent strategy related to protecting its security interests.

Finally, self-help would imply the deployment of military forces whenever China's interests are threatened, possibly in an attempt to train friendly armed forces and dissuade any challengers. Yet, such a Chinese military presence is negligible. China has no bases in Africa, as does the United States and France, nor has it trained African soldiers to counter threats to its national interests.

In Sudan, Zimbabwe, Cameroon, and Gabon, China has employed teams of three to ten instructors, but they are assisting in the maintenance of equipment, rather than providing training for combat missions. In Zambia and Algeria, similar examples of cooperation exist but are limited to medical activities. Other major powers deployed naval vessels in an effort to combat piracy and to maintain the maritime supply lines surrounding Africa. During such operations, the Chinese Navy has rarely shown its flag.

In 2000, China sent its newest *Luhai*-class guided missile destroyer and a supply ship to Tanzania and South Africa. A 2002 fleet composed of a guided missile destroyer, the *Qingdao*, and a supply ship, the *Taicang*, visited Egypt. These voyages were gestures of courtesy rather than a reaction to security challenges. They were limited in duration, and no actions were attempted against pirates or poachers. In December 2008, however, the Chinese government did deploy two destroyers and a replenishment ship in the Gulf of Aden to participate in the United Nations-backed mission against piracy. A mission that was only undertaken after receiving a positive signal from US Pacific Command chief Admiral Timothy Keating.

Instead of dealing with security threats unilaterally, China has resorted to bandwagoning. Although in the 1980s and early 1990s,

Beijing opposed attempts by the international community to intervene in African security issues, nowadays it tends to join them. Beijing is increasingly recognizing the United Nations' role in resolving the numerous conflicts and safeguarding the sovereignty of developing nations. In the 1990s, China began supporting United Nations (UN) missions designed to implement peace agreements between rivalling parties, on the condition that a well-defined and restricted mandate was included. Traditional peacekeeping operations such as those in Somalia (UNSOM I), Mozambique, Rwanda, and Sierra Leone all were supported. When the UN Security Council decided to dispatch forces to Liberia in 2003, China offered to support the mission and gradually increased the number of its peacekeepers to 1,300 in 2007.

At the same time, however, failed states and national governments that had actively participated in atrocities challenged the efficacy of many of the traditional UN operations. China's focus on the primacy of sovereignty, requiring at a minimum the state's consent, collided with the willingness of other nations to intervene aggressively under the UN Charter's Chapter VII mandate.

Beijing loudly opposed the move by European countries to push for Operation Turquoise in Rwanda, Washington's call to broaden the UNSOM mandate, or France's demand for a troop increase in the 2004 UN operation in Ivory Coast. Despite its strong concerns, China did not veto these interventions at the UN Security Council, but rather abstained and remained aloof from implementation. Sudan was the first instance where China actively lobbied an African government to permit a UN mission on its soil. Via active brokering and indirect pressure, China succeeded in neutralizing the incompatibility between its economic interests and the principle of noninterference on the one hand, and western appeals for intervening in Darfur and the need for long-term stability on the other.

That Beijing recognizes the importance of collective security became apparent in 2006, when China was the first nation to ask the UN Security Council for a peacekeeping mission in Somalia. In June that year, at a Security Council meeting in Addis Ababa, China's Permanent Representative to the UN, Wang Guangya, scolded other diplomats for neglecting Somalia and urged them to support the deployment of peacekeepers. "I was reluctant to take on this role," said Wang, explaining that African governments had been pushing China to raise the issue in the Council, "but there was a lack of interest by the other major powers."

Initially, the proposal was tentatively received by Great Britain and the United States, but after various talks in New York, Beijing and Washington jointly sponsored a resolution for the deployment of a UN mission. In 2007, in early consultations with France, China supported a French draft resolution on Chad calling for the dispatch of mainly European peacekeepers under the auspices of Chapter VII. It was significant that China approved the "close liaising" with the Hybrid Operation in Darfur (UNAMID), where earlier it had objected to the development of links between UNAMID and UN missions. "Our support for the resolution on Chad shows that we are prepared to cooperate to tackle security issues at a regional level and that our awareness on the increasing complexity of violent conflicts in Africa grows," a Chinese diplomat explained.

China is also turning to African regional organizations to collaborate on security issues. In the China-Africa Action Plan, approved in November 2006, Beijing vowed "to support Africa in the areas of logistics" as well as "to continue its active participation in the peacekeeping operations and demining process in Africa and provide, within the limits of its capabilities, financial and material assistance as well as relevant training to the Peace and Security Council of the African Union." In June 2006, the Chinese government granted the African Union's Mission in Sudan $3.5 million in budgetary support and humanitarian aid. Earlier, it provided financial and technical support to the Association for West African States.

Slowly but surely, China is showing itself ready to participate in international efforts to prevent conflicts, fuelled by the easy availability of small arms and illegally exported natural resources. In 2002, for instance, Beijing revised its regulation on the control of military products for export and published the "Military Products Export Control List" supplying guidelines for the export of military-related products. In the same year, it signed the "Protocol Against the Illicit Manufacturing of and Trafficking in Firearms," which committed the People's Republic to control the manufacturing, marking, import, and export of firearms, and to confiscate and destroy all illicit firearms. In 2005, the government launched a national information management system for the production, possession, and trade of light arms, and it introduced a system to monitor end-users of Chinese-made weapons to prevent the arms from finding their way to "sensitive regions" around the world via third parties. In 2006, China supported a draft UN resolution on the illicit trade of small arms and light weapons, in contrast to the United States. In 2002, China joined the Kimberley Process, a joint government, international diamond industry, and civil initiative designed to stem the flow of conflict diamonds originating from Africa. In 2005, China allowed a voluntary peer review of its support for the Kimberly Process. Although these actions still have many flaws, they seem to prove that China wishes to do more than just put "boots on the ground" in response to Africa's internal conflicts.

Despite the strategic importance of Africa, China does not try to safeguard its foothold in the region by unilaterally projecting military power. In Africa, its military diplomacy remains limited when compared with defence initiatives in other regions. If the PRC does pursue bilateral cooperation programs, these are more likely to be a part of its diplomatic charm offensive, rather than addressing threats to China's economic and security interests. Instead of relying on a military presence to counterbalance other powers, the PRC tends to join collective security efforts within the framework of the United Nations and African regional organizations. Over the past few years, this strategy of joint ventures has evolved from passive support to active cooperation. Beijing has softened its devotion to noninterference. While maintaining the primacy of sovereignty, it has become willing to support interventions whenever regional stability is at stake.

Although China has become a revisionist power in terms of its economic aspirations on the continent, it is acting as a status-quo power in terms of security objectives. There are several explanations for this stance. First, China only recently began its economic focus on the African continent. For the past two decades, China concentrated on curbing the military and diplomatic influence of Taiwan; the focus on "economization" of its Africa policy only began in the late 1990s. Hence, the security challenges it is facing now are a recent phenomena, and solutions to these challenges are just starting to be explored. The PRC is going through the early stage of resecuritization of its Africa strategy, and joining with other nations in an allied strategy can be considered the easiest immediate response. Second, and related to this point, China has not developed sufficient means to back up its security policy with military power. This is a matter of budgetary constraints. Building an independent and sustained military presence is a costly affair and would, at present, overstretch the PLA's capabilities, while Asia remains its primary focus. The PLA does not possess the logistical capacity to support sustained region wide deployment in Africa. Its long-range airlift and sealift, as well as its intelligence and command capabilities, are not up to the task. Third, the Chinese government wants to avoid the People's Republic being perceived as a hegemonic power.

In the initial stage of its economic charm offensive, the PRC tried to pursue a business-as-usual approach, maintaining a low profile and steering clear of political entanglements. That approach is no longer possible now that China stands at the forefront of Africa's political scene, actively altering the economic balance of power. Beijing is well aware of the dichotomy between its weak and strong identities and is reluctant to demonstrate any independent military capacity. Such a show of strength might reduce its diplomatic maneuverability, increase resistance from African nations-just as Washington is now experiencing-and raise suspicions elsewhere regarding Chinese intentions. Yet, as interests, perceptions, and capacities are susceptible to change, the question remains whether China will stay on this track of cooperative security.

China's interests in Africa have changed over the past decades and will undoubtedly continue to evolve. The concept for its security policy in the region will depend on the role that Africa plays as a supplier of natural resources. Africa currently supplies approximately 30 percent of China's oil imports. Beijing and its

African partners announced that they are preparing to increase bilateral trade to $100 billion by the year 2010. Most of this increase will come from the import of raw commodities. In recent years, Chinese companies have laid the foundation for a substantial increase in the production of resource industries. Exploration in the Gulf of Guinea, Angola, and the Horn of Africa have the potential for an increase in oil exports to China of more than 80 percent in the next ten years. Chinese companies are just starting to tap the large mines that were recently acquired in Gabon, the Democratic Republic of Congo, Namibia, and elsewhere on the continent. Given the fact that other emerging markets such as India and Brazil are shifting the use of their raw materials from export to domestic consumption, the economic relevance of Africa to China cannot be overstated.

How necessary it is to back up these Chinese economic ventures with more overt security measures is yet to be seen. The persistent instability in nations, as well as the weak position of amicable political leaders will undoubtedly position Africa higher on Beijing's foreign security agenda and require a more complete approach. The question again arises whether it is in China's best interest to apply its African policy independently or in synergy with other nations. The short-term costs of any unilateral action would certainly exceed those of collective action, but long-term uncertainty about the intentions of other major players might influence any concerns related to cost-effectiveness. If Washington or Delhi decides to change course and contain China's expanding influence in Africa by pursing a strategy of counterbalancing and sea denial, the repercussions for the People's Republic will be dramatic. The concerns of the national security establishments in India and the United States and their expanding military presence in Africa are not unnoticed in China, and they highlight the necessity for the PRC to build a legitimate capacity to deal with crises unilaterally.

China's diplomatic identity will help shape policy decisions in support of a more active and autonomous security strategy. Beijing is realizing that the comfortable cloak of frailty it previously presented to the world no longer fits. African partners do not attach much value to China's diplomatic schizophrenia and the complex image of an economic giant, political dwarf, and minor military player it projects. When mayhem erupts, China automatically ends up on the frontline, finding itself hounded by African governments asking it to exercise its leverage. The cases of Chad and Somalia are not the only examples of this. South Africa has accosted China regarding illegal immigrants from Zimbabwe. Central Africa has carefully examined the violent incursions from Sudan. The African Union has called upon China several times to play a more active role in promoting security. The possibility exists that individual countries may be compelled to form a closer alliance with China in order to reduce their current reliance on the European Union and United States for security. Nigeria's announcement that it would rely on China instead of the United States for military support hints at this direction. The ability of the PRC to keep a low military profile is diminishing.

On the other hand, China's self-perception is also in transition. The "Century of Humiliation" is far behind and is being replaced by a national attitude of confidence and assertiveness. Chinese leaders have built on the success of their policy of good neighbour diplomacy that resulted in fewer frictions and more influence in Asia. The People's Republic has drawn confidence from the successful launch of a number of new defence systems. As China sees its diplomatic leverage expanding geographically from the Strait of Formosa, via Asia to the rest of the developing world, its ability to deal with emerging security issues is likely to follow suit.

Finally, there is the factor of capacity. China is gearing its military for a greater deployment capability. Its large immobile army is gradually being converted into a highly specialized and flexible organization. Simultaneously, the PLA is launching new military systems that will enhance its capacity to transport these forces. In 2007, the Chinese government approved the development of large passenger jets, including military transport variants similar to the American C-17 Globemaster III. Beijing has also ordered several new ships in an effort to enhance its naval transport capacity. In 2006, the hull of the first T-071 vessel was laid. This landing-platform dock has a range that goes far beyond Taiwan, with the aim of providing sea-based support to operations on land, humanitarian aid, and assisting in evacuations and disaster management. These vessels will be supported by a new generation of large replenishment ships and could be escorted by advanced frigates and destroyers. The Chinese flotilla that was sent to Somalia demonstrates China's new blue-water capacity. The type 052C *Lanzhou*, for instance, is a showcase of the advanced detection capacity for China's Navy. Its multifunction, active phased-array radar has a detection range of 450 kilometers and is complemented with a long-range, two-dimensional air search radar that has a 350-kilometer range and three additional systems to detect incoming missiles and aircraft. China is advancing its ability to pursue a more confident and independent security policy in Africa.

Will all this newfound military activity be sufficient to offset the antagonistic response it is likely to provoke? Probably not. If China decides to go solo and to pursue a more aggressive security policy in Africa, it is improbable that it will be able to overcome countermoves by India and the United States. It will be difficult for China to safeguard maritime trade with Africa if India exercises its naval dominance in the Indian Ocean. The sheer geographical divide between the PRC and the African continent makes it extremely difficult to support military activities if the United States or India opposes them. Contrary to China's revolutionary phase of the 1950s and 1960s when trade and economic interests only played a small part, China's increasing reliance on Africa renders it highly vulnerable to sea denial operations or a *guerre de course*. The fragile Cold War balance between the United States and the Soviet Union that allowed Mao to meddle with America's interests in Africa without having to fear political or economic reprisals can no longer be counted on. These days China has much to lose if it provokes Washington or Delhi.

SOLVING THE SECURITY PUZZLE IN NORTHEAST ASIA: A MULTILATERAL SECURITY REGIME

The year 2000 marks a critical turning point on the Korean Peninsula. The June summit between North and South Korea may lead the United States, Japan, China, and Russia to establish increased consultation, discussion, and coordination, paving the way for the Korea issue to galvanize new cooperation among the concerned parties of Northeast Asia. Alternately, U.S. pursuit of missile defenses and its revised alliance with Japan may strengthen an inceptive strategic coalition between China and Russia. Korea's geographic location once again places the peninsula at the crossroads of these great powers and momentous events.

The process of managing transition on the Korean Peninsula holds the potential to create new patterns of cooperation that would lay the foundation for a 21st century security architecture in Northeast Asia. Establishing a six-party security regime centered on the Korean peninsula best captures this historic opportunity. Through confidence-building measures such a regime would draw in both Koreas while clearly defining the role of the major outside powers in resolving the Korea conundrum peacefully.

Nonetheless, the six-party formula has clear merits in its potential to promote peace and stability amid change on the peninsula. To generate more focused thinking on this proposal, this research examines the opportunities and prospects for a security regime in Northeast Asia. It begins with a summary of the origins and foundations for a multilateral security regime on the Korean peninsula, and then considers the interests, capabilities, and reservations of each of the six principle states involved. Finally, the chapter proposes a strategy for establishing this regime and evaluates its future prospects.

ORIGINS OF MULTILATERALISM IN NORTHEAST ASIA

The earliest inception of a Northeast Asian security regime began with U.S. proposals in the early 1970s for multilateral talks among all regional powers aimed at reducing tensions on the Korean peninsula motivated in part by a desire to gradually reduce U.S. troop deployments in East Asia. Despite subsequent similar proposals by South Korean and other U.S. politicians, the bipolar confrontation of the Cold War effective suppressed any efforts to implement these concepts. The advent of the post-Cold War era quickly expanded prospects for a regional security regime, as a number of multilateral fora were quickly established. These included: ARF (ASEAN Regional Forum), the official-level security forum for the Asia Pacific; CSCAP (the Committee on Security Cooperation in the Asia Pacific); the North Pacific Working Group of CSCAP as a track-II sub-regional security dialogue, which is attended by all the North Pacific countries, including North Korea; and the "ASEAN plus three," which has been held annually since 1997 with members of ASEAN plus China, Japan and South Korea.

However, such promising ventures as the Northeast Asia Cooperation Dialogue (NEACD), a "track two" conference proposed by Susan Shirk, and South Korea's proposed Northeast Asia Security Dialogue (NEASED), were stymied by a lack of regional consensus, their inability to develop into official level talks, and an inability to include the principle party of concern, North Korea. Finally, multilateral cooperation was almost accidentally created in the formation of the KEDO (Korean Energy Development Organization) operation.

KEDO was founded in 1994 to implement the Geneva Agreement signed between the United States and North Korea, but also included South Korea and Japan. By offering North Korea an incentive-access to heavy oil, and the construction of light water reactors-to negotiate with these three states, KEDO established a functioning model of multilateral cooperation in security matters in Northeast Asia-one that may lead North Korea to other forms of engagement with the outside world. KEDO thus laid the foundation for the Four Party Talks, proposed by the United States and South Korea in 1996, and held for the first time in 1997. These meetings were aimed at negotiating a formal peace treaty that would officially end the state of war that has existed on the Korean Peninsula for almost five decades. While critics argue that the Four Party Talks are mere ceremonial gatherings with little substantive impact, they have served at least as an important confidence-building measure in the uncertain Northeast Asian security environment.

Since its 1998 inauguration, the Kim Dae-Jung government in South Korea has taken numerous steps to promote cooperative security interests and dampen possibilities for a major power confrontation on the peninsula. Particularly, Seoul has taken numerous diplomatic initiatives to engage North Korea, Russia, and Japan. However, South Korea's effort at sub-regional multilateralism has taken an interesting turn in 2000. South Korea's strong support for six-party talks was to open a venue for official level dialogue with the North while involving neighboring powers. Yet the advent of an inter-Korean dialogue and exchange may free South Korea from the political burden of pursuing sub-regionalism. Moreover, since both Koreas support the idea of "achieving reunification independent of outside pressures," the value of a multilateral security regime may appear to have declined.

Nevertheless, in a multilateral, six-party framework for Northeast Asia, less politically sensitive issues such as disaster relief, coordination of the pending refugee issues, environment and energy, and other functionally oriented issues including joint investment and economic development, can be dealt with. In the absence of a comprehensive multilateral regional mechanism, sub-regional settings can also facilitate bilateral negotiation among countries and their representatives who may otherwise be unable or ill prepared to have direct talks with each other.

THE SIX PARTIES: OBSTACLES, INTERESTS, AND OPPORTUNITIES

South Korea - Motivated Middle-Power

Why does South Korea, a small power surrounded by the big powers, seek to establish multilateralism in Northeast Asia? There are three major reasons behind South Korea's support for multilateralism: its desire for reduced tension on the peninsula, its need to engage the surrounding powers, and domestic imperatives. At a minimum, South Korea seeks the amelioration of tension on the peninsula. By pursuing modest goals, such as expanding trade and facilitating the movement of people between the two Koreas, a multilateral forum might foster an initial atmosphere of modest détente between the two Koreas.

South Korea also recognizes that its future security environment is inextricably linked to the vicissitudes in relations among the four nearby great powers: China, Japan, Russia, and the United States. By seeking the endorsement or implicit understanding by the surrounding powers, South Korea improves its security environment while enhancing the durability of any agreement on the future of the Korean peninsula. A multilateral regime on the peninsula, such as NEASD (Northeast Asian Security Dialogue), would not replace the current bilateral security framework, but instead supplement it by engaging Russia, which remains the only major party outside current multilateral regimes on the peninsula.

Finally, domestic politics is also an important reason behind South Korea's pursuit of sub-regionalism. Inter-Korean dialogue, in whatever manner, is a sign of success essential to South Korean efforts to build domestic support for its engagement policy. Since North Korea had adamantly refused official level government-to-government talks with the South until recently, the multilateral framework became a convenient venue for the South to deal directly with the North. The Korean public wishes to see the Korean issue resolved by the Koreans, while the big powers' interests and calculations are kept at a distance. In this regard, South Korea's initiative and the ultimate establishment of a multilateral security regime strengthen its diplomatic credibility, both at home and abroad. A successful new multilateralism, functionally oriented and issue-centered on Korea, would thus strengthen domestic support in South Korea for the unification process.

In addition, current unilateral and bilateral movements such as the U.S.-DPRK talks, the inter-Korean summit, the DPRK-Russian summit, and the DPRK's diplomatic strides to break self-imposed isolation encourage progress on multilateral negotiations. Other bilateral policies, such as the recognition of the DPRK by both Japan and the United States, are also important interim steps toward eventual reunification. Multilateralism complements, but does not conflict with, such developments.

North Korea - A Constraining Element

Despite the South's numerous efforts, its diplomatic influence on major power relations is clearly limited. It is difficult to clearly identify North Korea's real interest in multilateralism. Overlapping interests among the major powers and the two Koreas are not enough to form a positive motivation, since the countries involved exhibit serious gaps in defining common interests and common aversions.

Despite the reduced tension on the Korean Peninsula in the wake of North Korea's omni-directional diplomacy and historical summit between the two Koreas, North Korea still shows little interest in the six-party security framework since it fears isolation in a de facto five plus one formula. In fact, ever since expressing interest in joining the ARF in 1994, North Korea has shown little interest in any kind of multilateral forum, including the Four-Party Talks. North Korea has denounced the South Korean government for seeking to win support from foreign countries, while characterizing its effort toward multilateralism as proof of its subordination to external forces. The DPRK has set two important preconditions for its support of a multilateral security dialogue: improvement of its bilateral relations with Washington and Tokyo; and that the dialogue not be directed specially toward (or against) them.

North Korea feels more comfortable with bilateral bargaining and track-two because of the sensitive, controversial issues with which it is involved. DPRK officials maintain that in order to ensure security in the region through multilateral negotiations, it is important to create an atmosphere of confidence building by resolving complicated issues bilaterally.

As implied in such a statement, the DPRK's resistance to four plus two settings also stems from their resentment, if not feeling of betrayal, over the lack of progress in establishing diplomatic relations with both Japan and the United States.

The key to success in creating and implementing a multilateral security regime in the region would be creating an irresistible stake for Pyongyang to be engaged in such a mechanism. Given North Korea's aversion toward multiparty regimes, South Korea planned to promote a five-party intergovernmental dialogue in Northeast Asia if North Korea continued to reject participation.

The United States - Uncooperative Hegemon

Ironically parallel to North Korea, the United States also has traditionally viewed a regional security regime with much skepticism.

The United States has remained concerned that the institutionalization of multilateral security mechanisms might unnecessarily constrain its freedom of action in dealing with regional security affairs.

Instead, the U.S. has repeatedly emphasized its bilateral defense relationships as the foundation of American security policy in Asia. More comfortable with one-on-one approaches to security issues in Asia, U.S. officials are rather hesitant to embrace and aggressively pursue a multilateral approach-particularly in addressing security concerns, and especially when the idea also draws skeptical responses from North Korea and China.

American distrust arises in part from the origin of the idea; it was originally proposed by the former Soviet Union during the Cold War in order to dilute American influence.

However, with the advent of the post-Cold War era, a tendency toward more senior-level, issue oriented multilateral security initiatives began to emerge. Since 1991, support from American intellectuals and officials for greater U.S. involvement in a regional dialogue process grew markedly.

The enhancement of multilateral security dialogue as well as a continued U.S. military presence and commitment was among the Clinton Administration's ten priority policy goals for Asia. Joseph Nye also emphasized the regional institution as a confidence building measure designed to complement the existing American alliance structure, not to replace it.

As Richard N. Haass recently pointed out, the success of a strategy encouraging cooperative multipolarity depends on the United States' ability to bring others on board on a regional scale.

Yet the United States still shows little willingness to lead such a venture, despite its primacy in world politics. U.S. reluctance also stems from its recent difficult lessons in multilateralism, such as in the 1994 North Korean nuclear crisis. When U.S.-North Korean talks were suspended and the issue returned to the United Nations Security Council, the expanded number of actors involved likewise enhanced the difficulty of reaching a negotiated solution.

Some Americans, including former Deputy Assistant Secretary of Defense Kurt Campbell, have proposed "minilateralism" as a secondary approach or stepping stone for more institutionalized multilateralism.

KEDO and TCOG (the Trilateral Coordination and Oversight Group of the United States, Japan and South Korea) are representative cases of this approach. So far, the minilateral setting has been proven an effective venue for negotiation and coordination, even though it has not, and may not, lead to the establishment of a multilateral regime in the region.

Overall, U.S. support for the development of multilateral cooperation on the Korean Peninsula has been ad hoc, opportunistic, and crisis-driven rather than conforming to pre-planned strategic objectives.

An underlying reason is that multilateral fora are not effective in responding to crises given their consensus-oriented operating style. In the event of military hostilities or a clear threat to U.S. national security interests in Asia, the United States is more likely to act in concert with its existing allies or through an ad hoc grouping of like-minded states.

Yet the lack of common interests and a common enemy in Northeast Asia render the establishment of a NATO-type security structure extremely unlikely.

With its bilateral military alliances and a healthy skepticism toward multilateral approaches, the U.S. is not eager to go down the path of multilateral security frameworks.

The problem is not that the U.S. has strong opposition to the idea of multilateralism itself, but that it has not paid real attention to the idea thus far. Multilateralism has been viewed by the United States as a nice thing to have if the international community is ready for it, but unfortunately, in most cases, the international community has proven itself to be rather unprepared. Yet if multilateralism in the region is going to move forward, it will require that the U.S. offer not only its support but also its leadership and vision.

China - A Reluctant Participant

In principle, Chinese officials support the idea of multilateral dialogues to exchange views and promote mutual understanding. In practice, they have been cautious at multilateral meetings, acutely sensitive to perceived intrusions into Chinese sovereignty, sometimes rigid in presenting their views, and frequently anxious about perceived coalitions operating against them.

China's participation in any kind of multilateral regimes tended to be reluctant and defensive. Frequently China wants a seat at the table but attempts to limit the pace and scope of discussions, especially in areas related to transparency and specific regional conflicts.

A key reason for China's lack of eagerness is its concern over Japan. China simply does not want to see Japan play an important role in security issues in a multilateral regional setting.

On the other hand, there is some evidence that the Chinese leadership has decided that multilateral security fora can be used to serve its own interests, in order to challenge the U.S. role, or undermine the U.S. bilateral alliance structure by emphasizing regional dialogues.

Thus, for Beijing, the multilateralism in Northeast Asia is a way to tie China in and to tie the United States down. Furthermore, China began to realize that it would help reduce fears of the "China threat" if China became actively involved in multilateral fora. In addition, China may see multilateral structures as support for its ideological insistence on the trend toward multipolarity, as opposed to an American-led Asian security order.

China presumably wields influence over North Korea, as North Korea depends upon China for a good part of its fuel and food supplies. Interestingly, China has kept some distance from KEDO (the Korean Peninsula Energy Development Organization), arguing that it can better contribute to the success of KEDO by remaining outside the organization. Perhaps the major reason for Chinese disinterest is the cost to be borne by KEDO members for building the two light water reactors in the North.

On the other hand, China has displayed deep interest and active involvement in the Four Party Talks, particularly after North Korea finally agreed to participate. Furthermore, when in early 1998, South Korean President Kim Dae-Jung asked his Chinese counterpart to accept the proposed six party declaration for peace and stability in Northeast Asia, China accepted it "in principle."

In the short to medium term, China has the most to gain diplomatically from radically improved relations between North and South Korea and so has thrived on the so-called "double-edged sword" approach of improving relations with both Koreas. As the secret visit by Kim Jong-Il to China only a few days before the summit reflects, China is back on center stage in Korean affairs.

China shares many of the same objectives as the United States regarding the Korean Peninsula. It wants to keep Korea nuclear-free. It wants stability and to prevent either a refugee crisis or an armed conflict that could draw China in. To Beijing, a stable and friendly but divided Korean Peninsula is more desirable than Korea's rapid unification. So far, China has played a constructive role on the Korean Peninsula, as demonstrated through the North Korean nuclear and missile issues of the past few years. Beijing does not oppose closer bilateral relations between North Korea and the United States, however several of its important interests do diverge from those of the U.S.. Most importantly, Beijing firmly opposes what it sees as Washington's troubling tendencies toward unilateral action. Like many other countries, China does not always support U.S.-led interventions in hot spots around the world. Therefore, China's position toward multilateralism will likely depend on three factors: the triangular relationship between the United States, Japan and China, progress in the U.S.-DPRK relationship, and the development of the situation on the peninsula.

Japan - Strong Advocate

Japan and Russia have thus far been left out of the ongoing four-party talks on the Korean Peninsula. Tensions could arise between the Four Party Talks mechanism and the other consultation mechanisms that have developed among the United States, Japan, and South Korea.

Comparatively, Japan has been more deeply involved than Russia in Korean affairs by virtue of its bilateral security alliance with the United States. Involved in both KEDO and TCOG (the Trilateral Coordination and Oversight Group), Japan also has shown interest in participating in the missile talks between the United States and North Korea.

Pursing cooperative security through multilateral security fora allows Japan to play a more active role in regional security while allaying the concerns of neighboring countries and surmounting constitutional limitations on the use of force overseas in situations other than for self-defense.

Since the intensive bilateral summits held in the fall 1997 between Northeast Asian countries, Japanese prime ministers have consistently encouraged the creation of additional multilateral dialogue processes.

Japan has shown interest in the so called four power talks (the United States, Japan, China and Russia), arguing that peace and stability in the Asia-Pacific region hinges upon these states building mutual ties based on confidence and cooperation.

In addition, Japan also seeks a version of minilateralism that would include a series of trilaterals and quadrilaterals. Trilateral dialogues, such as the Trilateral Forum on North-Pacific Security Problems (with the United States, Japan and Russia) or the JAC Conference (Japan, China and the United States), provide Japan with an opportunity to solidify its alliance with the United States while simultaneously improving relations with other leading powers.

In 1999, Korea and Japan agreed to creating a dialogue on regional security at their ministerial talks. The move followed Seoul's proposal for the establishment of a multilateral consultative body to deal with security problems in Northeast Asia. Japan has advocated an institutionalized six party talks to replace the existing Four Party Talks, whereas South Korea prefers to keep the two separate, assigning the six party dialogues to cover issues other than building a peace mechanism on the Korean Peninsula. Thus, among the critical issues to address is the need to distinguish between the role of a sub-regional security dialogue and the purposes of the Four Party Talks involving the two Koreas, China, and the United States.

Russia - Seeking To Retain Influence

Militarily and economically, Russia struggles to retain some level of parity with its neighbors. It remains highly dependent upon good relations with the U.S., China, and Japan, and so its foremost task in the region is preserving both the status quo and its own influence.

Russia has therefore continued the U.S.SR's support for a multilateral security cooperation regime. Russia's main concern regarding the Korean issue is not to be left out of the process and to prevent U.S. or Chinese dominance on the Korean Peninsula. Hence, in 1994 it proposed an international conference in connection with the North Korean nuclear issue. Needless to say, Russia was upset with its exclusion from the subsequent four-party proposal.

After Moscow established relations with Seoul in 1990, its previous influence over North Korea steadily declined. In response, Moscow has attempted a more balanced policy toward Seoul and Pyongyang, signing a new friendship treaty with North Korea during Russian Foreign Minister Ivanov's recent visit, and promoting again the establishment of a six party security mechanism. However, Russia today has only limited resources with which to help North Korea. North Korea, for its part, is concentrating its attention on the United States as a source of support and aid, while also trying to expand its own diplomatic ties to Japan, Italy, Canada, the Philippines, Brunei, Australia and France. To South Korea, however, full support from Russia would contribute greatly toward a truly effective arrangement on Korean peace. Hence, President Kim Dae-Jung requested Russia's understanding and cooperation in his engagement policy toward the North and suggested that a six party security framework be initiated in the future.

Russian President Vladimir Putin's visit to Pyongyang for talks with North Korean leader Kim Jong-il was an emphatic gesture of Russia's return to the Korea question.

Russia is now aiming at strengthening bilateral relations in the face of new developments springing from the June inter-Korean summit and is positioning itself to recover its leverage over the two Koreas.

Among the proposals suggested by Russia include working with South Korea to restart North Korea's idle thermal power plants and steel mills by providing technology to normalize the North Korean facilities while South Korea supplies capital for the project. Besides restarting moribund industrial plants, Russia has shown keen interest in connecting the TSR (Trans-Siberian Railroad) lines with the North and South Korean railroad networks. In addition, Russia is also seeking to form a new trilateral strategic partnership with China and North Korea while emphasizing anti-unilateralism in dealing with the Korea issue.

While welcoming the historic summit between the two Koreas and supporting the process of a Korea-led resolution, Russia has no reason to give up its support for multilateralism.

Conclusion: A Pragmatic Program for Multilateralism

Based on the preceding discussion, it may appear that the possibility of a sub-regional multilateralism remains slim due to some objections from the United States and a lack of common interest among the parties.

However, despite the ubiquitous pessimism toward using multilateralism to resolve the Korea issue, we can find at least one positive trend in development of the reconciliatory atmosphere between the two Koreas. The two bilateral alliances between the United States and Japan and South Korea have enabled the three countries to cooperate on security matters as if a trilateral security arrangement existed, particularly in their response to the North Korean nuclear and missile issues.

Despite criticisms that multilateral security institutions are unlikely to result in tangible results, they allow counterparts in the region to meet regularly and exchange views. For example, track-two processes have been instrumental in creating and supplementing track-one processes. Multilateralism has also helped foster bilateralism by accommodating bilateral meetings during the multilateral forums.

By the same token, the current bilateral structures of security relationships can advance multilateralism in the region by assuring a modicum of stability and creating imperatives for North Korea and China to participate in cooperative mechanisms. While multilateral cooperative security institutions are admittedly far less effective in defending against armed conflicts, they do have the ability to improve regional relations, promote confidence, and foster trust, which, in turn, should help ameliorate the security dilemma and the chances for accidental miscalculations.

Perhaps the most pragmatic solution is to pursue issue-specific and functionally-oriented ad hoc mini-multilateral institutions. This more limited approach, focusing on functional areas where cooperation could be expanded, offers states confidence that positive outcomes are likely, with only minimal costs if the process deteriorates.

A regional agenda that goes beyond helping North Korea rehabilitate its ailing economy and respond to urgent environmental and maritime issues would help expand multilateral dialogue. Economic growth in North Korea, China, and Russia will only flourish with the removal of the old Cold-War barriers and the promotion of greater cross-border contacts, as was visible in the local farmers' markets established in North Korea during the food crises of 1996 and 1997.

A multilateral dialogue might also address region-wide concerns such as implementation of the Law of the Sea Convention in Northeast Asia or multilateral approaches to nuclear reprocessing and plutonium management. The area of energy cooperation holds perhaps the most promise for multilateral cooperation in Northeast Asia. All the major actors have an interest in pipelines to transport natural gas from Russia and yet all have developed varying notions of how such a regional pipeline grid might work. There are adequate amounts of Russian gas from Iskutsk and East Baikal to meet long-term projected needs of Japan and Korea, as well as China, however such a project would require enormous financing. Other issues that lend themselves to multilateral cooperation are the development of the Tumen River Basin and the Yellow Sea area, natural gas pipelines from Siberia and the Sea of Okhost, and environmental pollution. All could be managed by such a Northeast Asian entity.

This promising, if limited, approach of "functional multilateralism" would also identify issues where there is an overlap of interests and finding mechanisms to address them. Such proposals as KADO (the Korean Peninsula Agricultural Development Organization) proposed by Ralph Cossa, PACATOM (the Pacific Atomic Energy Community) by Robert Manning, and other arrangements for economic and environmental cooperation are good examples. Another idea is that South Korea play the leading role in providing loans and credit guarantees to North Korea in exchange for concessions in the North's missile program. This proposal would build interdependence between the North and the South, reduce the U.S. economic burden, and possibly include future cooperation with Japan, China and Russia. Over the long-term, it may facilitate the conversion of North Korea's military sector into an industrial base.

Today's complex North-South Korean bargaining situation and the opening of more exchanges between the two will create greater opportunities for peaceful change on the Korean Peninsula. Functional multilateralism, with moderate ambitions and concrete proposals, can capitalize upon this historic diplomatic opportunity. By giving an indication of their flexibility and good will, and by demonstrating anew to the South Korean public the difficulties of dealing with the North, the South's leaders may also be able to gain public confidence-crucial to future efforts. Timing is important, and the stakes are high. Multilateral organizations seem to work when the underlying bilateral relationships are positive and when there are persuasive incentives for cooperation. Thus, the prospects for sub-regional dialogue will depend on national interests and on governmental will and leadership.

One final important element in the activation of multilateralism is the expansion of membership. Given that post-Cold War regional multilateral proposals emerged from such middle powers as Australia and Canada, and that North Korea currently places more weight on improving relations with these countries, it is vital to engage in any multilateral process countries as Canada, Australia and Mongolia. Despite cynicism dismissing these multilateral security dialogue processes as mere talk shops, the dialogues have been instrumental in reducing distrust and misunderstandings. It would be a good lesson to remember that history is created by vagaries, and not by status quo proponents. A multilayered, multi-dimensional forum of bilateral, trilateral, quadrilateral, and multilateral security dialogues will play a positive function in supplementing, if not supplanting, the existing bilateral security architecture.

8

North East Asia's Undercurrents of Conflict

Shifting power relations in North East Asia are spurring rising nationalism in China, Japan and South Korea, aggravating long-standing disputes over territorial claims and differing interpretations of history. Failure to bridge these differences could raise tensions and impede efforts to tackle the security and economic challenges confronting the region. While finding lasting solutions will be difficult, a series of practical confidence and institution-building steps should be taken immediately by the three states to keep the simmering disputes from boiling over.

The economic rise of China, generational shifts in South Korea, and the waning of Japan's economic dominance have spurred xenophobia that occasionally spills over into violence. All three need to work together to address their major challenges in security, non-proliferation, energy procurement and environmental protection, but North East Asia remains one of the least integrated regions, with no effective institutions to address its common political and security problems.

A number of events in 2005 illustrate the simmering tensions. In March, South Korean demonstrators cut off their fingers in protest over Japanese claims to a pair of small islets. The next month, Chinese demonstrators attacked Japanese businesses and diplomatic missions over a Japanese history textbook, while in June, Japanese Prime Minister Koizumi Junichiro and South Korean President Roh Moo-hyun spent most of a two-hour meeting discussing history, rather than current issues. China began drilling for oil in September in a disputed area of the East China Sea, over Japanese protests, and in November, as a result of the visit Koizumi paid to the Yasukuni Shrine, where Japanese war criminals are among the millions of honoured dead, President Hu Jintao refused to have a one-on-one meeting with Koizumi on the margins of the Asia-Pacific Economic Cooperation summit.

Most territorial disputes in the region are over uninhabited islands and partially submerged rocks, whose status remains ambiguous under international law, including Tokdo/Takeshima, jointly claimed by South Korea and Japan; Senkaku/Diaoyu, jointly claimed by China, Taiwan, and Japan; and the Kuril/Northern Territories, jointly claimed by Russia and Japan. The importance of most of these lies not so much in their intrinsic value, but in the surrounding economic zones. The best way to address the problems, therefore, would be to leave aside territorial issues and focus on joint exploitation and, as appropriate, conservation of the natural resources. A lesser, but longer-term, dispute involves the area in North East China (Kando in Korean, Jiangdao in Chinese) populated by ethnic Koreans and to which some groups in South Korea have begun to advance a historical claim that they hope to make good when Korea is reunified. In reality, however, ethnic Koreans in China have little interest in joining a unified Korea, and Seoul will likely need to renounce any such interests if it wants to gain Chinese support for any eventual unification of the peninsula.

Prime Minister Koizumi's visits to Yasukuni Shrine and attempts by right-wing groups to produce revisionist history textbooks have prompted alarm in both China and South Korea and added to the emotion with which they accuse Japan of failing to show contrition for its World War II crimes. While Tokyo has offered numerous official apologies and provided billions of dollars of aid to help spur the development of South Korea and China, it has failed to offer direct compensation to individual victims, and, unlike Germany, has shown little interest in continued, critical examination of its history. Combined with Japan's moves to become a more "normal" nation in terms of defence capabilities, these battles over history increase regional fears of reviving Japanese militarism. Japan has passed legislation to allow it to play a stronger role within the U.S. military alliance and in international peacekeeping operations, and the ruling Liberal Democratic Party is backing a constitutional amendment that would remove most of the restrictions imposed on the country's military after 1945. Hostile reactions to these moves by China and South Korea have created a backlash in Japan that goes beyond the extreme right.

History is an equally troubling subject, though in different ways, in South Korea, which is in the midst of leadership change and a re-examination of its relationship with the U.S. at the same time as it re-examines the national myths surrounding politically sensitive collaboration with and resistance to imperial Japan. And in China, history, not least the memory of the military struggle against that imperial Japan, is used to provide the legitimacy for its political order that communist ideology no longer can.

Attempts to address these emotion-laden and intertwined problems have led to some encouraging instances of inter-regional cooperation among scholars and civil society groups that suggest North East Asia's problems can be managed. Promising proactive measures include codes of conducts – one has already been effective in reducing tensions over the Spratly Islands; agreements on joint management of off-shore resources; regional institutions to address energy and historical issues; increased military-to-military exchanges; and historical memorials that focus on the universal suffering of war victims, rather than on national glory or shame.

Definitively resolving territorial and historical disputes that have been building for decades will not be easy or quick but failure at least to ameliorate them risks undermining the peace and prosperity of the region.

Recommendations:

To the Governments of Japan, China, South Korea and the United States:

1. De-link history issues from diplomacy by continuing contact among officials at all levels regardless of the fluctuating state of public opinion.

2. Refrain from unilateral military exercises in disputed areas.
3. Increase military-to-military exchanges, training and confidence-building measures.
4. Establish a regional institution for energy security and cooperation that would explore such issues as establishing a depository for spent nuclear fuel.
5. Set up regional cooperative mechanisms for disaster relief and environmental protection.
6. Start an East Asia Peace Institute for sustained Track Two dialogue, joint inquiries, scholarship and conferences.
7. Convene a committee of museum curators and scholars to develop agreed standards for historical exhibitions, with the goal of focusing displays on universal human suffering and accomplishment, rather than nationalism.
8. Increase support for NGO activity that promotes regional dialogue.

To the Government of Japan:

9. Set up a fund that uses public money to assist remaining individual victims of Japanese war crimes, in particular "comfort women", forced labourers, and subjects of biological warfare experiments.
10. Release into the public domain any remaining documents on World War II and colonial activities.
11. Build a new memorial to Japanese war dead to provide an alternative to official visits to Yasukuni Shrine.
12. Have cabinet members refrain from making public statements which praise or downplay Japan's colonial exploits.

To the Government of South Korea:

13. Conclude an agreement on allowable catches by South Korean and Japanese fishing boats in the median fishing zone around Tokdo/Takeshima.
14. Clearly state that the South accepts existing border treaties and will pursue peaceful reunification on this basis.
15. Establish a public fund to provide compensation for the victims of Japanese colonialism who were under-

compensated or not compensated by the 1965 Normalisation Treaty.

16. Publicly acknowledge and thank Japan for the economic aid provided under the Normalisation Treaty.

To the Government of the People's Republic of China:

17. Allow Chinese internet users greater access to Japanese and Western media to provide alternative views.
18. Accept in principle Japanese offers on joint development of oil and gas deposits in the East China Sea.
19. Develop a Code of Conduct with Japan over the Senkaku/Diaoyu dispute, using the China-ASEAN Code of Conduct on the Spratlys as a model.
20. Publicly acknowledge Japan's role in China's economic development.

To the Government of the United States:

21. Strengthen trilateral policy planning coordination with Japan and South Korea to develop more direct discussion on security issues between Seoul and Tokyo.
22. Release to bona fide researchers documents related to Japanese war crimes seized at the end of World War II and which until now have been withheld.

NORTH EAST ASIA'S UNDERCURRENTS OF CONFLICT

Simmering tensions between China, Japan and South Korea risk boiling over unless the three countries embrace confidence- and institution-building measures and put aside their arguments over history.

North East Asia's Undercurrents of Conflict, the latest report from the International Crisis Group, describes shifting power relationships that have contributed to the rise in nationalism, which is aggravating old disputes over territory and history and threatening to make progress on critical security and economic challenges more difficult. China's economic growth, generational shifts in South Korea and Japan's waning economic dominance have spurred xenophobia and occasional violence throughout the region. A dialogue that avoids extreme rhetoric on all sides is needed.

"Territorial disputes and revisionist history stoke the fires and undermine regional stability and prosperity", says Peter Beck, Crisis Group's North East Asia Project Director. "These countries need to develop a more sophisticated understanding of each other and build cooperative institutions that support, rather than undermine, regional progress".

Changes in Japan's defence policy, including reinterpretation of the constitutional clause renouncing use of force to solve problems, continuing leadership visits to a shrine where war criminals are among those interred, and controversial school history books anger and worry Koreans and Chinese with memories of Japanese imperialism. China's emergence as a global economic power has created new security, environmental and energy challenges, sometimes provoking direct competition with its neighbours. A younger generation of leaders in South Korea wants the country to develop a new identity as a regional "balancer" rather than a reflexive U.S. ally and to focus on reconciliation and reunification with the North.

To keep incidents from raising tensions to the boiling point, Japan, China, South Korea and the U.S. should refrain from unilateral military exercises in disputed areas, increase military-to-military exchanges and establish regional institutions to address common political and security problems. Japan should use public money to assist war crimes victims. South Korea should clearly state that it accepts existing border treaties as it pursues peaceful reunification. China should publicly acknowledge Japan's role in its economic development and accept Tokyo's offers to develop oil and gas deposits in the East China Sea jointly.

"It's overly ambitious to think long-standing, symbolic problems will be resolved anytime soon", says Beck. "But taking these steps would go a long way toward reducing tensions and allowing these countries to focus on more important issues like security, non-proliferation, energy procurement and environmental protection".

WHITHER NORTHEAST ASIA? MANAGING TENSIONS AND AVOIDING CONFLICT IN A TROUBLED REGION

Tensions are rising in Northeast Asia, threatening more than a generation of peace and prosperity that has made the region's growth and development the envy of the world. Regional reaction to China's declaration of an "air defense identification zone" encompassing areas controlled by South Korea and Japan is the latest sign that longstanding rivalries, territorial disputes, and historical antagonisms increasingly have the potential to result in conflict.

The downturn in relations between China and Japan and between Japan and South Korea represents a serious challenge to regional stability and a deep concern to the United States, which has a major stake in the region and important alliances with both Seoul and Tokyo.

Many of the Northeast Asia region's problems have deep roots and long histories, and emotion and resentment play a significant role in keeping old disputes alive. If the region is to avoid conflict, it must find a way to move past the often-tragic legacy of its history. China, Japan, and Korea must understand the seriousness of the situation and share responsibility for addressing it. Failure to do so is not an option, since the region's stability and prosperity are at stake.

This essay offers ten principles and guidelines for managing current tensions and creating a framework for intra-regional cooperation. The United States has a major role to play, including by reassuring its allies and by making clear to China that it is prepared to defend them. Those tasks will be high on Vice President Biden's agenda during his visit to Asia this week. Helping the region resolve its current crisis will be a major test of the credibility of the U.S. "rebalancing" policy and could bring about another generation of peace, stability, and prosperity in Northeast Asia.

Rising Tensions

Relations between China and Japan and between South Korea and Japan are deteriorating, escalating tensions in an already troubled Northeast Asia region. Now, China's declaration of an "air defense identification zone" (ADIZ) that includes territories controlled by Japan and South Korea is fueling concerns that things may be about to get worse among the three neighbors.

Rivalries and difficult relations are nothing new in a region marked by competing nationalisms, historical antagonism, a legacy of past invasions and occupations, and territorial disputes. Still, the region has managed to produce more than a generation of peace and unparalleled prosperity that has made it the envy of the world. However, there are signs that cooperation is fraying as old resentments dressed in new clothing are dominating regional relations.

In the late 19th and early 20th century, Northeast Asia witnessed a dramatic shift in power as a rising Japan sought to lead the region and replace a Western imperialist-dominated order with its own. This shift and Japan's ambitions led to a bitter legacy of invasions, colonialism, and war that eventually drew in the United States. Today, it may be fair to ask whether we are witnessing a 21st century version of this tragic drama, this time with China in the role of the region's ambitious rising force.

CHINA'S DOMESTIC ACID PRECIPITATION

Sulfur dioxide is the most important acid precursor in China, and coal combustion accounts for 94% of all atmospheric sulfur emissions. Total emissions have been rising nearly as fast as coal use, since mitigation efforts have been weak. Power plant boilers are collectively the single largest contributor, industrial boilers the second, and residential stoves and boilers third. Power plants are the largest contributors to pollutant emissions that are transported long distances, and thus to regional acid precipitation. Industrial and residential sources contribute mainly to local, particularly urban acid precipitation

Areas affected by acid precipitation are principally in southern China, with some areas experiencing precipitation with average pH below 3.5. The affected area has gradually expanded to include eastern and northern coastal areas. Until recently, acid precipitation was mostly restricted to cities, but it has been spreading to rural areas. Direct acid-rain damages in the worst affected areas were 16 billion yuan (US $2 billion at present exchange rates) annually by the end of the 1980s.

CHINA'S CONTRIBUTION TO ACID PRECIPITATION IN NORTHEAST ASIA

China officially recognizes that acid precipitation is a problem with regional dimensions, and that there is substantial transboundary transportation of acid precursors. The government remains noncommittal, however, on the relative contribution of each country's emissions to the severity of acid precipitation in other countries. A crucial gap in understanding of regional acid precipitation is the lack of empirical research on transboundary transport. Privately, some Chinese researchers may say they believe that China contributes more to other countries' acid precipitation burdens than those other countries do to China's, but this does not represent an official position. Whatever damage China's emissions may cause in other countries, it is far less than the damage China does to itself, since most emissions remain with the country's boundaries.

Legislation To Control Acid Precipitation

In August 1995, the National People's Congress (NPC) passed a new version of the Atmospheric Pollution Control Law, and it is expected to approve and issue regulations-drafted by the National Environmental Protection Agency (NEPA)-for implementation in the first half of 1997. Major provisions of the Law call for creating "acid rain control regions" and "sulfur dioxide control regions" in China. Power plants and other large coal users will be required to adopt measures to reduce emissions. Production of high-sulfur coal will be limited and new coal-washing facilities will be encouraged. A sulfur dioxide emissions permitting system will be extended to cover all major coal users, and emissions fees will be gradually raised to a level above the cost of control. The system for using emissions fees will also be reformed. The Ministry of Electric Power's plans call for desulfurization equipment to be installed at power plants totaling 10 GW (out of a projected total of about 200 GW of fossil fuel-fired generating capacity) by 2000.

In addition, NEPA is releasing new standards for power plant emissions rates.

Participants In Controlling Acid Precipitation In China

Setting and implementing China's policies to control acid precipitation involves a wide array of actors with divergent interests. Most deeply concerned are those involved with environmental protection: the State Council's Environmental Protection Leading Group, the NPC's National Committee on Environmental Protection, and NEPA, including all its local branches down to the county and township level. This set of organizations, however, is relatively weak compared to the others that also have a say in policy formulation. The State Planing Commission and the State Economic and Trade Commission, which have responsibility for coordinating activities in different sectors, try to integrate environmental goals with other crucial objectives, such as overall economic growth and poverty alleviation. Line ministries are powerful, and vigorously defend enterprises within their jurisdictions against regulation. Provincial and lower-level administrations are crucial to implementation. Local environmental protection bureaus (EPBs) that carry out regulatory activities report both to NEPA and to local administrations, which are typically concerned mainly with local economic development, and often restrain EPBs' activities.

Regional And International Cooperation To Control Acid Precipitation

China is far from ready to consider an international agreement on limiting transboundary pollution, but there are some positions that China would likely take. Since coal will continue to dominate the primary energy consumption mix for many decades, and since coal consumption will likely continue to grow by several percent annually, China's sulfur dioxide and other coal-related pollutant emissions sources will keep growing. So long as control of emissions remains expensive, China will likely maintain that, given its relative poverty, sulfur dioxide emissions controls can only be phased in slowly. China may be willing to discuss limits to the rate of growth of emissions, or limits to per capita emissions, but talks about reducing total emissions would be unlikely. At least initially, officials would probably prefer to discuss acid precipitation issues with other Northeast Asian countries on a bilateral basis, or through existing multilateral fora, rather than through a newly created organization.

For the time being, China is likely to reject any calls to begin drawing up a framework for joint action on transboundary pollution in Northeast Asia. It's willingness to cooperate on joint research efforts and on technology transfer and development projects in support of domestic efforts to mitigate acid precipitation, however, indicate that China could be slowly drawn into such a process.

In the early 1980s, China's central government recognized acid precipitation resulting from coal-related sulfur emissions as a serious and growing problem. Sulfur dioxide emissions from power plants and other sources have risen quickly along with the expansion of economic activity, and some parts of southern China are experiencing damages from acid rain similar to those found in the most severely affected regions of Europe and North America. The government established monitoring networks to study trends in emissions and acidity of precipitation, and supported numerous empirical and analytical studies designed to deepen understanding of the causes and effects of acid rain. The government has gradually raised the priority accorded to this key environmental problem, and is now devoting substantial economic and political resources to mitigation efforts. Officials and others in China are very open to international exchanges to address the problem, and actively seek technical and financial assistance for controlling sulfur dioxide emissions.

Although it is the largest contributor to regional acid precursor emission, China has not shown great interest in joint international efforts to address the larger problem of acid precipitation in Northeast Asia. The government would likely be unwilling to consider an agreement on control of transboundary pollutants in Northeast Asia. Some in China may not even see the need for such an agreement, since the domestic incentives to control sulfur emissions-both to reduce acid precipitation and human health impacts-are already very strong. On the other hand, China has shown a willingness to participate in joint research efforts.

CHINA'S DOMESTIC ACID PRECIPITATION

Sources Of Acid Precursor Emissions

Sulfur dioxide is by far the most important acid precursor in China (although nitrogen oxides are rising in relative significance), and coal combustion provides 94% of all atmospheric sulfur emissions. Basically, then, those sectors and equipment categories that use the most coal also contribute the most to sulfur emissions. Power plant boilers are collectively the single largest contributor, and industrial boilers the second. Furnaces and kilns are also important contributors. Less than half a dozen of the country's hundreds of power plants is equipped with desulfurization equipment, and virtually no industrial boilers are. Only 20% of coal is washed, and nearly all of that in coking for the metallurgical industry. Thus, almost none of the coal used in utility and industrial boilers is washed, sorted, or matched to improve efficiency and remove sulfur and ash.

Residential stoves and boilers are also important, mainly in terms of locally transported pollutants, but total coal use in the household sector has been declining since 1990. Many households have switched partially or completely to gas and electricity for cooking and water heating. Those households that continue to use coal increasingly use honeycomb briquettes in specially designed stoves, increasing the efficiency of coal use. Moreover, many briquettes incorporate sulfur-fixing additives, further reducing emissions.

While particulate emissions from fuel combustion in China have been rising much more slowly than fuel use (mainly because air pollution control efforts to date have focused on controlling particulates), sulfur dioxide emissions are rising, and in 1994 reportedly stood at nearly 19 Mt (Figure 1). Official reports of sulfur dioxide emissions understate the total, however, because they do not include rural industry, which consumes a growing share of China's energy. Actual emissions rates may be about 20%

higher.1 Chinese estimates of total emissions are due to be published soon.

Besides efforts to control sulfur emissions in combustion chambers and smoke stacks, two trends will fundamentally affect China's sulfur dioxide emissions. Most important is the continued growth of coal use, from 1.2 billion metric tons (Gt) currently, to about 1.5 Mt in 2000, and up to 2 Mt in 2010. Absolute consumption of coal will continue to rise in industry, and especially in the utility sector, since electricity is the fastest growing form of energy in the end-use mix. Utility boilers will take an increasing share of coal use, and much of that rise in use will be at plants located near coal mines and major coal transfer facilities.

The other major trend is the change in average sulfur content of coal. Despite little change in the rate of washing, the sulfur content of coal is declining; in the early 1990s, delivered coal contained over 1.1% sulfur, whereas the average is now about 1.0%. One reason has been the Ministry of Coal's policy of conserving coking coal to restrain non-metallurgical use of this relatively less plentiful resource. Since coking coal has a higher average sulfur content than steam coal, this has reduced the sulfur content of coal available on the market. The recent greater availability of low-sulfur (0.5%), low-ash coals from large surface in Shanxi, Shaanxi, and Inner Mongolia has also been important. The economic reforms that have pushed mines to become more financially independent may also have played a part. Underground mines, in order to reduce mining costs, have begun to exploit shallower resources, which tend to have lower sulfur content.

Affected Areas And Severity

According to the National Environmental Protection Agency (NEPA), the main affected areas include the area to the south of the Yangtze River and to the East of the Tibetan Plateau, and the Sichuan Basin (see map in appendix).2 Until recently, acid precipitation was mostly restricted to urban areas, but it has been spreading to rural areas. Southern central China (Guizhou, Hunan, and Jiangxi) is afflicted with the country's worst acid rain, experiencing precipitation with an average pH of under 4.0, with more than four-fifths of precipitation episodes considered acid (i.e., below pH 5.0). Some areas regularly experience precipitation with pH under 3.5, and episodes of rain with pH as low as 2.8 have been recorded. The Southwest is also seriously affected, with areas of Sichuan receiving precipitation with an average pH of under 5.0. In 1993, most major municipal areas in Guizhou received precipitation with average pH under 4.0, with some as low as 3.2.3

The problem is less acute in eastern China, but the affected area is large, covering the heavily populated lower reaches of the Yangtze River and coastal areas as far south as Xiamen in Fujian. Some cities in southern China, particularly in the Pearl River Delta (the area surrounding Guangzhou) and in eastern Guangxi, have very acid precipitation (ranging from 4.5 to 5.0 pH), and rural areas are increasingly affected. Only a few cities in the North and Northeast-notably Qingdao in Shandong, Shijiazhuang in Hebei, Taiyuan in Shanxi, and Tumen in Jilin-regularly experience acid precipitation. Acid rain in the north is likely to intensify, especially if construction of mine-mouth power plants accelerates as planned.

An assessment of acid-rain damages in the four most affected provinces (Guangdong, Guangxi, Guizhou, and Sichuan) concluded that, in the latter half of the 1980s, direct damages were 16 billion yuan (about US $2 billion at present exchange rates) per year. Another source places the annual damage to forests alone near 1 billion yuan or more. Certainly, damages are likely to be near levels experienced in very acidified regions in Europe and North America, since many areas of southern China experience similar precipitation pH levels.

Dry deposition is also a large source of damage. Ambient levels of sulfur dioxide give an idea of the severity of this problem, as well as the direct health problems resulting from this pollutant. Figure 2 shows the range of annual average sulfur dioxide levels for nearly 90 Chinese cities. The average level for all cities regularly exceeds the U.S. annual standard of 80 ug/m^3, and for some cities the annual average is many times that. Despite increases in total sulfur emissions, ambient level have remained stable, in part thanks to efforts to switch away from coal and to introduce low-sulfur briquettes to households and the food service industry, which typically account for a large fraction of emissions to ambient urban environments.

CHINA'S CONTRIBUTION TO ACID PRECIPITATION IN NORTHEAST ASIA

China officially recognizes that acid precipitation in Northeast Asia is a problem with regional dimensions, and that there is substantial transboundary transportation of acid precursors. The government remains noncommittal, however, on the relative contribution of each country's emissions to the severity of acid precipitation in other countries, noting that further study is needed to develop a more quantitative understanding. Modeling exercises to date suggest that a substantial fraction of the acidity of precipitation in Japan and the Korean Peninsula is attributable to emissions from China. Research on acid aerosols found on mountains in Japan seems to confirm that some acid precipitation in that country originates in the East Asian continent. Privately, some Chinese researchers may say they believe that China contributes more to other countries' acid precipitation burdens than those other countries do to China's, but this does not represent an official position. Whatever damage China's emissions may cause in other countries, it is far less than the damage China does to its own southern central and southwestern regions, since most of China's emissions remain with the country's boundaries.

A crucial gap in understanding of regional acid precipitation is the lack of empirical research on transboundary transport. Since the second half of the 1980s, China has expended considerable effort to characterize weather and atmospheric transport patterns within its borders, but has not done similar work on the Northeast Asia region (which would have to be conducted in collaboration with other countries). Such research, along with more work on source analysis of acid precipitation in the countries of Northeast Asia, is needed to complement the extensive computer modelling of regional weather patterns and pollutant transport that has already been done. Officials at NEPA reportedly have discussed with Japanese counterparts the possibility of mounting a joint empirical study of regional pollutant transport, but the political sensitivity of the issue has prevented any action to date.

LEGISLATION TO CONTROL ACID PRECIPITATION

In August 1995, the National People's Congress (NPC) passed a new version of the Atmospheric Pollution Control Law (Daqi Wuran Fangzhi Fa), originally passed in 1987. Implementation regulations for the Law have already been drafted by an expert group appointed by the National Environmental Protection Agency. State commissions, line ministries, and local administrations are currently commenting on the regulations. The NPC is expected to approve and issue revised versions of the draft regulations in the first half of 1997.

Major provisions of the Law call for creating "acid rain control regions" and "sulfur dioxide control regions" in China. Power plants and other large coal users in these regions will be required to gradually adopt measures to reduce sulfur emissions. Coal mines are also covered; production of high-sulfur coal will be limited and construction of new coal-washing facilities will be encouraged. Other provisions require that a sulfur dioxide emissions permitting system be extended to cover all major coal users, and that emissions fees gradually be raised to a level above the cost of emissions control. In addition, NEPA is releasing new standards (in three classes) for power plant emissions rates, based on stack height.

Within the "acid rain control regions", regulations will be designed to address long-range transport of acid precursors, and will therefore focus on large end-use facilities like power plants, as well as coal mining and processing facilities. Standards will be set for sulfur content of coal used. Those facilities that use coal that exceeds the standard will be required to adopt flue-gas desulfurization and other measures to reduce emissions. New mines that produce high-sulfur coal will be required to invest simultaneously in coal-washing facilities, and existing mines will be required to build washeries within a limited time. Overall levels of production of high-sulfur coal will be limited in some districts, based on an overall evaluation of all emissions sources and coal characteristics. In the "sulfur dioxide control regions" the focus will be more on local transport of pollutants and on controlling impacts to human health. In these areas, measures to control sulfur emissions from household and restaurant stoves (e.g., coal briquettes with sulfur-fixing additives) and residential boilers will receive more attention.

Provincial and municipal governments will be allowed to set rules that are more stringent than the ones applied to their jurisdictions by national authorities. Guangdong, for instance, is implementing special rules for the Pearl River Delta area. Like the national regulations now being drawn up, Guangdong's rules require coal-fired power plants to adopt measures to reduce sulfur emissions, but the timetable for implementation is more rapid than the national rules are likely to require.

The boundaries of acid rain control regions will be set according to average acidity of precipitation. The threshold level is likely to be set at pH 4.5, although it may be as low as 4.0. A threshold level of pH 5.0 has been discussed, but is not likely to be adopted, in part because the area subject to precipitation with that average level of acidity is quite large and would strain already limited resources for implementation.

China has had an emissions fee system in place for many years, but air pollution fees were levied only on particulate emissions, and collection has been uneven. The new legislation calls for phasing in fees on other pollutants as well, beginning with sulfur dioxide. China has already implemented a sulfur dioxide emissions fee system on a trial basis since 1992. Major coal consumers in two provinces (Guizhou and Guangdong) and nine cities (Chongqing and Yibin in Sichuan; Nanning, Guilin and Liuzhou in Guangxi; Changsha in Hunan, Yichang in Hubei, Hangzhou in Zhejiang; and Qingdao in Shandong) were required to pay emissions fees of 150 to 200 yuan per ton of sulfur dioxide emitted. The new law requires that the emissions fee system be extended to the rest of the country, and that the fee be gradually raised to a level higher than the cost of emissions control. The regulations currently under consideration will lay out a timetable for phasing in the higher fees and means for enforcing collection.

The disposition of funds from emissions fees will also change under the new air pollution control law. Formerly, up to 80% of emissions fees were returned to the same enterprises from which they were collected, often in the form of direct subsidies. The new system will no longer guarantee that the fees revert to polluting enterprises. Instead, the money will be used to fund a credit facility that will provide loans to all enterprises for environmental protection projects. Those enterprises that "contribute" more to the fund will not necessarily be entitled to greater amounts of credit.

Aside from the recent legislative activity, NEPA has worked jointly with the Ministry of Electric Power (MOEP) to address sulfur dioxide emissions from power plants. MOEP is involved in desulfurization technology development and demonstration projects (including the foreign-funded projects mentioned below). The Ministry's plans for the Ninth Five-Year Plan call for flue-gas desulfurization equipment to be installed at power plants totaling 10 GW (out of a projected total of about 200 GW of fossil fuel-fired generating capacity) by 2000.15 Sulfur dioxide emissions from power plants alone would be near 11 Mt per year.

PARTICIPANTS IN CONTROLLING ACID PRECIPITATION IN CHINA

Setting and implementing policy for addressing acid precipitation involves first the bureaucratic apparatus for environmental protection. The State Council, the Chinese government's highest administrative body, is home to the Environmental Protection Leading Group, which sets the general direction for environmental policy and coordinates overall activities. NEPA is under the direct authority of the State Council (as are all other state agencies, ministries, and bureaus), and NEPA in turn has branches at each lower level of government, including provinces, cities, most counties, and some townships.

The NPC is the country's highest legislative body, and has responsibility for considering and passing environmental legislation. Until recently, the NPC largely signed off on legislation passed to it through the State Council, but has begun to take a more active role. The NPC has a National Committee on Environmental Protection (headed by former NEPA administrator Qu Geping), which has a brief to develop new laws and to formulate effective implementation mechanisms. In practice, the NPC does not have the wherewithal to formulate environmental policies, and typically provides guidance to NEPA for drafting policies and rules.

Like most organs of the central government, NEPA has a relatively small staff given its responsibilities, and it usually creates an expert committee, with many members drawn from research and academic organizations, to draft legislation. The scientific basis for NEPA's policy recommendations generally comes from work (including joint international projects) done by NEPA, its research arm, the Chinese Research Academy of Environmental Sciences, the Chinese Academy of Sciences, and the China Energy Research Society. Research projects directly related to policy also involve staff of state commissions and line ministries.

Since environmental policy touches on so many spheres of activity, policy formulation and implementation is coordinated with other parts of government. Those national organs with economic and financial responsibilities-the State Planning Commission (SPC), the State Economic and Trade Commission (SETC), the Ministry of Finance, and the major banks-have input into the process. If, as is often the case, policies and rules involve requirements for developing new technologies, the State Science and Technology Commission will become involved. Particularly for environmental issues that arise primarily from energy use, such a acid precipitation, ministries and state corporations in the energy sector will be involved. They include especially the Ministry of Electric Power and the Ministry of Coal, and in some cases the China National Petroleum Corporation and regional coal and electricity authorities. For legislation affecting major energy-using sectors (e.g., the metallurgical, building materials, and machine-building industries) the relevant line ministries will have a say as well. Should policy involve agreements with other countries or multilateral organizations, the Ministry of Foreign Affairs will play a part, and participation by the state commissions will be stronger.

Most of the actors just mentioned are relatively more powerful than NEPA and can therefore have considerable influence on the content and strength of environmental regulations as they are written and implemented. They can be expected to work hard to protect their respective spheres of influence from perceived intrusion by environmental regulators.

The SPC and the SETC have responsibility for coordinating activities in different sectors, try to integrate environmental goals with other crucial objectives, such as overall economic growth and poverty alleviation. Those organs responsible for energy and industrial sectors often resist new and more stringent environmental control requirements as an undue burden on sectoral economic performance.

Just as important as the national actors, in many ways, are the local actors, particularly in view of the continuing process of decentralizing authority that has been a key feature of economic system reforms.

Provincial and some municipal administrations, whose top priority is typically local economic development, have direct input into drafting of environmental legislation, and have primary responsibility for carrying out monitoring and regulation. They also have considerable influence on how monitoring and regulatory activities are carried out.

Local environmental protection bureaus have difficulty functioning as regulators because, in addition to their responsibility to the national environmental protection system, they are also subject to the authority of local administrations, which allocate their funding. There is considerable variation among localities, with some vigorously pursuing environmental protection objectives.

In some areas, there is a virtual vacuum in implementation, with only one or two part-time staff in country environmental protection offices, and sometimes no staff whatsoever. On the other hand, local administrations that are supportive of environmental protection efforts can be crucial to the success of regulatory actions. Zhangjiagang in southern Jiangsu, for instance, is an extremely clean city by Chinese standards, mainly due to the support of the mayor, who has taken Singapore as a model.

REGIONAL AND INTERNATIONAL COOPERATION TO CONTROL ACID PRECIPITATION

Terms Of Engagement

The Chinese government currently views the problem of transboundary acid precipitation as a subject for scientific research rather than for a binding international agreement. While willing to admit that the problem exists, and that acid precursors move between countries, China remains unwilling to discuss relative contributions, let alone targets and methods for emissions controls.

On the other hand, China is very willing to engage in many of the kinds of aid and trade activities that would be adopted under almost any regional agreement to control acid precipitation-so long as the rationale for such activities does not include statements about responsibility for transboundary pollutants and targets for control. For instance, China's Agenda 21 Office actively seeks foreign participation in projects oriented towards sustainable development, but does not tie the projects to any specific commitments to meet targets that would measure progress towards sustainability. China has been very responsive to Japan's Green Aid Program, which has included demonstration and design of utility and industrial boiler desulfurization equipment and transfer of energy-efficient equipment. Sino-Japanese desulfurization projects announced to date. Some Japanese-funded research projects conducted by Chinese organizations have been aimed (both directly and indirectly) at characterizing the markets in China for Japan's clean-coal and energy-efficient technologies. These have been characterized as aid and trade promotion programs with multiple benefits for all parties, including unquantified contributions to controlling emissions of acid precursors and greenhouse gases.

The only other countries with flue-gas desulfurization demonstration projects in China are Germany and Finland. China's State Council recently approved a project, partially funded by a $300 million loan from Germany, to install desulfurization units on two 200 MW generating units in Chongqing. The terms of the project will allow the power plant to charge a higher rate for its electricity to cover operating costs and depreciation of the scrubbers. Since the region is short of generating capacity, customers are willing to absorb the increased cost of electricity. Lack of similar provisions have hampered operation at the Japanese-funded demonstration plant in Chonqing; that plant reportedly runs its desulfurization equipment only during the day in order to reduce its high operating costs.

In general, China is very interested in technical cooperation projects aimed at adapting flue-gas desulfurization technologies. In particular, researchers and officials feel that Japanese and American wet lime injection technologies are well-suited to Chinese conditions, and would like to find ways to develop cheaper, perhaps marginally less effective, and smaller-scale versions of Japanese and American equipment. Technical cooperation of this sort with no more than vague mention of its relevance to regional acid precipitation would be ideal, from China's point of view.

As with any other area that touches on development, China is very keen to attract foreign financial support for environmental protection. China simply does not currently have the capital to finance its own, very rapid growth, nor the production capacity. Approximately one-third of the investment funds for power projects in China, for instance, already comes from overseas, and by 1998 China will probably have exceeded the capacity of its equipment manufacturers to fill orders for utility boilers and generating sets. China would probably be very receptive to finding ways to tie funding for sulfur emissions controls to funding for power projects.

China has also shown a good deal of willingness to conduct joint research projects (except in certain sensitive areas, as noted above). The participation of Chinese government organs and research organizations in numerous bilateral and multilateral studies of greenhouse gas emissions sources and mitigation strategies provides ample evidence. Chinese researchers have been involved in studies of Asia's regional acid rain problems (both in multinational studies like the RAINS-ASIA modelling study and in internally financed and conducted studies) since the early 1980s. Most of the joint research projects have been done in collaboration with Japanese and South Korean researchers. China very likely would view expanded joint research efforts as a prerequisite to any official discussions on a framework for controlling transboundary air pollution.

Regional Vs. Subregional (Bilateral) Fora

Chinese researchers and officials recognize that there are a number of important transboundary environmental problems, including acid precipitation, that would be best solved through joint regional approaches. China already participates in some regional fora that address environmental problems in Northeast Asia, setting a precedent for possible future participation in a regional organization to address acid precipitation. China would probably prefer to deal with acid rain through an existing regional forum, like APEC, rather than through a newly created organization.

On the other hand, China has given some signals that it prefers to deal with regional issues on a bilateral basis. In the dispute over the Spratley and Paracel Islands in the South China Sea, for instance, China has preferred to deal directly with the parties to the dispute in bilateral talks rather than through a multilateral forum like the Association of Southeast Asian Nations (ASEAN). Bilateral negotiations give the parties much greater control over the process of negotiation, and agreements, once reached, can be used a precedents when dealing with other parties regarding similar issues.

Convention To Control Transboundary Pollution

China is far from ready to consider an international agreement on limiting transboundary pollution, but there are some positions that China would likely take. Since coal will continue to dominate the primary energy consumption mix for many decades, and since coal consumption will likely continue to grow by several percent annually (even if the energy consumption elasticity of economic growth remains under 0.5, as it has for years), China's sulfur dioxide and other coal-related pollutant emissions sources will keep growing. So long as control of emissions remains expensive, China will likely maintain that, given its relative poverty, sulfur dioxide emissions controls can only be phased in slowly, and that absolute levels of acid precursor emissions will rise. China may be willing to discuss limits to the rate of growth of total sulfur dioxide emissions, but talks about reducing total emissions would be unlikely in the near future. China may be willing to consider limits to or reductions in per capita sulfur dioxide emissions, particularly if such limits allowed total emissions to grow.

Many of the issues that would be dealt with in a transboundary pollution control agreement (and many of the mitigation measures) would be similar to those contained in a regime for limiting greenhouse gas emissions, but China would probably find the latter easier to agree to. One reason is that acid rain is already viewed as a serious domestic problem, and substantial resources are being devoted to its mitigation. Concern about global climate change is far weaker. Another reason is that, compared to carbon dioxide, sulfur dioxide is somewhat easier to deal with: available technologies can reduce sulfur content at any stage of fuel extraction and use, while this is simply not possible for carbon (except through switching to non-carbon-based energy sources and measures that raise energy efficiency). Limiting sulfur dioxide emissions could be very expensive indeed and possibly affect economic growth, but hard limits to greenhouse gas emissions could deprive China of its cheapest form of energy and severely hamper the rapid economic growth China so strongly desires.

For the time being, China is likely to reject any calls to begin drawing up a framework for joint action on transboundary pollution in Northeast Asia. It's willingness to cooperate on joint research efforts and on technology transfer and development projects in support of domestic efforts to mitigate acid precipitation, however, indicate that China could be slowly drawn into such a process.

NATIONAL IDENTITIES, HISTORICAL MEMORIES, AND RECONCILIATION IN NORTHEAST ASIA

No one can dispute that nationalism is a key factor in provoking tensions between Japan and Korea; however, this is such a broad concept that one must consider specifically what triggers "nationalist" sentiments in both Japan and Korea. Here I focus on the role of historical memory in shaping national identity, which, in turn, affects regional relations. Questions about history touch on the most sensitive issues of national identity, including the national myths that play a powerful role to this day. Whether it be Japanese atrocities in Korea and China or the US decision to drop atomic bombs on Japan, no nation is immune to the charge that it has formed a less-than-complete view of the past. All share a reluctance to fully confront the complexity of their past actions and blame others for their historical fate. Divided historical memories or a gap in identities separates nations, resulting in distinct, often contradictory, perceptions deeply embedded in the public consciousness transmitted to succeeding generations formally by education and informally through the arts, popular culture, and mass media. They can become central to a population's sense of its shared identity, superseding all other identity themes.

Why have these nations developed different, distinct, and incomplete historical memories? One common answer would be that Japan is an aggressor and Korea/China is a victim. While this is historically true, a closer examination reveals that the aggressor-victim dichotomy is too simple to explain the complexities of modern history and collective memory in Northeast Asia. Historical memories and reconciliation are rooted not only in colonial and Pacific war injustices but also in much deeper and more complex historical, cultural, and political relations. We need to understand the crucial imbalance in each country's formation of historical memory that leads to the gap in national identities. Certain past experiences symbolize how the identities of two nations differ, shaping how other eras in bilateral history are viewed and how cultural or political divisions are seen.

Different factors figure in the formation of historical memory in each of the involved countries in the region. For example, for China and Korea, Japanese acts of aggression—such as the Nanjing massacre or forced labor and sexual slavery—constitute the most crucial element in their wartime memories, while for Japan, memories related to US actions, such as the fire-bombings of Japanese cities or the nuclear attacks on Hiroshima and Nagasaki, are the most crucial in their memories of the war. This imbalance in focus is also noticeable in each country's history textbooks. In Japanese ones, only 4 percent of the coverage of Japan's modern history (1868-1945) is devoted to Korea, while the United States is the main player. In contrast, in Korean ones, Japan occupies a quarter of the coverage of its modern history. Korea and China are a less significant element in Japan's wartime memories, while Japan figures most prominently in their memories.

This imbalance in focus helps to explain the formation of historical memory in each nation. Japanese focus on US actions in war memory both reflects and explains Japan's victim identity and reluctance to fully engage Asian neighbors regarding colonialism and issues of wartime aggression. Unlike Germany, postwar Japan developed a mythology of victimhood in which many innocent civilians were sacrificed as a result of the massive and destructive atomic and fire bombings of its cities. Many Japanese charge that the United States did not address its own "crimes against humanity." Memory based on victimhood then pardoned the Japanese of their guilt, fostered an already ubiquitous sense of self-pity, and impeded the search for historical truth. Victim consciousness provided fertile soil for the growth of postwar neo-nationalism that denied Japan's responsibility for wartime atrocities. This imbalance in historical memory formation produces misperceptions and misgivings among the parties, hindering reconciliation.

Historical disputes did not emerge as a key foreign policy issue until the 1980s. During the Cold War years, they were put aside, as in the normalization of relations between Japan and South Korea in 1965 and between China and Japan in 1972. Japanese wartime atrocities and compensation were not to be raised, as governments focused on economic development, which was heavily dependent on Japanese capital and investments. The need to appease Japanese sensibilities (and US interests) meant that it was considered unwise or impractical to recall the horrors of the war or the colonial period in official discourse. The history question began to surface in response to the 1982 controversy, in which Japanese authorities attempted to distort the connotations of some words in its sixteen types of history textbooks, e.g., removing the term "invasion" and replacing it with "advance," or replacing "exploitation" with "transfer." Up to this point, textbooks were almost purely a domestic issue, mainly within Japan. Yet with the emergence of civil society in the 1980s, issues of historical injustice were no longer monopolized or controlled by governments. Following South Korea's democratization and the "comfort women" issue's resurfacing as part of a "transnational memory with social, legal, and moral consequences that transcend national or cultural borders," the emergence of a new "community of memory" in Korea recast the war in international rather than purely domestic terms. These changes in domestic and international environments brought the history question to the forefront of Northeast Asian relations as the Cold War ended.

National identity is not necessarily obsessed with the past. In the past decade there were times when attention focused on other dimensions, such as the East Asian community and shared universal values. Even if the United States is inclined to set the past aside, East Asian states are not, and they bring previous US behavior into their identity concerns. In this chapter the identity gaps between Japan and China and Korea, respectively, are linked to identity gaps with the United States, as we consider ways to narrow the sharp divides. A framework of interconnected identity gaps is proposed, leading to suggestions to deal simultaneously with multiple gaps as a way to overcome barriers to narrowing each one.

The Complexity of the History Question

The growing complexity of the situation in Northeast Asia does not bode well for the future. First, tensions over history and historically rooted claims to territories are not occurring simply among adversaries. Conflict exists also between two key allies of the United States, Japan and South Korea, taking a turn for the worse in recent years, making the United States increasingly concerned and frustrated: "This has now emerged as the biggest strategic challenge to American interests in Asia," said Kurt Campbell, who served as assistant secretary of state for East Asian and Pacific affairs during President Obama's first term. Daniel R. Russel, Campbell's successor, has also voiced his concern that "the headwind created by these tensions over history raises the political cost of Japan-Korea cooperation that should be a given."

Some experts approach the history question from a realist perspective. Victor Cha, for instance, poses what he calls the *quasi-alliance paradox*—that the two unallied states will better align and cooperate when there exist concerns of abandonment and entrapment by a common third-party ally, that is, the United States—and argues for a gradual and calculated disengagement from the region by the United States. However, this approach cannot adequately explain the Japanese-Korean antagonism because the United States is not just a common great-power protector, but an integral part of the problem itself.

Second, tensions over the past have not improved with the passage of time. Those who did not experience war years are seemingly more critical of the history issues than those who did. According to a 2013 survey of Koreans, 42.8 percent of respondents in their twenties—who have no firsthand experience of Japan's past wrongdoings and perhaps are more familiar with Japanese cultural influence—identified the question of history as the most critical issue to be resolved, while only 34.6 percent of those in their sixties who lived through the period in question viewed it as the most pressing problem in relations. This points to the importance of political leadership and education, official and unofficial (such as media or cultural and educational exchanges). Not only are identity gaps best addressed at many levels, they lend themselves to an inclusive identity approach with multiple "significant others" entering the picture in search of a comprehensive strategy.

"The Asian paradox" clearly attests to the power of historical memories and national identity in shaping regional relations in Northeast Asia. Realist scholars argue that Japan and other governments are behaving "rationally" to maximize their current interests through manipulation of public sentiment over the history issues. Alexis Dudden counters that this line of reasoning treats history as occurrences in "homogenous empty time," where past events are measured as equal to events occurring in the present; from the past, moments, heroes, and villains are selectively chosen for the present. She contends that this overlooks history—as if it were yet another factor of the present, like a trade imbalance or background music—and limits our understanding of why the historical problem weighs so heavily on Japanese-Korean relations, among others in the region.

LIMITS OF PAST EFFORTS AT RECONCILIATION

Divided historical memories have hindered efforts at reconciliation, even as there has been widespread recognition of the need for final resolution of historical injustices. In fact, all involved countries have, to a certain extent, sought to achieve this goal through various means—apology politics, litigation, joint history writing, and regional exchanges, etc.

Apology

Apology diplomacy has been a major tactic in the reconciliation process. Since 1984, Japanese heads of state or government have issued a number of direct apologies to China and Korea. Until the 1990s, the key terms used were "regret" or "remorse," which did not necessarily signify an apology, a term that first appeared in 1992, when Miyazawa Kiichi meeting with Roh Tae-woo, stated, "I, as prime minister, would like to once again express heartfelt remorse and offer an apology to the people of your nation." Despite Japan's repeated use of the term "apology" from that point on, its neighbors have continued to respond with skepticism. As Caroline Rose points out, Japan's various efforts to "apologize" have not been backed up by actions to "reinforce the apologies"; instead, they are often coupled with ambiguous wording and counterproductive statements and behavior on the part of the government. In fact, throughout the 1990s, Japanese political elites vacillated between formal apologies and frequent statements glorifying their colonial rule. Repeated statements by right-wing officials, such as Abe, denying war crimes—"there is no evidence that comfort women were coerced through violence or coercion by military or government authorities"—aroused severe criticism.

Along with Abe's attempt to revisit the Kono Statement and his recent visit to the Yasukuni Shrine, the outpouring of ultra-nationalist Japanese books, films, and magazines raising doubts about the veracity of their past aggression has led neighbors to question the sincerity of the Japanese apology. People in Korea and China have gradually realized that the formal ritual of apology is but one element in the politics of remembrance with questionable utility as a means of furthering historical reconciliation. According to Dudden, politics surrounding state-issued apologies have largely negated the putative intent of apologizing and, if anything, have set Japan back in terms of actually reconciling with its neighbors. She sees "apology failure" (apologizing for the past as a means to capitalize on it in the future)—not failure to apologize—and asserts that the general effect has only "perpetuated a disastrous policy failure." Decades of this have created a deadlock in the East Asian reconciliation process that will not be broken until Japan addresses its "identity mythmaking."

Joint History Writing

As history education plays such a powerful role in the formation of collective memory and national identity, collaborative history writing has been another approach toward narrowing the gap in views. The frequent clashes over history textbooks in Northeast Asia—in 1982, 2002, 2005, and 2011, for instance—demonstrate that history is not simply about the past. Government oversight makes textbooks a natural and legitimate subject for debate and it is no coincidence that textbooks have become a nexus for tension in the region. One approach has been to form official and unofficial committees to produce jointly written accounts of history.

The first official attempt to deal jointly with history textbooks occurred in Oct. 2001 when Koizumi and Kim Dae-jung established the Japan-ROK Joint History Research Committee, a state-sponsored effort toward placing a reconciled view of the past in a new regional history framework. The committee, while not entirely a failure, has yet to attain the success envisioned. Although it adopted the UNESCO model of writing a "parallel history" in

May 2005, the two sides failed to come to a consensus on what should be incorporated into the textbooks, disagreeing over how to interpret Japan's colonial rule, including its role (or lack thereof) in Korea's modernization. Following Koizumi's visits to the Yasukuni Shrine, the work of the joint committee was put on hold until October 2006 when Abe and Roh Moo-hyun re-launched its efforts. In April 2007 a new subgroup—in addition to existing groups studying ancient, medieval, and contemporary history—formed to study history textbooks to try to narrow differences between the textbooks of the two nations. Another report was released in 2010 but still failed to reach a consensus on Japan's 1910-1945 colonial rule, notably on recruitment of Korean laborers and comfort women as well as on drafting Koreans into the Japanese military.

Japan and China launched a similar effort as part of the thaw that followed the leadership transition from Koizumi to Abe. Modeled after the Japan-ROK format, the Joint History Research Committee of twenty leading historians from both countries aimed to write parallel histories. They agreed to conduct a joint study and produce an account of 2,000 years of Sino-Japanese interaction by 2008. Not surprisingly, the Japanese wanted to focus on the postwar era, while the Chinese were more interested in taking inventory of the colonial and wartime periods. Each side was to separately write its own version of bilateral history texts and exchange written comments on controversial issues. They agreed on a list of major historical events to be discussed, including the Nanjing massacre and Japan's Twenty-One Demands. The final report was made public in January 2010, after one and half years' delay, only to show that the two sides could not resolve differences on controversial modern events including the 1937 Nanjing massacre.

Writing a shared history has offered important lessons for the nations involved. It seems impossible to arrive at a common rendition of events, particularly regarding the most controversial aspects of history. A shared regional history is not feasible politically. Northeast Asian governments have considerable influence in textbook production, and these books have become a nexus of significant tension in the region. The experience of the past two decades underlines how profoundly historical writing—especially the writing of history texts—is affected by nationalist politics.

THE US ROLE

Even when the governments of Japan, China, and South Korea have tried to stop being held hostage to history, public perceptions have not always followed. This tension is increasingly unfavorable to US strategic interests. According to a May 2013 report by the Congressional Research Service, "Comments and actions on controversial historical issues by Prime Minister Abe and his Cabinet have raised concern that Tokyo could upset regional relations in ways that hurt U.S. interests." There has been ongoing debate in US academic and policymaking circles about the role that the United States might play in helping to resolve historical disputes and achieve reconciliation. A predominant view is that this is primarily a matter for Asians and better left to historians. Many fear that the United States could be forced to choose between its key allies in the region, The State Department has consistently taken the position that the San Francisco Treaty protected Japan from demands for compensation from victim nations.

An emerging view contends that the United States can hardly afford to stand outside these disputes, particularly as it was a key player in their formation. Referring to the recent dispute over the naming of Dokdo/Takeshima, Dudden aptly points out that it has "brought us back to 1952, when America's occupation of Japan ended, and the United States determined who owned what in East Asia and the Pacific." She asserts, "Washington must not overlook its place in the problem now." Gilbert Rozman argues that US efforts need to be directed more toward narrowing the historical divide in East Asia, while acting as the impetus for increased mutual understanding. He writes that "benign neglect of Japanese nationalism threatens to unravel the spirit of reconciliation in East Asia." Daniel Sneider contends that the United States must "abandon its position of neutrality on wartime history issues, as it is not really a neutral party, and step forward," and play the same central role it played during the Clinton administration in the complex negotiations with governments and citizen groups that led to the formation of the German Fund for the Future—a joint project of the German government and the German private corporations that used forced labor during World War II to compensate survivors in almost one hundred countries.

As the history conflict has become an increasingly vexing problem, the United States has tried various ways "to create the conditions where both sides can find a solution to this." However, any attempt, as a "neutral" player, to broker a deal between Japan and South Korea will prove to be insufficient, It can hardly afford to act as a mere bystander; it was the US-led Tokyo War Crimes Tribunal and the San Francisco Peace Treaty that largely failed—albeit not always intentionally—to address the sufferings and grievances of Asian victims of Japanese aggression.

Unlike the Nuremberg court, only three of eleven judges at the Tokyo trial represented Asian countries, and there was no representative from Korea. The US-led tribunal failed to appreciate the massive suffering of Chinese and Koreans at the hands of Japanese invaders and colonizers and the need to dry up the deep well of anger left behind. Instead, the tribunal focused on the Japanese actions that had most directly affected the Western allies—the surprise attack on Pearl Harbor and the mistreatment of Allied prisoners of war. The failure to address the issue of Emperor Hirohito's war responsibility greatly shaped the ways in which the Japanese would remember the war years and later approach reconciliation issues with their Asian neighbors. Encouraged by the American decision, the Japanese elite promoted a myth of the Emperor's innocence that only strengthened Japanese victim consciousness and impeded the search for historical truth. A report noted "the absolution of the Emperor left the country without anyone to blame" and "provided fertile soil for the growth of a postwar neo-nationalism." Acknowledging that it paid scant attention to Asian issues during the Tokyo Tribunal, the United States could set a new tone for recognizing the linkages in historical memories.

As Japan's importance as a bulwark against communism increased in the Cold War, the United States sought to quickly put aside issues of historical responsibility. It did not press Japan to reconcile with its neighbors as it had Germany. The San Francisco Peace Treaty of 1951 formally ended the war, settling Japan's obligations to pay reparations for its wartime acts. But neither China nor Korea was a signatory, and Japan's responsibility toward those nations was left unresolved. Drafted at the height of the Cold War, it denied countries legal means to obtain redress. In 1965, under heavy pressure from a United States anxious to solidify its Cold War security alliance system, the ROK agreed to normalize relations with Japan despite strong domestic protests. Issues such as disputed territories and Japan's colonial rule were again overlooked. Unlike the push for Franco-German reconciliation to establish a multilateral security system in Western Europe, in Northeast Asia the United States established a bilateral "hub and spoke" alliance system with Japan and the ROK and did not press for historical reconciliation between the two US allies. "Normalization" occurred at the governmental level but without addressing popular demands for redressing historical injustices. As one former US senior diplomat points out, "for American policymakers, strategic considerations have consistently trumped issues of equity in historic disputes involving Japan since Word War II."

Looking back, the US approach made sense from a geopolitical perspective, but not in terms of historical reconciliation. It played a crucial role in the rise of Northeast Asia as a powerhouse but sowed the seeds for current tensions over the past. This gave Japan the leeway to escape the responsibilities and penalties of a war that left unhealed scars in China and Korea, while also deliberately leaving the status of Dokdo/Takeshima in a gray area. Taking a self-critical approach by acknowledging, if not necessarily apologizing for, the mishandlings of history issues in Northeast Asia, will endow it with moral power to facilitate a larger process of historical reconciliation in the region as a responsible stakeholder. Focusing national identity on linkages between historical memory gaps in three pairs of states and universal values, which can be reinforced in all of the states, the United States can play a leadership role that transforms the way recent disputes over symbols of history are seen.

Looking Forward

Despite significantly increased regional interactions, the importance of the past has not diminished. On the contrary, it has become even more contentious as nations vie for regional leadership, and there exists an urgent need to find a Northeast Asian strategy of reconciliation. Sustainable reconciliation is inherently a complex process that involves a multitude of actors from the state, civil society, and international organizations. The United States can play a facilitating role. In the Cold War era it put priority on geopolitical concerns over historical reconciliation, but it is becoming increasingly difficult to pursue this strategy. As recent tensions between its two allies show, the history question may no longer be separated from the security question.

Efforts to bridge gaps in understanding history and forge a balanced perception should be underpinned not only by relevant governments but more importantly by civil society. Joint efforts such as group discussions by young people from China, Japan, and Korea, as well as joint study of past issues and visits to such historic sites as the Nanjing Massacre Memorial Hall, Hiroshima Peace Memorial Park, and Seodaemun Prison History Museum in Seoul would prove valuable to developing comparative and ultimately more comprehensive views of the region's history. Such gatherings would be a region-wide attempt to share and heal pains of the past. By bringing history more to the forefront, they would, arguably, serve to reduce its relevance in national identity and bilateral relations.

Deng Xiaoping said, "It does not matter if this question is shelved for some time, say, ten years. Our generation is not wise enough to find common language on this question. Our next generation will certainly be wiser. They will certainly find a solution acceptable to all." Contrary to his expectations, Northeast Asian nations find themselves in a worsening situation involving history and territorial disputes, and their history education tends to be more nationalistic. Today's youth, armed with universal values that underscore democracy, human rights, and peace, have a foundation capable of reducing the gap in national identities. Overcoming the history gap with Japan by placing the past in the context of universal rights, as championed by the United States, would be a force for refocusing each country's identity and promoting regional reconciliation. Three identity gaps placed in this context through an active US role can be addressed together.

RECONCILING JAPAN AND CHINA: A FRAMEWORK FOR TRANSFORMING SINO-JAPANESE CONFLICT

China-Japan relations constitute a long-running, dangerous, and seemingly intractable conflict. The relations are not immune to positive change, but they are constantly vulnerable to backtracking and intensification of rivalry. Both kinds of changes have occurred since normalization of relations in the early 1970s. The issues in dispute are well known and are therefore not the primary subject of this chapter. Instead, the aim here is to explore areas of potential cooperation that may ease tension and eventually lead to reconciliation.

This aim, almost needless to say, is more easily written about than accomplished in fact. Intractable conflicts by their nature acquire a life of their own; the longer they go on, the more vested in conflict do the parties become. In the case of China and Japan, moreover, history envenoms the relationship to an extraordinary degree, infecting both high-level dialogue and public opinion. Official rhetoric about the importance of Sino-Japanese peace and cooperation notwithstanding, in the public arena it is rare to find groups or individuals speaking out on behalf of reconciliation, even when (as in the case of business leaders, for instance) they benefit from it.

In fact, influential people in both countries have been attacked for advocating reconciliation. Governments always devote more resources to conflict than to conflict resolution.

Because China-Japan conflict operates at so many levels—it is at once structural, societal, psychological, and of course political—any effort to move it toward reconciliation needs to look at both *policies* and *processes*. Moreover, we should be audacious in thinking of reconciliation as involving something more than "simple coexistence." As David Crocker has written with respect to warring parties, reconciliation is a healing process:

In the most minimal account... reconciliation is nothing more than "simple coexistence" in the sense that former enemies comply with the law instead of killing each other. Although this *modus vivendi* is certainly better than violent conflict, transitional societies... should aim for more... Among other things, this implies a willingness to hear each other out, to enter into give-and-take about matters of public policy, to build on areas of common concern, and to forge principled compromises with which all can live. The process, so conceived, may help to prevent a society from lapsing back into violence as a way to resolve conflict.

Yet, if *transformation* of the parties is the ultimate goal of reconciliation, there is a long road to travel when it comes to China and Japan.

This chapter contends that to travel that road, the appropriate starting point is not continuing debate over grievances but practical steps that serve common interests. There is a school of thought that argues that until Japan fully acknowledges its past transgressions against China and, like post-war Germany, makes apologies and amends, no progress is possible.

But such an approach may add to the problem of conflict resolution. Dealing with the proximate causes of conflict is often more productive than attempting to resolve past grievances. As we have seen many times in the China-Japan case, whenever Japanese politicians reopen the wounds of war, they invite a Chinese response, thus feeding competitive nationalisms and pushing the history issue to center stage—precisely where it should not be. History is better off being shelved until such time as a sense of true partnership emerges—that is, when concerted cooperation occurs over a lengthy period. Only then, when mutual trust is implicit because of habitual dialogue and policies that serve common interests, is reconciliation possible and apologizing politically feasible.

For reconciliation to happen, the tools of both political science and conflict resolution need to be used. Most analysts favour one or more of the three now-standard approaches in political science:

- *Liberalism*: the role of multilateral regimes and commercial ties in promoting irreversible interdependence;

- *Realism*: the impact of power differentials and power transitions on policy making;
- *Constructivism*: addressing issues pertaining to cultural and psychological differences, and the politics of identity (nationalism in particular).

Analyses grounded in political science, however, are insufficient when it comes to reconciling states and societies in conflict. For one thing, they have a strong tendency to fish for trouble: They mainly seek to identify the causes and consequences of conflict rather than focus on preventing, managing, and resolving conflict. For another, they are in sharp disagreement with one another on basic premises. Realist analysis typically sees China-Japan rivalry as an enduring feature of the East Asian strategic landscape, and discounts economic engagement as likely contributing to China's military as well as economic superiority. Constructivists often point to nationalism and history as being able to overwhelm any common ground Chinese and Japanese diplomats may find. The Liberals' response—that strong business ties, coupled with China's deepening involvement in Asian multilateral groups, will diminish rivalry and promote further cooperation with Japan—is appealing but not easily testable. On one hand, business ties have grown in spite of disputes over history and territory; but on the other, those disputes have persisted. Moreover, strong economic relations sometimes create new disagreements of their own, such as over technology transfers, trade imbalances, and development assistance.

If scholars are to contribute to China-Japan reconciliation, as I believe they should, they will need to dig deeper into the tool box and exploit the conflict-resolution literature. Three areas seem particularly pertinent:

- *Dialogue*: focus on the legitimacy of the parties, the diversity of formats for discussions, and the process of "getting to yes";
- *Engagement*: techniques, such as use of positive incentives, for bringing parties to the table or otherwise making contact;
- *Confidence building*: the use of preventive diplomacy and transparency to build trust.

The vantage point of conflict resolution is its focus on establishing greater trust, widening common ground, and managing differences between disputants. Rivalry is not treated as unalterable, nor is one side to a dispute assumed (for purposes of a settlement) to bear greater responsibility than the other. Approaches to resolving conflicts and reconciliation must take place at several different levels, from the personal to the regional and global. Of central importance, and often neglected, is the domestic political element. In the case of China and Japan, the roles of powerful bureaucracies, parties, and political leaders, as well as of public opinion and civil society, must weigh in any usable approach to conflict management. Of cardinal importance, as stressed below, is the widespread understanding that each leadership and society must come to about the virtues of their mutual dependence, as a source of common prosperity and as a restraint on nationalistic outbursts.

PROBLEMS OF SINO-JAPANESE CONFLICT MANAGEMENT

The contribution and piece together a menu that might be seized upon by Chinese and Japanese at various levels to design a new relationship with each other. These ideas are essentially building blocks, in which synergy and consistency rather than a carefully calibrated strategy is the key. The essential argument is that peaceful, cooperative relations are in China's and Japan's (not to mention the United States' and everyone else's) best interest, and that there is a high and increasing price to be paid for indifference to the consequences of ongoing rivalry—among which is a new cold war in Asia.

Managing Sino-Japanese differences presents a number of special problems, however. One is that neither Beijing nor Tokyo seeks an honest broker who might mediate the conflict. Another is the lack of self-criticism in each society, hence also the seeming inability of each to establish a new domestic consensus regarding the other party. Third is that neither of the multilateral forums to which Japan and China belong—Asia-Pacific Economic Cooperation (APEC) and the various offshoots of the Association of Southeast Asian Nations (ASEAN)—has the capacity or the authority to act preventively or as conciliator in the dispute. Nor does Northeast Asia, unlike Southeast Asia, have a security dialogue mechanism that the two countries might use to discuss their disputes.

Fourth is the asymmetry of Japanese and Chinese power. While much is made these days of the fact that the two countries, for the first time in their modern history, are simultaneously strong, their strengths lie in different areas. Fifth, is the consistent inconsistency of China-Japan dialogue. It seems that every positive step is quickly undermined by a negative one—sometimes deliberately, one suspects. One recent example is when Koizumi expressed "deep remorse" to Hu Jintao in April 2005 for Japan's aggression in China. Hu accepted; but once Koizumi announced in Japan that he would visit the Yasukuni Shrine, all the goodwill dissipated. A second such instance occurred following Chinese defense minister Cao Gangchuan's visit to Japan in August 2007. It was the first such military exchange in nearly ten years, and it may lead to the setting up of a hotline. Thereafter, China's foreign ministry informed the UN secretary general that it would resume reporting of arms exports and imports after a decade-long break, and would give a breakdown of its military budget. But these two steps were undermined when Japan's navy joined U.S., Indian, and Australian ships in war games, part of a major security initiative under Abe to become a strategic partner with Australia and other states with "democratic values."

One other formidable obstacle in the path of China-Japan reconciliation is the United States. Positive U.S.-China relations are central to the resolution of most of East Asia's security issues. But while the United States and China have found common ground lately in a number of policy arenas, such as terrorism and nuclear nonproliferation, Japan and China have not. In the eyes of many Chinese specialists, U.S. partiality to Japan is a major reason why. Their argument is that Japan's deployments in the Middle East, its enhanced military firepower, its interest in constitutional revision, its strategic partnership with Australia, and its revival of national spirit have all come at the behest of the United States and thus have the appearance of balance-of-power politics directed at China. Yet, as one Chinese specialist on Japan has admitted, Beijing must choose between the lesser of two evils:

> The Chinese academic community is somewhat conflicted about the future of the U.S.-Japanese alliance. On one hand, although it does not expect the alliance to become stronger, an invigorated U.S.-Japanese alliance may join hands against China. On the other hand, a looser U.S.-Japanese alliance may lead to its ultimate collapse, leaving a Tokyo unbound by Washington. It remains uncertain whether an independent Japan would employ a friendly China policy. The direction and future of the alliance, however, is ultimately up to Washington and Tokyo.

The Costs of Avoidance

A serious potential consequence of the continuing rift is that a new cold war will break out in East Asia. The longer the rift simmers, the more likely it is that the so-called security dilemma will come to pass. While Japan has extended its security ties, Beijing is busy cultivating its own alignments: the Shanghai Cooperation Organization, ASEAN+3, and Russia. As China's military modernization proceeds and issues of transparency go unresolved—the 17.8 percent boost in military spending announced in 2007 represented the seventeenth year in the last eighteen in which a spending increase reached double digits; and China's ASAT test in January 2007 may have revealed the secretiveness of the military even within China's own bureaucratic ranks—Japanese leaders will justify countermeasures, such as increases in military spending and force acquisitions, and revision of Article 9 of the constitution.

Accenting the Positive

Up until now, the official bilateral level has been the locus of most discussions of problem areas in China-Japan relations. There is a positive side to this reality, however. First, Japanese and Chinese leaders have embraced East Asian regionalism, at least in terms of deepening economic integration and joint consultations (mainly in ASEAN+3); and they along with all the other key actors in Northeast Asia have also accepted the idea of creating a regional dialogue mechanism for dispute resolution. Second, as discussed further below, Prime Minister Abe Shinzo's trip to China and South Korea soon after succeeding Koizumi Junichiro in October 2006, and the reassurances to China of his successor, Fukuda Yasuo, may open the door to further and more concrete dialogue. Third, the high and growing degree of economic interdependence between Japan and China—in trade, direct investment, and official development assistance (ODA)—remains the crucial asset for preventing open conflict.

Viewed from the perspective of conflict management, moreover, another source of optimism is that the same issues that divide the two countries and peoples may be turned into arenas of cooperation.

Why do Chinese and Japanese leaders eye each other so warily? The reasons are easy enough to list: geographic propinquity, historical animosity, unequal power, concern about alliance relationships. All these concerns can be turned around, however, so that the key issue becomes not sources of endless rivalry but ways in which China and Japan need one another. For indeed they do—such as to control environmental destruction, to promote China's "peaceful rise" in ways conducive to both domestic and international stability, to restrain military growth, and to sustain regional political and economic stability. Such mutual dependence helps neutralize potentially aggressive forms of nationalism. Thus, rather than interpret China-Japan relations exclusively in terms of competition for influence, we might think about the significant opportunity costs that occur as the result of China-Japan friction.

Fortunately, in recent times the China-Japan relationship has not been all about competition and heated words. In October 2006, on the occasion of Prime Minister Abe Shinzo's official visit to the PRC, the two sides proclaimed that they would "strive to build a mutually beneficial relationship based on common strategic interests..." "Contact and dialogue," including "frequent" talks between the top leaders, would take place. Explicit references were made to four areas of cooperation: the East China Sea negotiations, "Japan-China security dialogue," ASEAN+3, and the

Six-Party Talks. Last, Japan and China promised to "strengthen mutually beneficial cooperation particularly in the areas of energy, environmental protection, finance, information and communication technology, and protection of intellectual property." Then, in April 2007 Prime Minister Wen Jiabao returned Abe's visit and won great applause with a speech, "For Friendship and Cooperation," before the Japanese Diet. As he had in the past, Wen stressed looking ahead rather than backward, common development, and "seeking agreement while minimizing differences" (*qiutong cunyi*). Mention was again made of energy and environmental cooperation.

Some specific follow-ups to those promises have since emerged. First, Prime Minister Fukuda immediately proclaimed interest in improving China-Japan as well as Japan-Korea relations, starting with the assurance that he would not visit the Yasukuni Shrine for war dead. On visiting China in December 2007, following a visit to the United States, Fukuda (like Abe) again stressed mutual interest. Second, the two governments reportedly reached a basic understanding on global warming, with Japan agreeing to provide China with technological assistance to help cut greenhouse gas emissions. Third, on the military side, the Chinese missile destroyer *Shenzhen* visited Tokyo Bay in November 2007, with a Japanese return visit scheduled for sometime later. Fourth, the first China-Japan High-Level Economic Dialogue was held in December 2007. China's delegation leader spoke of how trade with Japan was of mutual benefit: "China's development is not a threat to Japan but an opportunity, and Japan's development is advantageous for China's uninterrupted economic progress."

The restoration of high-level diplomacy was in itself an important act, and the promises made as the result of Abe's visit were all to the good. Japan-China relations have had their best moments when dialogue has focused on functional areas such as those mentioned in the joint statement on military, economic, environmental, and other concrete subjects. Still, one wonders how much wider and deeper cooperation might be if dialogue were more culturally informed. How does dialogue actually take place between Japanese and Chinese officials, journalists, historians, and environmental and energy experts? Are there missing ingredients that reduce the opportunities for creating greater trust, such as mutual respect and acceptance of the other's legitimacy? Intercultural research has shown that insensitivity in international relationships can be a major contributor to tensions, or can limit progress in dialogue. Likewise, the choice of format, procedures, and participants in international dialogue may also have much to do with outcomes.

RECONCILING: POTENTIAL AVENUES AND RESOURCES

Tracks I, II, III Options at Three Levels

Below I consider just a few possible steps on three tracks—governmental, mixed governmental and nongovernmental, and popular (civil society)—and at three levels: unilateral, bilateral, and multilateral. *Track I* consists of official declarations, confidence-building measures (CBMs), and negotiations. *Track II* includes activities such as workshops, conferences, and other gatherings that bring together NGOs, business, parliamentary, and other officials speaking in their private capacity. *Track III* activities are entirely in the public (civil-society) domain—e.g., professional and popular associations, media and labor groups, and businesses.

Unilateral Steps are those that either of the parties, or an important outside party such as the United States, might take to reduce tensions. These include policy initiatives such as statements of noninterference, arms reductions, and apologies for past conduct. *Bilateral Steps* are those the parties take together, such as joint research, environmental cooperation, and energy development, as well as pledges and statements of principle. *Multilateral Steps* bring the parties together in larger cooperative networks, such as regional and global organizations devoted to security dialogue, energy, arms transparency, labor, health epidemics, and other transnational issues.

The steps I have chosen may not stand much chance of being implemented any time soon, but each one may generate the kind of goodwill and trust that will lead to other positive steps. Thus, I have stepped around issues of historical grievance, which are the most difficult to address, in favour of those where mutual interests coincide—the well-known win-win approach.

Regularization of High-Level Diplomacy (Track I, Bilateral)

Now that direct dialogue has resumed, Chinese and Japanese leaders should pledge to make it a regular occurrence. In addition, they should issue a new joint statement of friendship and cooperation to upgrade both the sentiment and the functionality of the 1998 joint declaration. A counterpart of such diplomacy might be creation of a prevention-focused bilateral group to provide advance notification (for instance) of troop or ship movements, somewhat like the Organization for Security and Cooperation in Europe (OSCE).

Mutual Appreciation (Track I/Unilateral and Track II)

Chinese government, media and other institutions (including schools) can contribute to a positive atmosphere by expressing appreciation for Japan's contributions to China's economic rise. Some Chinese commentators agree that China has been lax in this regard. Japan has been very generous with yen loans, for example—over $14 billion from 1990 to 2005 alone—and has directly invested over $51 billion in the same period. Although expressions of appreciation have been made from time to time, they have often been diluted by bitter reminders of the past and suggestions that Japanese business has also benefited from the aid and investments. The Japanese side therefore has an obligation too: to acknowledge the benefits it has received, and to consider new ways to contribute to China's development, such as an extension of environmental protection programs when ODA ends in 2008.

Affirmations of Good Intentions (Track I, Bilateral)

Although words can never replace deeds, professions of friendly intentions and mutual respect, apologies for past conduct, and a positive common vision of future relations do serve good purposes. A negative example to demonstrate the point is the November 1998 China-Japan joint declaration of friendship and cooperation, which left both leaderships very upset: Jiang Zemin, because the Japanese side failed to provide an apology for the past, unlike in the Japan-ROK joint declaration that had been concluded the previous month; and Obuchi Keizo, because of Jiang's immoderate criticisms of Japan. The China-ROK agreement, and the Sino-Indian joint declaration of November 2006, are models of forward-looking statements: They specify areas of actual and potential cooperation, as well as the agencies that will undertake it; they assign roles for specialists; and they stress mutual involvement in regional and global activities. These functional areas are framed with rhetoric suggesting positive intentions toward the other party: India and China "are not rivals or competitors" but rather have a "strategic and cooperative partnership," says the joint declaration. It therefore might be time for China and Japan to renegotiate or update the 1998 agreement, with a new spirit of cooperation and attentiveness to specific areas of cooperation.

Creating a Northeast Asia Security Dialogue Mechanism (Track I, Multilateral)

All the recent agreements reached during Six Party Talks on North Korea—the September 2005 joint statement of principles and the agreements of February and October 2007—held out the prospect of a multiparty security forum that might evolve from the Talks and the establishment of a "permanent peace regime" on the Korean peninsula. Although implementation of each party's commitments remains to be seen, preliminary discussion of the scope and organizing principles for a dialogue mechanism could begin now.

A dialogue mechanism would provide China and Japan with an opportunity to work together on any number of common security issues, such as their long-running dispute in the East China Sea, security guarantees for the Korean peninsula, and a Northeast Asia nuclear-weapon-free zone. The common forum would also provide an institutional basis for greater transparency in military affairs, such as arms acquisitions and deployments. The Japan-China Fisheries Agreement that went into force in June 2002, and ongoing bilateral "security consultations" since 1994, provide positive reference points and building blocks for a regional dialogue mechanism.

Putting Balance into U.S. Policy

As two knowledgeable experts have argued, the United States has a large stake in a moderation of China-Japan relations. If U.S. policy continues to promote "normal nation" status for Japan in ways that seem to China to amount to containment, a new cold war in Asia might result, with the two countries engaged in arms racing, forcing other countries (notably in ASEAN) to take sides. Rather than promote an expansion of Japan's international security role and sound alarm bells about China's military modernization, the United States "should declare its unambiguous opposition to worsening Sino-Japanese relations and exert its considerable influence with both Tokyo and Beijing to establish a cooling-off period."

One major Japanese newspaper, worried about a new cold war in Asia, offered several concrete suggestions, all of which require U.S. support in multilateral settings: creating a Northeast Asia security "entity" (such as the security dialogue mechanism discussed above), convening regular U.S.-Japan-PRC summits, and obtaining U.S. and Chinese signatures on a protocol to the Treaty on the Southeast Asia Nuclear Weapon-Free Zone (the Treaty of Bangkok) that bans the use of nuclear weapons. Other ways the United States can help improve Japan-China relations are by moderating Japanese expressions of a security interest in Taiwan (contained in the "2+2" joint U.S.-Japan statement of February 2005), not supporting constitutional revision of Article 9, and not calling upon Japan's military in support of U.S. collective-security missions far from Japan, and inviting China to take part in the trilateral security talks that take place between Japan, the United States, and South Korea.

All these policy changes can be taken with assurances to Japan that the security alliance remains strong and that the United States is not moving to a "pro-China" policy—shifts that Japanese leaders have feared in the past but that Chinese analysts themselves do not demand. What they want, and what is surely in Japan's interest as well, is *cooperativeness in U.S.-China relations, which is vital to East Asia's future*. For history shows that when their relations are cooperative, difficult regional issues can be dealt with effectively, as the Six Party Talks on North Korea have abundantly demonstrated. Japan may well need to hedge against a rising China, but it should not be perceived as seeking to contain it. U.S. and Japanese policies would do better to focus on seeing that China's modernization proceeds along environmentally sustainable lines.

Track II Gatherings

Apart from high-level diplomacy, Chinese and Japanese media, business, academic, and scientific circles have much that they could explore with each other. A gathering of such specialists, drawn from private and public institutions, might promote mutual understanding, reduce stereotyping, and change popular opinion in both countries.

For example, a scientific meeting might be arranged to come up with initiatives on global warming and energy cooperation, or a joint plan for dealing with transboundary pollution. A joint East Asia television history project is a second example, following on publication in 2006 of a joint Chinese-Japanese-Korean history text. Track II gatherings might also encourage particular groups to lobby their governments for improvements in China-Japan relations—as Japanese business groups have already done on the Yasukuni issue. The two governments might convene an eminent persons group to advise on solutions to specific issues in dispute.

Track III - Civil Society and People-to-People Exchanges

Improving mutual perceptions and counteracting distorted imagery require remedies at the grassroots level as well as among political leaders.

For policy makers, nationalism is a two-edged sword; if they appear to be going against it, they face domestic opposition to "softness" when dealing with the enemy. Thus, Hu Jintao is sometimes said to have been a target of the April 2005 demonstrations against a permanent Japanese seat on the UN Security Council for not being as tough with Japan as Jiang Zemin had been; and the China hands in Japan's foreign ministry have often been criticized in the Japanese press for being too "pro-

China." At the popular level, the problem is more complex. In China's case, anti-Japanese nationalism clearly has grassroots dimensions; the fact that the 2005 protests were driven by the Internet showed that new reality very plainly.

But official approval of anti-Japanese feelings (so long as they do not get out of control) is just as clearly involved, not only in popular demonstrations but also in the "patriotic education campaigns" carried on numerous television stations. Japan has its counterparts when it comes to playing to or promoting anti-Chinese feelings.

Japanese courts consistently reject suits that challenge officially sanctioned history textbooks and ask for compensation for Chinese (and all other) war victims; revisionist historiography still has an audience (and is rarely criticized by public officials); the arch-conservative *Sankei News* and popular comic books often depict China in the most evil terms.

Civil society, though nascent in China and still rather weak in Japan, needs to be encouraged to explore, systematically and practically, how Chinese and Japanese can learn at least to be more accepting of one another. At least one study of Japanese NGOs in China—which are far more numerous there than in any other country—suggests that they can be very effective people-to-people diplomats, particularly in the environmental field.

Yomiuri's reevaluation of Japan's war responsibility exemplifies what the mass media can do to dispose of historical myths. *Yomiuri* and its liberal newspaper counterpart, *Asahi Shimbun*, might co-sponsor a media summit with their Chinese counterparts on ways to avoid stereotyping and report objectively on events in the other country.

The editors of these two newspapers have already joined in calling for building a secular war memorial to replace the Yasukuni Shrine. In academia, the appointment of scholarly panels to reevaluate historical sources of grievance has already occurred twice, in the first instance (in 2005) ending with the production of a joint textbook in Chinese, Japanese, and Korean. Such scholarly gatherings should be regularized.

If some of the above ideas are implemented, they may lead to other positive developments. For example, China might support a Japanese seat on the UN Security Council. The two countries might find agreement on the purposes and membership of the East Asian Community. Suspicions about the force modernizations of their militaries might abate as new CBMs are devised. They might establish a standing crisis-management body. Private groups might be prevented by their governments from interfering in territorial disputes. In the end, China and Japan must reach the point of recognizing that security for one is really security for the other—just as happened between the United States and the Soviet Union during the Cold War, and as the previous two South Korean governments decided in seeking to engage the North.

9

The Russia-China-India Triangle Moves Forward

Soon after Russian Prime Minister Yevgeni Primakov arrived in New Delhi on Dec. 21 for a two-day official visit, a sensational piece of news sounded across the globe: Primakov had publicly called for the formation of a "strategic triangle" among the three giant nations of Russia, India, and China. Encouraging India to see itself more as a world power, and calling for closer relations not only between India and Russia, but also between India and China, Primakov reportedly stated, "A lot in the region depends on the policies pursued by India, Russia, and China.... If we succeed in establishing a triangle, it will be very good." As the Indian newspaper The Hindu commented, "The concept of a 'strategic triangle' covering India, China, and Russia, spelt out by the visiting Russian Prime Minister, Mr. Yevgeny Primakov, is of immense significance since this is perhaps the first time that a senior leader from Moscow has made such a statement."

Wasting no time to research the real background of Primakov's remarks, Western and other media were quick to impose their own distorted, mechanistic interpretation. The new "strategic triangle"—they intimated—was Russia's reply to the U.S.-British bombardment of Iraq, the attempt of the weakened and frustrated former superpower to put together a new, anti-Western bloc. When a spokesman of the Chinese Foreign Ministry, reacting to such press reports, emphasized China's strictly independent foreign policy and China's policy not to participate in any sort of blocs or alliances, the headlines of the British press proclaimed triumphally: "You see! China rebuffed Primakov"!

In reality, the Russia-China-India triangle is no new invention made under the pressure of the Iraq crisis, but a crucially necessary feature of the entire Eurasian Land-Bridge development strategy, as repeatedly emphasized by Lyndon LaRouche and others in the pages of EIR. For competently informed persons, the actual emergence of the "strategic triangle" Russia-China-India, became virtually inevitable no later than Chinese President Jiang Zemin's historic speech at the Russian Science City Akademgorodok in Novosibirsk on Nov. 24, 1998.

There, Jiang Zemin put forward the basic principles of a policy to harness Russia's enormous scientific and technological potential, as typified by the "closed cities" of the military-scientific-industrial complex, for the economic development of the entire region. This policy, as Jiang emphasized, is integral to creating a "new, just, and rational world economic order," guaranteeing the sovereign economic rights of the world's developing countries. That same concept was affirmed in the official declarations of both the Chinese-Russian and Russian-Indian summit meetings.

The most appropriate comment to these developments, interestingly enough, came in the pages of China's official foreign press review, Reference News (Can kao xiaoxi) on Dec. 24. Reference News published on its front page a detailed summary of a speech given by Helga Zepp-LaRouche in early December at a conference in Mexico City.

Her speech laid out the background and implications of Jiang Zemin's Novosibirsk speech, and predicted that Primakov would push for the inclusion of India in the new China-Russia development partnership during his (then forthcoming) visit to New Delhi.

What was most significant in the Reference News coverage of Mrs. LaRouche's remarks, however, was her emphasis on the difference in attitude between the Chinese government—which paid attention to LaRouche's analysis and warnings on the financial crisis—and the attitude of most other governments. That fact, indeed, uniquely coheres with China's role as a centre-point of a growing circle of nations

devoted to real development around the Land-Bridge policy, at a time when the United States and western Europe are plunging toward a self-imposed "dark age" of financial and socio-economic collapse.

Collision ahead?

It is only in this context, and not from some mechanistic geopolitical standpoint, that can one speak of the Russian-Chinese-Indian triangle as an "answer" to what is increasingly perceived in Asia and elsewhere as a dangerous pattern of insanity coming from the West. The turning-point in that perception was doubtless the outrageous, disgusting performance of Vice President Al Gore at the Kuala Lumpur meeting of the Asian Pacific Economic Cooperation (APEC) forum on Nov. 17. Gore's "globalist" ravings and his brazen attack on Malaysia for asserting its sovereignty against international speculators, are increasingly viewed in Asia as a signal for the same insane, destructive policy and mind-frame, which characterize the Anglo-American attack on Iraq and the closely related escalation of the fraudulent "legal coup" against U.S. President Clinton. All add up to an unprecedented assault against the very institution of the sovereign nationstate—including, emphatically, against the constitutional system of the United States itself. Going handin-hand with a major escalation of British geopolitical destabilizations in the Near East and elsewhere, and a coming, new global financial earthquake of unprecedented dimensions, that assault has already brought the world closer to nuclear war, than anyone could have imagined a mere 12 months ago.

One should not forget, that it was China and India's stubborn insistence on maintaining their sovereignty in the face of "financial globalization," that has so far permitted those two countries to weather the so-called Asian financial crisis, while less prudent nations went under. The striving to restore to Russia a modicum of national sovereignty, is key to the constellation of forces behind the Primakov government. It is above all this issue of national sovereignty and economic development that is placing China, Russia, India, and other Asian nations—despite the repeated, and doubtless sincere affirmations that their growing partnership is not directed against any third party—on a collision course with the "globalist" policy championed by Gore.

The sharp reaction to the Iraq bombing, by Russia and China particularly, is a mild foretaste of what may come. Unequivocal condemnation of the Iraqi bombing was a major point of the Russian-Indian joint declaration signed during Primakov's visit. In an unprecedented action, Russia recalled its ambassadors from the United States and Great Britain, while at the same time calling a limited military alert. Soon afterward, Russia gave the world a pointed reminder of its continued existence as a nuclear superpower, by deploying the first of its new generation of mobile, high-precision ICBMs. China's representative at the United Nations did not mince words in ripping apart the fraudulent basis for the whole operation, naming UNSCOM director Richard Butler in public. And after the Dec. 28 incident in which U.S. planes enforcing the so-called "no-fly zone" fired on an Iraqi anti-aircraft position, the speaker of the Chinese Foreign Ministry, Zhu Bangzao, declared: "The Chinese side has many times declared that the sovereignty, territory, and independence of Iraq must be fully respected. China regards the action of creation of a 'no-fly zone' in Iraq as contrary to the United Nations Charter and to standards of international relations." Another, increasingly angry message is implicit in the sharp statements and actions of the Chinese government, in dealing with the Western-supported political opposition movement in China itself.

A growing community of interest

Russia, India, and China make up 22% of the world's land area and over 40% of its population. As the world's largest and most populous developing nations, whose very maintenance requires enormous inputs of science and technology, India and China have a strong common interest in stabilizing and developing Russia. Russia, for its part, can only survive by bringing its scientific and technological potentials into full economic play, which in turn requires large and stable markets for the kinds of industrial goods it can best produce. All three nations have a vital joint interest in Central Asia, and so forth.

They also share, in different ways, the experience of significant joint development in the 1950s. At that time, both India and China profitted greatly from close scientific and technological cooperation with the former Soviet Union—a partnership which was also key, in its direct and indirect effects, to the relatively rapid rates of industrial growth in the Soviet Union in that period. In a limited, but significant way, the transfer of industrial technology and know-how from the Soviet Union to China and India, in that period, helped shape the Non-Aligned Movement's later striving for a "new, just world economic order."

For all these and other reasons, a profound community of interest now exists among the three giant nations. That community of interest is by no means limited to the three alone, but explicitly includes the concept of joint cooperation in other developing countries. It should be noted, for example, that the Russian-Indian agreements signed during Prime Minister Primakov's visit, provide for joint exploration and exploitation of oil and gas resources not only on each other's territories, but also in Kazakstan, Central Asia, and Iraq. Iraq has already been an important oil supplier to India, and India and Russia both have considerable interest in developing petroleum resources there.

But the pathway to consolidation of the Russia-China-India triangle is by no means an easy one. It will be necessary to overcome a long heritage of British geopolitical manipulation in Eurasia. That heritage is lodged above all in false axioms and habits of thinking among the elites, which have permitted the nations of the region again and again to be manipulated against each other in the name of falsely defined, so-called "competitive national interests." The earlier triangle was effectively smashed in the late 1950s and early 1960s, by geopolitical manipulations whose fruits included the Sino-Soviet split, the Sino-Indian war, the apparently "insoluble" Indo-Pakistan conflict, and so on.

One of the notable tools in those British-directed manipulations, incidentally, was none other than the late Armand Hammer, sponsor of the Gore family and supposed "great friend" of the Soviet Union. Some painful rethinking of old mistakes will be needed on all sides, if Russia and its partners want the "Great Triangle" to succeed today. That means above all gaining a more competent under-standing of the historical conflict between the United States and Britain—or in other words, why Lyndon LaRouche has the friends and foes he has.

BUREAUCRATIC POLITICAL LANDSCAPE

China

It is difficult to accurately sketch the bureaucratic/political landscape in China regarding nuclear policy making and the institutional and individual proponents and opponents of nuclear disarmament. Overall, nuclear policy remains under the purview of the highest policy-making bodies in China: the Standing Committee of the Chinese Communist Party Politburo and the Central Military Commission (CMC). The actual process of policy making on nuclear strategy and disarmament appears to be more complex and involves a multitude of governmental agencies whose input varies depending on the specific issue; debates are usually conducted behind closed doors, and what little information about them that becomes public is not always reliable. Research institutes and think tanks affiliated with government ministries and universities also provide some input into the process via analyses that are funnelled into the decision-making system either through their supervisory organizations, if engaged in interagency processes, or through the China Arms Control and Disarmament Association (CACDA). The CACDA yearbook on international arms control and disarmament, published since 2004, provides an overview of such analyses.

In doctrinal and operational terms, the General Staff Department (GSD), and to a certain degree, the Second Artillery Corps (SAC), play the key role. The General Armaments Department (GAD) of the People's Liberation Army (PLA) is responsible for nuclear weapons programs and provides important input on nuclear arms control and disarmament, especially from a technical perspective. In recent years, with the elevation of the

PLA Navy (PLAN) and the PLA Air Force (PLAAF) commands to the CMC, there is speculation that the two services may also have a say in decisions on nuclear doctrine and nuclear weapons use. In arms control and disarmament matters, a number of important stakeholders in China are periodically engaged in review and discussion of major issues, provide input in the policy-making process, and are charged with implementation of policy.

These actors include government ministries, PLA general departments, nuclear laboratories, and occasionally, research and academic institutions. On the civilian side, the Department of Arms Control and Disarmament in the Ministry of Foreign Affairs (MFA) remains the lead agency in stipulating and implementing government policies. Some of the government-affiliated think tanks, such as the China Institutes of Contemporary International Relations (CICIR) under the Ministry of State Security, the China Institute of International Studies (CIIS) under the MFA, and CACDA, play important advisory roles and are actively involved in research, analysis, and outreach activities. CACDA in particular serves as a bridge between the Department of Arms Control and Disarmament and the research and academic communities at large, organizing research projects and outreach activities and disseminating government policies. Outside this group, individuals who are leading experts, such as Li Bin of Tsinghua University and Shen Dingli of Fudan University, may also be involved in advising on these matters.

On the military side, GAD has an important part as a strong voice in arms control and disarmament debates and deliberation. Its Science and Technology Committee and Lieutenant General Qian Shaojun (now retired) have played major roles in representing the PLA in interagency arms control and disarmament consultations. The China Defence Science and Technology Information Centre (CDSTIC) under GAD provides valuable advice to the Science and Technology Committee and therefore exercises some influence. Some of the centre's core staff members, such as Liu Huaqiu and Zou Yunhua, both semi-retired major generals, have been actively involved in research and analysis of crucial arms control issues affecting China's security. The nuclear weapons laboratories, such as the China Academy of Engineering Physics (CAEP) and its affiliate, the Beijing Institute of Applied Physics and Computational Mathematics (IAPCM), provide technical advice on many nuclear weapons–related issues and negotiation, in particular on CTBT-related issues. CAEP was formerly under the Commission on Science and Technology in National Defence but now is under GAD, although most of its staff wear civilian rather than military uniforms. The GAD Foreign Affairs Bureau does not play a significant role, but its Arms Control and Disarmament Desk is responsible for documentation and policy implementation. Finally, the Academy of Military Sciences (AMS) also provides input and analysis, as do to a lesser extent the National Defence University (NDU), SAC Command College, and the China Institute of International Strategic Studies (CIISS) under GSD.

Although GAD's positions on various disarmament issues remain unclear after a review of open sources, one can glean insights about its perceptions through the publications of CDSTIC analysts. These analysts tend to be unenthusiastic about disarmament given their concerns over U.S. missile defences, space dominance, and perceived development of new nuclear weapons, which they view as potentially threatening to China's limited nuclear deterrent. Some members of the CDSTIC staff 's arms control group have been CNS visiting fellows over the years, including Liu Huaqiu, Zhu Qiangguo, and Ma Chunyan. NDU, CIISS, AMS, and the China Foundation for International & Strategic Studies (CFIIS) provide research and analyses for the military on arms control and disarmament issues; CIISS staff members often serve in Chinese delegations to the Conference on Disarmament (CD) and other international/multilateral fora.

Outside access to Chinese governmental agencies and departments is severely limited, and their representatives tend to toe the official line during interactions with foreign experts. At the same time, they eagerly follow international debates and new proposals, although it is difficult to judge how these proposals are processed in internal deliberations. It is clear that new concepts and initiatives get into the system, but response is often delayed due to a complex assessment and interpretation process. Take for example the debate in the late 1990s and early 2000s over whether the Chinese government should always link the Taiwan issue to Sino-U.S. bilateral discussions on non-proliferation issues. Because several Chinese governmental agencies are involved in setting policy on interactions with the United States on Taiwan—the Chinese Communist Party Centre/State Council Taiwan Affairs Office, the Department of North American Affairs, and the Department of Arms Control and Disarmament, as well as the relevant PLA departments—policy formulation necessitated drawn-out interagency deliberation and bargaining. It was not until 2002 that the Taiwan issue was more or less de-linked from the other Sino-U.S. bilateral issues. Other new proposals are likely to involve similarly lengthy and complex interagency bargaining processes.

Semigovernmental and nongovernmental actors offer a more available avenue of access to the Chinese decision-making system, both in terms of understanding the current debate and in terms of influencing it. The most important of these actors include CACDA, CICIR, the Centre for Arms Control Studies affiliated with the Institute of American Studies at the Chinese Academy of Social Sciences (CASS), Tsinghua University, Fudan University, NDU, the Academy of Military Sciences, CIISS, CFIIS, and the Chinese People's Association for Peace and Disarmament. CACDA, for instance, essentially plays the role of an outreach arm of the MFA's Department of Arms Control and Disarmament. It typically performs the role of coordinating nongovernmental organizations (NGOs) in providing expert opinion on a range of arms control, disarmament, and nonproliferation issues, and it organizes activities that aim to improve dissemination and implementation of government policies. CICIR, under the Ministry of State Security, assesses international and regional security and arms control developments and provides advice to the government.

At the university level, members at a number of arms control and disarmament programs, such as those at Tsinghua and Fudan (and to some extent NDU), and individuals who actively monitor international and regional arms control developments, such as

Major General Pan Zhenqiang (retired), Li Bin, and Shen Dingli, interact with their international counterparts.

Through their connections with people who have played or still play important roles in government, they may participate in debates that could indirectly influence policies. More importantly, given their exposure and their nongovernmental affiliations, these individuals can be more receptive to new ideas and open to advocating positions that may not be identical with those maintained by the government.

However, the extent and frequency of these organizations' and individuals' participation in the policy debate within China remain uncertain.

Therefore, their abilities to influence policy deliberation and formulation are similarly unclear. Out of this group, one could generalize that CACDA and CICIR closely follow Chinese government positions, while CASS, Tsinghua, and Fudan express more independent views. The military institutions are more suspicious of nuclear disarmament concepts although some analysts (especially those considered retired) offer interesting perspectives and at least conditionally support the idea of nuclear zero. However, they tend to emphasize the missions of nuclear weapons and resist numerical reductions or limits on modernization as long as nuclear weapons remain a critical component in other states' national security policies and defence doctrines.

Interestingly, discussions with Chinese analysts affiliated with CAEP/IAPCM revealed that weapons scientists and/or nuclear physicists–turned–arms control analysts may be very engaged in discussion of arms control matters. Many of them have participated in discussions with their American and other foreign counterparts, and some have also had stints as visiting fellows at Stanford, MIT, Princeton, and the Union of Concerned Scientists, among other places. For example, Li Bin and Shen Dingli—among the most active and well-known Chinese arms control analysts—were postdoctoral fellows at MIT and Princeton and are relatively open-minded, can assess issues from both technical and policy angles, take the lead in training the next generation of arms control specialists in China, and occasionally are called upon to advise government officials.

Russia

The Russian decision-making system with regard to national security and disarmament became considerably more closed after Vladimir Putin's ascendance to the presidency than it was under Boris Yeltsin. During his two terms as president from 2000 to 2008, Putin built a decision-making pyramid that consolidated power in his hands. Today as prime minister he retains much of that power as half of a duumvirate with his successor, President Dmitri Medvedev. It does not appear, however, that they delve into the details of the Russian position on disarmament issues: rather, they set the tone and respond to proposals, initiatives, and analysis provided by the government machine. For them, disarmament seems to serve as a tool in a broader foreign and defence strategy to be advanced or withheld as grand strategy requires.

Formally, at the top of the pyramid is the Security Council (a close analogue of the U.S. National Security Council), but its actual role varies depending on the person who occupies the position of its secretary. The Security Council played a prominent role in formulating nuclear strategy and nuclear disarmament policy during the tenure of Sergey Ivanov until his appointment as minister of defence. Currently, the Security Council takes a more passive stance. The only exception appears to be former chief of the General Staff Yuri Baluevski, who continues to play an important role as a "brain" behind military policy, offering advice independent of the formal military establishment. Baluevski primarily looks after the interests of the military, but he is also generally supportive of limited nuclear arms reduction.

As in any large bureaucracy, decision-making on disarmament is built around an interagency mechanism, which is apparently similar to the one that existed in the Soviet Union and was behind arms reduction initiatives of the 1980s. As in the past, the key players in the field are the Foreign and Defence Ministries, the Foreign Intelligence Service, and, since 2006, the Military-Industrial Commission, which represents the interests of the defence industry, including the weapons component of the nuclear industry. The relative influence of various agencies has waxed and waned mostly as a result of the stature of their heads and their degree of access to Putin (and more recently, Medvedev).

It appears that two agencies play pivotal roles in disarmament decisions: the Foreign Ministry and the Defence Ministry—or, rather, the Defence Ministry's General Staff, since both the current and the former defence ministers, Anatoly Serduykov and Sergey Ivanov, respectively, lack expertise in the area. However, the appointment of a new chief of General Staff, Nikolai Makarov—and the replacement of several key figures whose portfolios include nuclear policy and arms control—is likely to result in the General Staff 's decreased capacity and diminished willingness to entertain changes in arms control and nuclear policy. Within the Defence Ministry, arms control is the prerogative of the General Staff 's Main Operations Department and the Main Directorate for International Cooperation (which is formally charged with participation in all arms control and disarmament negotiations). Several key services (the Strategic Rocket Forces, the Navy, and the Air Force) and research institutes of the Defence Ministry (such as the 4th Institute, which supports operations of the Strategic Rocket Forces) play a pivotal role in the development of the Defence Ministry's position on disarmament and to a large extent dominate the discourse because of their monopoly on technical expertise.

Closely associated with the Defence Ministry is the Academy of Military Sciences, which is staffed primarily by retired, high-ranking military members. The academy tends to take a very hardline position on key international security and military posture issues, including nuclear strategy. Yet, contrary to common perception, only two or three experts get a hearing in the military establishment; the academy's role is thus very limited.

The enhanced role of the Foreign Ministry is a relatively new phenomenon and can be attributed primarily to the success of Minister Sergey Lavrov in strengthening his position in the Russian bureaucracy. While the rising profile of the Foreign Ministry is a welcome sign, its willingness to push forward the disarmament agenda should not be overestimated, as over the past ten years high-level diplomats have been reluctant to challenge the military's control over that issue area.

Compared to China, Russian governmental agencies have greater experience and expertise in all matters pertaining to nuclear policy and disarmament. Although the turmoil of the 1990s created a partial breakdown in institutional memory, the depth and breadth of experience generated by almost uninterrupted arms control negotiations since the 1960s make Russian military and civilian policy makers highly informed and experienced in both technical and diplomatic details. The downside of that experience is relatively low interest in outside proposals.

The role of the nongovernmental community in decision making on nuclear arms control and disarmament matters has significantly decreased in comparison to the 1990s as a result of Putin's efforts to control information. Still, NGOs continue to participate in discussion of arms control matters and can serve as a useful conduit for innovative approaches.

The Russian NGO scene includes a number of well-established academic research centres, such as the Institute of USA and Canada Studies, as well as the Institute of World Economy and International Relations; it also includes some new organizations established in the post-Soviet era, including the PIR Centre and the Moscow office of the Carnegie Endowment for International Peace. These organizations continue to maintain close contacts with governmental agencies, often through personal relationships; their expertise and ability to contribute to policy deliberations are enhanced by the presence on their staff of retired military and foreign policy officials with insider knowledge and good bureaucratic connections. NGO publications oft en reflect debates that are taking place within the Foreign and Defence Ministries. While direct NGO input into policy formulation is limited, they can provide a useful alternative channel for raising issues with decision makers.

Russian officials are reasonably open to contacts with foreign counterparts and NGO experts. The system is therefore open to Track 2 and even Track 1½ contacts. The responsiveness of officials to proposals about nuclear disarmament is, obviously, limited by general political guidelines, but at a minimum this channel can be used to raise new ideas and explore possible alternative approaches.

A WEAK RUSSIA'S FUTURE

Rely on China

China has made highly optimistic forecasts about Russia's prospects for recovery and return to the ranks of the top five powers in the future security environment. Few analysts in the United States share this optimism about Russia's future, nor would Americans agree with the proposal of some nationalistic Chinese authors, like He Xin, that China must form a long-term strategic partnership with Russia in order to balance the rise of a militaristic Japan. One orthodox senior analyst explains that the geopolitical thinking is, "Russia needs to rely on China. Because both the United States and Japan regard Russia as a potential force to reduce their influence in the Asia-Pacific region, and Japan has territorial disputes with Russia, Chinese-Russian cooperation can, to a great extent, resist U.S. and Japanese forces, as well as maintain the power balance in Asia."

Chinese military estimates of Russian national power by 2010 to 2020 place Russia as the second-or at least the third-ranking country in terms of overall military power. Applying the ancient statecraft of the Warring States, Chinese authors refer to the geopolitical nightmare of a powerful predatory Japan joining with a declining but still powerful America to isolate and contain China. A strong Chinese partnership with a recovering Russia is the preferred countermeasure. This chapter, which introduces the views of 55 Chinese authors on Russia, lists the factors they foresee Russia will face in its future dangerous security environment.

In spite of these dangers, they believe Russia also has advantages, such as its potential partnership with China and advanced military concepts and technology, which cause China to assess the Russians as far more likely to exploit successfully the revolution in military affairs (RMA) than the United States. One military author argues that "Russia will use the RMA to maintain its military superiority... and is taking aim at America's commanding position in the RMA." Another military author states that the Russian General Staff Academy is focusing on the RMA. Ancient Chinese statecraft warns that a state needs powerful "partners" to survive in a multipolar environment. China's authors seem to see a rewarding Russian "partnership" in the decades ahead. This chapter also describes Chinese sympathy for the dangers that a weak Russia will face from Japan, Europe, and the United States as these three powers attempt to carve out part of the former Soviet sphere of influence in Central Asia and Eastern Europe.

Debates on Russia

According to interviews with civilian experts, after the collapse of the Soviet Union, it took 2 years for Chinese analysts to reach a consensus on the causes and future significance of the Soviet collapse (addressed at the end of this chapter). It is apparent from Chinese articles written since the consensus was reached that China has decided Russia's decline will end and that it will be able to play its assigned role as one of the five poles in the multipolar world foreseen by Deng Xiaoping and Huan Xian in 1986. Indeed, Russia may be aligned with China in the future multipolar world, now that Moscow is somewhat weakened from its Soviet days and has a smaller gross national product (GNP) than China.

According to one author, Russia's GNP is fifth in Europe, or "the level of a medium country." Additionally, because Russia has forsaken Marxism, Marxist ideology cannot be a source of conflict between the two countries, nor can Russia realistically ever again seek to dominate China.

The new consensus on Russia's promising future contrasts with past debates. Since the early days of the Chinese Communist Party, even before Mao was Chairman, party leaders have debated the nature of the Soviet Union. The subject of Soviet communism and the Russian nation may be the most controversial among Chinese strategists. From alliance with the Soviets in the 1950s, to estrangement and then border clashes in the 1960s, Moscow has proved "hard to understand," in the words of one People's Liberation Army (PLA) officer interviewed for this study.

In spite of the collapse of the Soviet Union, Chinese analysts "officially" continue to portray the future role of Russia as one of the five equal "poles" (along with China, Japan, Europe, and the United States) that will shape the future world balance of power.

Nevertheless, a few years ago, China's analysts saw Russia's immediate future as uncertain. At least four scenarios were mentioned, although none of them would upset the "inevitable" trend toward a five-power multipolar structure laid down by Deng Xiaoping:

- *Further fragmentation* could bring warfare within and between many republics, including an independent Siberia.
- *Chronic crisis* might bring neither a full collapse nor any real progress, but just gridlock and a continued limping along.
- *Successful transformation* built around the old Russian core, with stable relations among the republics and a territorial settlement with Japan, would bring investment and trade opportunities, keeping Russia in play as a pole in the five-pole multipolar world structure and as a coalition partner to Japan or China.
- *Nationalistic regression* would resemble the results of the coup in 1991 against Gorbachev, had it succeeded. Hardliners impose martial law, followed by a halt to market reforms and democracy.

By 1995, Chinese writings about Russia became more optimistic. Chinese military authors envisioned Russia increasing its military power in future decades by exploiting the RMA ahead of other nations. In any event, Chinese authors deny that the collapse of the Soviet Union caused future trends in world politics to "break" or be "transformed."

They asserted China had anticipated the end of the bipolar world as early as 1986, 5 years before the Soviet collapse. Although there is a general consensus among Chinese authors about Russia's position as a pole in the future multipolar world, Chinese analysts suggest there are dangers to Russia in the decades ahead:

- The United States will continue to exploit a weakened Russia still coping with short-term domestic economic and political problems.
- Russian success in implementing the RMA ahead of others is not certain.
- As Russia rebuilds its Comprehensive National Power (CNP), it will be under pressure from the United States and Europe to the West and Japan to the East.

Development and Recovery

Chinese authors recognize that Russia will continue to have economic, political, and social turbulence in the short term but do not foresee these problems preventing Russia from assuming its position as a pole in the future multipolar world. Although its influence has weakened and it no longer is a superpower, Chinese analysts emphasize that Russia remains a major nation with extensive military strength. While today's crises have contributed to a decline in Russia's CNP, in the long run they forecast that its domestic difficulties will gradually be overcome. At present, however, the Chinese view Russia as a factor of instability during the period of transition to a multipolar world. When assessing the overall situation in the Asia-Pacific, Zhang Changtai, a Research Fellow at the China Institute of International Strategic Studies (CIISS), writes:

Russia remains an uncertain factor where there are still ups and downs in the political arena.... For the future, the struggle among all political factions around redistribution of powers will continue to develop and even intensify; the position of the military has declined with growing dissatisfaction, and it is a severe test for President Yeltsin and his government whether they can maintain stability in the armed forces. Chinese analysts also see economic problems precluding stability in Russia's current development and do not believe the economy will recover quickly. A Shanghai Institute for International Studies (SIIS) analyst estimates, "In the short term it will be difficult for the Russian Federation's economic situation to take a turn for the better, economic recovery will necessitate a very long period of time... by the year 2005 it has become able to break even with the economy in 1990. The necessary time for Russia to build a comparatively complete and developed market economy will probably be even longer."

A study of Russia's current and future development by the China Institute of Contemporary International Relations (CICIR) provides a representative orthodox view of Russia's overall near-term prospects. It both acknowledges serious problems and predicts a trend of inevitable gradual recovery and restoration. Stating that "for many years Russian society has accumulated a huge number of complex contradictions and problems," the study lists some of the most critical issues it is currently facing:

- "Economic depression has endangered political stability."
- "The state of social political order is becoming seriously worse," with the pervasive spread of crime and terrorist activities.
- "The trend of local independence and localities acting on their own is difficult to contain."
- The uncertainty of President Yeltsin's health.

According to the study, the combination of the above problems "makes it very difficult for people to make an optimistic appraisal of Russia's political situation and the entire country's situation at the end of the century." However, at least with regard to Russia's economic prospects, CICIR was more positive and put forwarded a timetable predicting future development and reconstruction. It forecasts that 1997-98 will be "the true turning point for Russia's economy," 1999-2005 brought "stable recovery," and after 2005, Russia saw "sustained growth." This growth will permit gradual progress in attaining strategic goals to "restore its position as a great nation," to "contain regional separatism," and to prevent "external forces" from penetrating Russia's sphere of influence.

What Chinese analysts emphasize is that despite Russia's current and short-term difficulties, the "framework" of its former power and status still exists, and the country has definite potential for future development. The CICIR study concludes, "Currently, Russia's domestic political and economic relations still are not smooth and the restoration of its Comprehensive National Power still requires time.

However, the framework of Russia as a major nation and the factors of its actual strength have not disappeared; in particular, Russia possesses a huge nuclear weapons arsenal and armed forces that can not be belittled." Similarly, Chen Qimao, former president of SIIS, writes, "In the short term it will be difficult for Russia to revive, but its potential cannot be underestimated.... From the long-term view, Russia will gradually recover and develop, and although it can not again become a superpower, it still will be a global power." Yu Sui, of the Central Committee International Liaison Department, sums up Chinese analysts greater optimism about Russia's mid-to long-term prospects, saying, "We would rather assess that Russia will rejuvenate at an earlier date and at a quicker pace."

Dangers in the Future Security Environment

Not only do Chinese analysts predict continued domestic problems during Russia's path to establishing its position as one of the five poles of the future multipolar world, but they also examine the numerous threats to its external security environment. One author writes,

> The correlation of forces is moving in an unfavourable direction for Russia.... Russia's geopolitical environment is becoming worse.... The western area of Russia has lost its strategic defence line by over a thousand kilometres.... Even more serious, the Pan-Turkic and Islamic Fundamentalists that tend to be against Russia are rapidly developing, which may possibly cause new conflicts and endanger the security of southern Russia.

In general, most Chinese analysts focus on the United States and NATO as being the biggest challenges currently endangering Russia's security environment. In fact, some have blamed the West for contributing to Russia's continued domestic problems. For example, several authors assert that one of the reasons that Russia has not recovered more rapidly is "the stingy financial assistance provided by the Western powers." The insufficient aid is explained by Chinese authors as the West's desire to keep Russia weak, so that it will not grow and once again be a challenge to America and NATO. "The United States and other Western countries... (have) continued their Cold War mentality, trying to take advantage of Russia's current political, economic and military weakness to pursue a policy of containment in order to weaken, westernize and split Russia and prevent it from restoring its position as a big power."

However, Chinese analysts note that the West wants Russia to be "weak but not chaotic," and therefore must temper its efforts to inhibit the country's power. Xue Gang, a Research Fellow at CIISS, explains, "The present U.S. attitude toward Russia is like this: on the one hand it continues to assist and support the present government in Moscow in order to stabilize the situation in Russia, but on the other, it attempts to prevent Russia from becoming truly powerful so that Russia will not become a threat to it again in the future."

The main thrust of the West's "policy of precaution, containment, and enfeeblement" toward Russia is through the NATO eastward expansion. Feng Yujun of CICIR writes, "There are three objectives for the West to extend eastward: to fill up the security vacancy in Eastern and Central Europe so as to consolidate its victory won in the Cold War; to give an impetus to Westernization of the former Warsaw Pact nations so as to 'enlarge the community of democratic countries' and to complete strategic encirclement of Russia so as to prevent Russia from staging a comeback." Consequently, Chinese analysts assert, "It is not a simple policy regression for the Russians to redefine NATO as its chief threat. It is an inevitable result of the fierce strategic collision between Russia and the Western powers to protect their respective strategic interests.... Containing NATO expansion naturally becomes a major goal of Russian military strategy." However, the Chinese forecast that the prospects for Russia's ability to prevent the eastward expansion are dim. A CICIR analyst, discussing how Russia was already forced to accept that Poland, Hungary, and the Czech Republic will join NATO, writes, "Confronted with such a powerful offensive, Moscow has evidently soft-pedaled its resistance. Acutely aware of the latent threats to its security, yet unable to reverse the trends, Moscow had no alternative other than swallowing the bitter pill." Some analysts do not foresee that

Russia will do much better at thwarting new Western aggression in the near term either: "Short of an evident increase in economic and military strength in the near future, Russia will still be in a passive position before the NATO eastward expansion."

Chinese authors often seem genuinely worried and even sympathetic to the hostile security environment in which a weakened Russia will find itself for decades ahead until its comprehensive power is rebuilt. For example, Russia's current weakness in the face of NATO seems exaggerated in this statement:

> The disintegration of the Warsaw Pact Organization and the Soviet Union had already inflicted upon Russia a loss of a strategic depth of more than one thousand kilometres, and now NATO expansion would further push its military frontier eastward by more than 700 kilometres. It is known that the current strength of NATO conventional forces is three times that of Russia. If that of the first batch of members-to-be are also reckoned in, NATO would be militarily stronger than Russia by nearly 4 times, which would be a tremendous military pressure on Russia's western border.... Russia's position is restrained by its worsening national power. Politically, economically and militarily, NATO enjoys overwhelming advantage. The total GNP of its member states is 20 times that of Russia, and its military expenditure is 10 times Russia's. On the part of Russia, the erstwhile superpower is now not only crisis ridden economically and drastically weakened militarily, but also bogged down in domestic political strife. In consequence, its opposition to NATO expansion to Eastern and Central Europe is almost tantamount to a hope for the impossible, at least for the time being.

Chinese analysts suggest that the real threat to Russia's security would occur if NATO decided to infiltrate the nations of the former Soviet Union, incorporating the Baltic states and Central Asian nations into its sphere of influence. They assert that such a move is part of the final NATO aim to completely encircle Russia and that the United States and Western European nations have already begun to lay the foundation for the ultimate stages of the eastward expansion. At present, they claim the West is penetrating the region through economic and military means. "The United

States has decided to play a more active role in the ethnic and local conflicts in the region, and has refused to let Russia have special peacekeeping privileges in the region."

A Senior Research Fellow at CIISS, Wang Naicheng, even argues that if NATO did eventually incorporate this area, such a development could mean the end of Russia's hope to becoming a pole in the future multipolar world. "Further NATO expansion to the Baltic nations, Ukraine, and other Commonwealth of Independent States (CIS) countries will make Russia's space for strategic survival contract to the maximum. This would be no less than to strike at the root of Russia, for she might finally lose the important base upon which she could be an independent pole in the world." However, Wang asserts that Russia is doing its utmost to prevent this worst case scenario. "With the first line of defence in Central-Eastern Europe broken through, Russia is exerting every effort to build and entrench on the second line, tolerating no entry into the 'forbidden zone.' "

Two articles written in 1998 foresee the three Baltic Nations— Lithuania, Latvia, and Estonia— becoming the next in line to fall into NATO clutches, citing the signing of the "U.S.-Baltic Charter of Partnership" in January and the first meeting of the Partnership Committee in July as preliminary steps. "The formal launching of NATO eastward expansion shows that East Europe is being drawn into the west European sphere of influence and will not longer be under Russian control. Against this background, the United States has decided to push on in the flush of victory and regards the countries of the former Soviet Union as the next targets in expanding its influence." According to the chapter, the three Baltic states are the natural choices of NATO because they "were the first to break away from the Soviet Union and have never joined the CIS." Additionally, they have already tried to "fuse into Europe" in an effort to maintain their independence from Russian control.

Other analysts see the Central Asian nations as the main countries targeted by the West. A CICIR study holds that "Western nations, with the United States at the head, have stood in the way of the CIS integration process, particularly toward Ukraine, and have actively carried out efforts to divide and disintegrate." U.S.

invitations to Ukraine and Uzbekistan to join NATO are extremely dangerous to Russia's security interests, for Uzbekistan is considered to be an "important strategic partner" by the West, and in 1996, the Ukrainian Minister of National Defence expressed that at a necessary time, Ukraine "would not eliminate the possibility of entering NATO." Additionally, Ukraine and a few Central Asian countries have signed "Peace Partnership Relationship" documents with NATO. One chapter asserts that it is through these Peace Partnerships that the United States will be able to increase its infiltration of the region, "on the pretext of 'mediating' regional conflicts, and, in the name of 'maintaining peace', dispatching U.S. and Western military forces to weaken and push out Russia's forces in this region." It concludes, "In essence it is a repeat of the 19th century 'fierce rivalry' among the great powers for Central Asia, and a way to turn Central Asian countries into the United States 'chess pieces.' "

The future U.S. challenge to Russia is even more serious than efforts to contain Russia's power. In addition to luring former Soviet republics to join NATO, the United States has targeted Central Asian oil and natural gas and is already "squeezing Russia out." Yang Shuheng, of the Chinese Academy of Social Sciences (CASS), asserts, "The rivalry over the Caspian Sea region's oil and natural gas is... part of the U.S.-Russian rivalry over strategic interests and spheres of influence in the Eurasian hinterland.... The number of countries involved (in the struggle) will increase.... International forces covet the treasure chest that is Central Asia."

Russia's Response

While some Chinese authors regard Russia as passive and weak in the face of these threats, others see Russia as taking a stand and adopting countermeasures against U.S. and NATO policies. For example, Li Qinggong, a Research Fellow at CIISS, states, "The plan of 'NATO eastward expansion' pursued by the United States and other Western countries has entered the stage of implementation, but Russia has not weakened its opposition; it has taken new countering actions in an attempt to build the Russia-France-Germany axis to oppose the control of the United States over European security affairs and offset the impact of 'NATO eastward expansion.' " Liu Guilin, an Associate Research Professor in the Division for Russian and East Europe Studies at CICIR writes, "Clearly, Moscow intends to rely on the CIS as both the basis for its great power strategy and the bulwark against NATO eastern expansion." He believes that despite drawbacks and problems that exist in inter-CIS relations, such as worries about "Moscow's possible domineering intention," Russia will not lose out to the West in the struggle for influence over the nations of the former Soviet Union. "Shared interests will sustain the CIS in the face of difficulties... (and) cooperation will remain the mainstream due to economic and security interdependence.... Russia still retains strong deep-seated influence in the CIS in the forms of geographical proximity, traditional economic ties, and a Russian community of some 25 million scattered all over the region. All this cannot possibly be replaced by the West." He writes that even the "strongly independence-minded Ukraine will still depend on Russia for a long time to come," citing the fact that 40 percent of its foreign trade is with Russia, and that Russia supplies much of its oil and gas. Therefore, Liu predicts that CIS integration will proceed, although it will be gradual. Finally, he concludes.

Looking beyond the current Russian financial crisis, it can safely be estimated that along with further improvement in overall conditions, the stronger Russia's urge to make bigger strides in winning back its original big power status in international life, the greater CIS cohesion and the higher the organization's profile in a multipolar world of the 21st century. Chinese analysts recognize that on international issues other than NATO eastward expansion, Russia also has strategic interests that conflict with those of the West. In the Iraqi weapons inspection crises, they assert that Russia came out ahead in its dispute with the United States over how to handle the problem:

In resolving this conflict, there has been practically a struggle between Iraq and the United States, or a struggle between Russia and the United States, and Moscow has scored the most points... . All these efforts were made by Russia in an effort not only to head off a war in the Gulf region, but also to pave the way for strong economic ties with Iraq when the U.N. sanctions are eventually lifted.... Russia is, of course, aware that Washington does not like the strengthening of Russia's position in the Middle East and the increasing role of its diplomacy in the region.

RUSSIA, CHINA, AND INDIA OVERCOME FRICTION IN THEIR RELATIONS

The Russia-China partnership has clearly helped to foster bilateral relations after more than two decades of tension and hostility. This partnership has also enhanced the international standing of both countries. At the same time, however, political trust is still rather weak. Moscow and particularly the Russian Far East are clearly worried that the further economic decline of that region will lead to its abandoning by Russians and even Chinese occupation.

China is not perceived by the majority of Russian experts as an immediate military threat, because it is not expected to close the gap with Russia in nuclear and conventional weapons anytime soon. However, more and more Russian commentators, including in the military, are worried about the consequences for Russia of arming China with sophisticated Russian weapons while the Russian army itself cannot afford to have them.

Russia's growing political, economic, and military dependence on China has provoked a certain alarm and anxiety in Russia's academic and political circles. Alexei Bogaturov believes that in spite of impressive rapprochement, Russia and China remain countries that have historically been in conflict and that the geopolitical source of the conflict has not been removed or reduced. Hence, he argues against attempts to pick China as an ally or key partner in the region. Such views are not rare in Russia, even among government officials, in spite of a general official euphoria and an informal taboo on anti-Chinese comments. Common views toward US politics and close military cooperation may not be enough to sustain and enhance the "strategic partnership" between Russia and China. To make it complete, the two countries will have to get rid of their traditional suspicion of each other and engage in a stable and long-term economic cooperation.

The relationship between India and China also has an important influence on the character of regional order and significant geopolitical implications. Friction in this bilateral relationship could have direct effects on China's relations with other neighbours. Stable and cooperative relations between India and China build trust and contribute to Beijing's own sense of security and confidence, providing a counterbalance should other important relationships deteriorate.

The near-rapprochement of relations (driven by the mutual consensus that economic development should have priority) between India and China diffuses, but does not dispel, three decades of friction. Four of the five primary causes of disquiet in India-China relations have been addressed by both powers: India's values-driven Tibet policy has ceased;

Chinese support for secessionist insurgents in Assam and the North East has been withdrawn; the collapse of the Soviet Union reduces Chinese fears of a containment-driven strategic nexus; and, most important, tensions stemming from border disputes between India and China are addressed, though not resolved, through the negotiation of confidence-building measures and agreements. The principal friction in contemporary relations between New Delhi and Beijing is India's belief (apparently well-founded) that China provides nuclear-related military technology and hardware to Pakistan. This abrasion is compartmentalized from India's overall bilateral relationship with Beijing. (New Delhi may be reassured by China's decision to join, and work constructively with, the Non-Proliferation Treaty Exporters Committee [or Zangger Committee].) New Delhi's preference for longer-term prudence in its relationship with China is one consequence of China's military nuclear exports to Pakistan.

India's approach to the management of tensions with China offers important lessons for other regional actors in how to manage relations (especially on sensitive issues) with China. New Delhi has handled Beijing more successfully than Washington has during the corresponding period. India and China have established and maintained regular reciprocal high-level personal visits between political leaders. Both states have improved trade relations and take care to compartmentalize intractable issues that continue to irritate long-standing tensions. Such a policy has perhaps returned dividends of its own with China in turn assuming a "position of `careful neutrality' on Kashmir." In contrast to recent US policy on China, India takes care to respect the principle of noninterference in the internal affairs of another state and eschews a values-driven foreign policy. These developments are especially significant given the depth of India's embedded longer-term strategic concerns with China and the record of mutual tension that has only eased in recent years. India's democratic status also may make it an attractive partner to those East Asian states condemned by the United States for abusing human rights or for falling short of democratic standards.

The renewed Russian-Indian strategic partnership, fuelled by common concern regarding Islamic revivalism, has thwarted Moscow's initial intention to follow a more balanced policy in South Asia, improving in particular its relations with Pakistan. Instead, Moscow-Islamabad links have further deteriorated, especially because of the latter's pro-Taliban role in Afghanistan prior to recent events.

Moscow's strategic interest in India motivates Moscow to promote India's inclusion into the leading forums and institutions of the Asia-Pacific. Having become a member of the Asia-Pacific Economic Cooperation (APEC) organization, Moscow is now backing New Delhi's bid for membership in this regional body. During consultations with the Indian Foreign Ministry in November 1998, Russian Deputy Foreign Minister Grigory Karasin noted that "Russia will try its best to help India develop ties with APEC and eventually to join the organization."

Although Russia and India have renounced an openly anti-Chinese policy, both countries continue to share suspicion and fear toward China. In spite of Moscow's public denunciation of India's nuclear tests in 1998, Russia appreciates India's concern about adequate military preparation in case of Chinese aggression. Moscow supports India not only morally, but also through the resumption of arms supplies, which, after a brief pause in the early 1990s, have been steadily increasing.

Challenges to US International Strategy

Some US officials admit that closer ties between Moscow and Beijing are cause for concern. They say, at the very least, debates are more complicated now on the UN Security Council, where Russia and China frequently make common cause against interventionist initiatives favoured by the United States and Britain. Deadlock on the UN Security Council reminiscent of the Cold War era is becoming a regular occurrence.

For instance, knowing that both Russia and China would probably veto military intervention in Kosovo, the Clinton Administration decided to work through NATO. Both Moscow and Beijing were concerned about external intervention on humanitarian grounds, which would be relevant to conflicts within Russia such as Chechnya, and within China such as its claims over Taiwan. Further, NATO was again conspiring to force the US value system on a Third World state.

Russia, China, and India watched the United States in conflicts throughout the 1990s and each learned the same lessons. Indian military and political sources were among the first to react to the Kosovo operation and to speculate on preliminary lessons to be learned. "We are studying what's going on there [in Kosovo] and drawing our lessons from it." A common theme in Indian, Russian, and Chinese thinking since Operation Desert Storm has been the importance of "force multipliers" provided by information technology, AWACs, mid-air refuelling, unmanned aerial vehicles, and electronic warfare capabilities. Analysts in all three countries believe their armed forces can succeed against a high-technology foe if they use these force multipliers in combination with clever low-technology tactics, urban guerilla warfare, financial terrorism, computer hacking, media warfare, diplomatic actions, and psychological warfare.

In light of the new "interventionist-oriented NATO doctrine" and the new capabilities of long-range precision conventional weapons, Indian military thinkers recommend upgrading its nuclear arms to deter Western intimidation and attack. This is a prime example of the drive toward nuclear weapons and its cascading effects predicted by

General Makmut Gareyev, President of the Russian Academy of Military Science. He believes that countries, including Russia, that are unable to match an opponent in high-technology conventional weapons will resort to nuclear weapons in order to deter conventional strikes. Until 1998, India held the principled position that nuclear deterrence was abhorrent to human sentiment, since it implies that if required to defend its own existence, a state will act with pitiless disregard for the consequences of its own and its adversary's people. But in remarks made on 15 March 1999, Prime Minister A. B. Vajpayee asserted: "The nuclear weapon is not an offensive weapon. It is a weapon of self-defence. It is the kind of weapon that helps in preserving peace. If in the days of the Cold War there was no use of force, it was because of the balance of terror." It is also true that India has begun revamping its conventional forces to push the nuclear threshold upward, creating more options with those conventional forces before resorting to nuclear weapon use.

Many scenarios that would present a challenge to the United States could arise from the triangular strategic partnership. One possible conflict scenario is that of China and Taiwan. This is a possible conflict for several reasons. First, China is going through an economic modernization. This is good over the long run for encouraging political liberty. In the short run, however, as large state-owned enterprises are disestablished, the Chinese may have unemployment of millions to tens of millions and social and political disruption of one kind or another.

For thousands of years dictators have responded to domestic problems by playing the nationalism card and focusing attention on a foreign enemy or foreign problem. Taiwan will be front and centre because now it is a thriving, prosperous, free-enterprise democracy. Taiwan inescapably disproves those people in Southeast Asia and in the PRC who have said for years that Asians do not have an aptitude for democracy and need to be ruled with a firm hand. Taiwan is an affront to the leaders in Beijing the same way Poland's Solidarity movement in the summer of 1989 was an affront to the leaders in the Kremlin and the dictators in Eastern Europe. The Taiwan Strait is one of the most likely places over the next five to ten years where the United States might end up in a clear confrontation with another nuclear power.

How would such a conflict evolve? Top echelons of the PLA officer corps do not necessarily share a common point of view with regard to Taiwan, and the advice they give is not necessarily militaristic. However, a Western intelligence source surmises that high-ranking naval and air force officers support a militant stance in Taiwan. They, rather than the ground forces, have received the benefits of increases in the defence budget and are eager to test their new capabilities.

Beijing is not likely to haphazardly lob a few missiles over to Taiwan and see what happens. Beijing would have a plan and expect to win. The more probable scenario would be for the Chinese to effect simultaneous crises to distract the United States, forcing the Americans to choose between Taiwan and another ally. This quote from Chinese ultra-nationalist author He Xing lends credence to the "simultaneous crises" theory:

China must pay close attention to those countries that are opposed to American interests, or are potential strategic enemies. It must be borne in mind that the enemies of enemies are one's own allies.... Know this: the more the United States encounters trouble in other places in the world, the more difficult it is for it to concentrate its power on dealing with China and the greater the opportunities for China's existence and development.

Hypothetically, Beijing might cooperate with Moscow on the timing of an attack on Taiwan. Moscow could simultaneously start a conflict with emerging democracies in the Baltics or the Caucasus. Or Beijing and New Delhi could cooperate on timing, with India engaging Pakistan, perhaps with the support of Moscow. Both Russia and China are arming other enemies of the United States such as Iran and Iraq. Iraq could be persuaded by Beijing or Moscow to simultaneously start a conflict with Kuwait, Saudi Arabia, or Israel. China could concurrently attack Taiwan and stop the food flow to North Korea, forcing millions of refugees into South Korea, and causing the United States to choose between helping Taiwan and assisting South Korea.

The possibility of a nuclear dimension to a conflict between China and Taiwan is all too real. On 2 December 1998, the Defence Intelligence Agency (DIA) reported that the PLA had conducted exercises that included simulated nuclear missile attacks on Taiwan and on US military forces in the region. DIA analysts determined that the missile units were conducting mock nuclear attacks on Taiwan and against US Army troops based in South Korea. US marines on the Japanese island of Okinawa and mainland Japan also were targeted.

The missile exercise directly threatened the 37,000 troops based in South Korea and the 47,000 troops in Japan, including about 25,000 marines on Okinawa. All of these China-Taiwan scenario options are conjecture, but they are not beyond the realm of possibility and are worth considering. That may be particularly so in the aftermath of the terrorist strikes on the United States on 11 September 2001 and the US response. The volatility of the current situation calls into question many of our previous assumptions about stability and the likely course of international and regional relations.

OTHER AREAS OF POTENTIAL CHINA-INDIA CONFLICT

Energy also is increasingly becoming a source of friction between China and India. They are two of the world's fastest-growing energy consumers, with China importing about 50 percent of its energy needs and India importing 70 percent. China has consistently outbid India in the competition for energy sources, and these bidding wars have inflated prices for energy assets, prompting the two countries to agree to joint bidding on some contracts. The Chinese provide monetary and diplomatic enticements to secure energy supplier contracts and largely ignore international concerns over issues like human rights and democracy.

Burma represents one country where the India-China energy competition is playing out. In the fall of 2007, attempts of the Gas Authority of India Limited (GAIL) and other Indian companies to tap Burmese oil and gas were thwarted by Chinese pressure on Burmese authorities. India was a strong proponent of the democracy movement in Burma throughout the 1980s and gave sanctuary to thousands of Burmese refugees following the military junta's assumption of power in 1988. India changed its position, however, to one of "constructive engagement" when it sought Burmese cooperation against insurgents across their porous frontier in the mid-1990s and has more recently sought oil and gas deals there to fulfil its growing energy requirements.

It is important to note that India's Burma policy may be changing yet again. In response to the September crackdown on pro-democracy demonstrators, India put arms sales to Burma under "review," at least temporarily halting them.

Energy competition between India and China is also reflected in their assertions of naval power. As India reaches into the Malacca Straits, Beijing is creating a "string of pearls" surrounding India by developing strategic port facilities in Sittwe, Burma; Chittagong, Bangladesh; and Gwadar, Pakistan to protect sea lanes and ensure uninterrupted energy supplies.

Water also has the potential to become a divisive issue in India's bilateral relations with China. New Delhi is concerned about the ecological impact on India of Chinese plans to divert the rivers of Tibet for irrigation purposes in China. With China controlling the Tibetan plateau, the source of Asia's major rivers, the potential for conflict over increasingly scarce water resources remains a concern.

Russia-China-India Trilateral Cooperation?

China is beginning to embrace the idea of a China-India-Russia trilateral axis to further its strategic aims in the region. Both China and India were initially cool to the idea of China-India-Russia trilateral cooperation when Russian Prime Minister Primakov began pushing the idea in the late 1990s. However, as Indian strategists see the economic balance of power shifting to Asia, they also have increased their support for China-India-Russia cooperation.

India last year hosted a trilateral meeting of the foreign ministers, marking the first time that it has hosted such a high-level China-India-Russia meeting. The meeting was welcomed by

Indian leftists opposed to India's increasingly cozy relations with the United States. In the February 14, 2007, joint communiqué, the ministers said that "trilateral cooperation was not directed against the interests of any other country." U.S. policymakers should nevertheless caution India that such a tripartite axis has the potential to undermine the shared U.S. and Indian objectives of supporting democracy, free trade, economic prosperity, and nuclear nonproliferation in Asia.

The trilateral axis idea could also raise suspicions among the Southeast Asian states about New Delhi's ultimate objectives in the region. The nations of Southeast Asia seek a greater Indian political and economic role in the region to ensure that China does not dominate the region. India has become a full dialogue partner with the Association of Southeast Asian Nations (ASEAN) and joined the East Asia Summit in 2005.

China-Pakistan Ties

Pakistan and China have long-standing strategic ties. China is Pakistan's largest defense supplier, and the Chinese view Pakistan as a useful counterweight to Indian power in the region. China transferred equipment and technology to Pakistan's nuclear weapons and ballistic missile programs throughout the 1980s and 1990s, enhancing Pakistan's strength in the South Asian strategic balance. U.S. scholar Steve Cohen describes China as pursuing a classic balance of power by supporting Pakistan in a relationship that mirrors the relationship between the U.S. and Israel. The most significant development in China-Pakistan military cooperation occurred in 1992 when China supplied Pakistan with 34 short-range ballistic M-11 missiles.

China has helped Pakistan build two nuclear reactors at the Chasma site in thc Punjab Province. In the run-up to Chinese President Hu Jintao's visit to Pakistan in November 2006, media reports speculated that Beijing would sign a major nuclear energy cooperation agreement with Pakistan. In the end, however, the Chinese leader provided a general pledge of support to Pakistan's nuclear energy program but refrained from announcing plans to supply new nuclear reactors.

Although the fate of the U.S.-India civil nuclear deal is uncertain, if it does reach the Nuclear Suppliers Group (NSG) for consideration, the Chinese may insist that any changes in the NSG guidelines must not be "country-specific," but rather "universal" or "criteria-based" so that all countries, namely Pakistan, can benefit from the peaceful use of atomic energy. This formulation, outlined by Chinese Foreign Minister Yang Jiechi, would pave the way for the Chinese construction of additional nuclear reactors in Pakistan. China also is helping Pakistan develop a deep-sea port at the naval base at Gwadar in the Pakistan province of Baluchistan on the Arabian Sea. China is seeking to secure oil and gas supplies from the Persian Gulf and has financed 80 percent of the $250 million project. The complex will provide a port, warehouses, and industrial facilities for more than 20 countries and will eventually have the capability to receive oil tankers with a capacity of 200,000 tons.

One source of tension between Beijing and Islamabad that has surfaced in the past has been the issue of rising Islamic extremism in Pakistan and the ability of Chinese Uighur separatists to receive sanctuary and training among other radical Islamist groups on Pakistani territory. The Chinese province of Xinjiang is home to 8 million Muslim Uighurs, many of whom resent the growing presence and economic grip of Han Chinese. Some have agitated for an independent "East Turkestan." To mollify China's concerns, Pakistan in recent years has begun to clamp down on Uighur settlements and on religious schools used as training grounds for militant Islamists. Tensions over Islamic extremism surfaced when Islamic vigilantes last summer kidnapped several Chinese citizens whom they accused of running a brothel in Islamabad. China was incensed by this incident, and its complaints to Pakistani authorities likely contributed to Pakistan's decision to finally launch a military operation at the Red Mosque in Islamabad, where the militants had holed up since January 2007.

Bibliography

Ajey Lele: *Strategic Technologies for the Military : Breaking New Frontiers*, Sage, Delhi, 2009.

Alexander Wendt: *Social Theory of Internationl Politics*, Peking University Press, 2005.

Allan, P. & Schmidt, C.: *Game Theory and International Relations*, Hampshire, Edward Elgar, 1994.

Anil, K.C.: *Military and Democracy in South Asia : Challenges, Politics and Power*, Sumit Enterprises, Delhi, 2009.

Atar Singh Jadoan: *Military Geography of South East Asia*, Anmol, Delhi, 2001.

Bhat, T.P. : *India and China : Trade Complementarities and Competitiveness*, Bookwell, Delhi, 2008.

Burchill, S. & Linklater, A.: *Theories of International Relations*, Hampshire, Palgrave Macmillan, 2009.

Byung-Joon Ahn: *The Rise of China and the Future of East Asian Integration*, Asia-Pacific Review, London, Carfax Publishing Company, 2004.

Deepak, B R : *India and China : 1904-2004 : A Century of Peace and Conflict*, Manak, Delhi, 2005.

Digumarti Bhaskara Rao: *Military Conversion : Impact on Science and Technology*, Discovery, Delhi, 2003.

Dixit, A.K. : *Military Wars and Rescue Techniques*, Cyber Tech Pub, Delhi, 2010.

Friedman, G.: *The Future of War: Power, Technology and American World Dominance in the 21st Century*, N.Y., Random House, 1996.

Gautam, P.K. : *Environmental Security : New Challenges and Role of Military*, Shipra, Delhi, 2010.

Hagström, Linus: *Japan's China Policy: A Relational Power Analysis*, London and New York: Routledge, 2005.

Huntington, S.P.: *The China Modernisation Military and the State*, N.Y., Vintage Books, 1964.

Ian Storey: *ASEAN and the South China Sea: Movement in Lieu of Progress,* Washington, D.C., Jamestown Foundation,2012.

Iriye, Akira: *China and Japan in the global setting,* Harvard University Press, 1992.

Itoh, Mayumi: *Pioneers of Sino-Japanese Relations: Liao and Takasaki.* Palgrave-MacMillan. 2012.

Jagannath P. Panda: *China's Path to Power : Party, Military and the Politics of State Transition,* Pentagon, Delhi, 2010.

Kapur, C.K. : *Chinese Military Modernisation,* Manas, Delhi, 2003.

Kenneth B. Pyle: *The Japanese Question: Power and Purpose in a New Era,* Washington, DC: American Enterprise Institute, 1996.

Marie Lecomte : *Hindu Kingship, Ethnic Revival, and Maoist Rebellion in Nepal,* Oxford University Press, Delhi, 2009.

Michael Schaller: *Altered States: The United States and Japan Since the Occupation,* Oxford: Oxford University Press, 1997.

Moulder, F. V.: *Japan, China, and the Modern World Economy.* Cambridge: Cambridge University Press, 1977.

Raj Kumar: *Weapons and Military Technology,* Sumit Enterprises, Delhi, 2009.

Rose, Caroline: *Sino-Japanese Relations: Facing the Past, Looking to the Future?* Routledge. 2005.

Rosen, P.: *Societies and Military Power: India and its Armies,* Ithaca, Cornell University Press, 1996.

Samuel P. Huntington: *The Soldier and the State : The Theory and Politics of Civil-Military Relations,* Natraj Pub, Delhi, 2005.

Selig Harrison: *Japan's Nuclear Future: The Plutonium Debate and East Asian Security,* Washington, DC: Carnegie Endowment, 1996.

Shaun Narine, *Explaining ASEAN: Regionalism in Southeast Asia,* Boulder, CO: Lynne Rienner Publishers, 2002.

Stegewerns, Dick : *Nationalism and Internationalism in Imperial Japan,* Routledge, 2003.

Storey, I.: *Southeast Asia and the Rise of China: the search for security,* New York, Routledge, 2011.

Storry, R.: *A History of Modern Japan.* Rev. edn. London: Penguin, 1961.

Tarling, N.: *Southeast Asia and the Great Powers,* London, Routledge, 2010.

Thapa, Deepak : *Understanding the Maoist Movement of Nepal,* Centre for Social Research and Development, Delhi, 2003.

Index

❑❑❑